# THE SELECTED WRITINGS
## OF
# John Jay Chapman

# THE SELECTED WRITINGS OF

# John Jay Chapman

### EDITED WITH AN INTRODUCTION

### BY

## Jacques Barzun

FARRAR, STRAUS AND CUDAHY / NEW YORK

## ACKNOWLEDGMENT

The editor is much indebted to Olivia Chapman, who years ago gave him several of John Jay Chapman's otherwise unobtainable books; to Chanler Chapman, whose friendly assistance supplemented M. A. DeWolfe Howe's encouragement in the preparation of this anthology, and to Robert Giroux, who from the outset was strongly in favor of the undertaking.

Copyright © 1957 by Farrar, Straus & Cudahy, Inc.
Introduction copyright © 1957 by Jacques Barzun

Library of Congress catalog card number 57-10319

First Printing, 1957

Manufactured in the U. S. A.
American Book–Stratford Press, Inc., New York

# Introduction

## by Jacques Barzun

THOUGH FEW AMERICANS KNOW IT, Coatesville, Pennsylvania, is an historic name in the annals of both the country's social evolution and its literary biography. Two events, a year apart, give Coatesville this singular distinction. The first occurred in the month of August, 1911. On Saturday night the twelfth, a Negro named Zacharia (or Ezekiel) Walker was brought under police guard to the Coatesville Hospital after a series of incidents which remain shrouded in doubt. The clear facts that emerge are that he had shot and killed a special officer of the Worth Steel Company and was himself wounded in the head. Almost at once a mob stormed the hospital, dragged Walker outside the town, bound him to his cot, and put both on a pile of rubbish to which they set fire. When the ropes burned away, Walker made a dash for freedom and tried to escape over a fence. But he was recaptured and thrown back into the flames.

The news first reached the New York papers on August 14th. The next day the *Tribune* reprinted a local account which said: "For hours today the scorched torso, the only thing left of Negro Walker, was kicked around by children on the highway a short distance from where he met his death." Later the remains were put into a box marked "To be claimed by relatives" and taken to the morgue. The mob was still in control and attempts made to identify the lynchers and sift testimony proved useless. According to some reports, Walker had been holding up a man when he was surprised by the company officer he killed. According to others, Walker confessed in the hospital to having drunk too much and in his elation fired three shots near the steel plant, which led to a challenge and a fatal scuffle with the officer. After his confession Walker is said to have begged, "Don't give me a crooked death because I am not white."

These are the facts and allegations on which John Jay Chapman, then almost fifty, brooded during the ensuing year. As he wrote later: "I was greatly moved at the time the lynching occurred, and as the anniversary came round my inner idea forced me to do something. I felt as if the whole country would be different if any one man did something in penance, and so I went to Coatesville . . ."

As a young man Chapman had had several years' experience in New York politics on the side of reform. But his mood when he decided to do penance for the country at Coatesville was not that of agitation. Leaving his understandably apprehensive wife at Islesboro, Maine, Chapman went to New York and discussed his intention with a friend, Miss Edith Martin, who read with approval the address he had prepared and offered to accompany him. This, as Chapman wrote to his wife, "puts my mind at ease as if I had a big bulldog to guard me, not from lynchers but from—I don't know what . . ." The next day Chapman set out to reconnoiter alone; he reports: "Very hard to get a hall—the prejudice against the subject. I have hope to get the City Mission (sort of Salvationists) but naturally can't get it Sunday, therefore try for Saturday."

He made other plans and on Friday, August 15th, the citizens of Coatesville could read in their afternoon *Record* the notice of Chapman's meeting:

### In Memoriam

A Prayer Meeting will be held
on Saturday morning at 11 o'clock,
at the Nagel Building

Silent and aral [*sic*] prayer:
Reading of the Scriptures:
Brief address by John Jay Chapman

In memory of the Tragedy of August 13, 1911
O Lord receive my prayer.

The details of Chapman's efforts to publish this announcement are given in a letter of the same day to Mrs. Chapman:

By good luck the local newspaper is a daily which appears in the afternoon, so—having hired my room by 9.40 this morning—(and most grateful to get a room—which I succeeded in by slightly changing my policy. It occurred to me that it was *not necessary*—nor morally right—to *burden* the conscience of the real estate men with my plans and purposes. By not knowing them *they* remained innocent). Curious experience in the backward working of principles in moral force:—I was a little afraid last night that perhaps I wasn't quite sincere—and really was after an agitation and not a prayer meeting—so I resolved it must be real, and drew the notice so. Well, at the newspaper office there was some doubt and trouble and the head man was called in. (Everybody says he's a tremendous shouter for peace and not an honest man.) But as I stood waiting for him to decide I thought to myself—'If the *Record* refuses to print that notice—the Philadelphia papers will give Coatesville such a hammering as they have never received'—(the hammering by the press of the country is what has injured them and pained them) and I was just going to suggest this when he saw his way to print the ad. He somehow saw it. He must be an able man. The room will hold 20 people but is very conveniently situated. If there should be a crowd, we can always move to a larger place. What I mean about principles is that by really abandoning politics I had bungled into the astutest thing I could have done.

No one who has not been up against it can imagine the tyranny of a small town in America. I believe a good old fashioned Medicean, or Papal, or Austrian tyranny is child's play compared to it. There's a dumb, dead, unlistening decision to do what it *has been decided* must be done—what business demands—e.g. to not raise the lynching issue in Coatesville today—by Jove, it's amazing! It doesn't irritate me—as the old political tyranny and hatred of opinion. Merely because the battle is won. It's a joke, this idea of Coatesville—whereas there was a good deal of seriousness in the successful way they used to put down independent ideas in New York. The great men of Coatesville are not so heavy. . . .

I haven't suffered from either fatigue or change of climate. I got into a nasty old hotel yesterday—didn't like the morale of it either—filthy room and no air—piazza in front, and a bar room as big and desolate as a dream. My, what that long dreadful stretch of stinking bar implies—one hundred men could drink there—fifty anyway, and what ruffians! Now, I've come across the street to an airy, clean, large, comfortable room and have nothing on my mind and nothing to fret about. I have sent for Miss Martin, though I *almost* didn't—because it's so long a journey—and then I thought after all that was her mission.

Yours<br>Jack

By Saturday the 17th Chapman was convinced that the inhabitants *"rather like* the idea of a prayer meeting. I get this in the air. 'Who's back of this?' said the editor of the *Record* fiercely. 'No one,' said I; 'at least, I am.' This satisfied him as he didn't know what kind of a feller I was, but I looked meek.' "

If the Coatesvillians liked the idea, they visibly did not like the reality, for besides Miss Martin from New York only two people came—"one an anti-slavery old Negress, who lives in Boston and was staying in Coatesville; the other a man who was, I think, an 'outpost' finding out what was up. We held the meeting just as if there was a crowd, and I delivered my address. There was a church meeting going on opposite us, and people coming and going and gazing, and our glass front windows revealed us like Daniel when he was commanded to open the windows and pray."

2.

How Chapman prayed and what passages he read from Scripture, we do not know, but his address remains under the sufficiently evocative title "Coatesville." * Like all of Chapman's work, it is an image of him and it contains things which tell us why he was at once a superior critic of his America and quite incomprehensible to it. He had not spoken two minutes at Coatesville before he

---

* See below p. 253. The present account of the sequence of events and the quotations from Chapman are based on the indispensable source book for Chapman's life: M. A. De Wolfe Howe, *John Jay Chapman and His Letters,* Boston, 1937. Permission to quote was kindly given by Mr. Howe and his publishers, Houghton Mifflin Company.

pierced through to the core of the mystery, the secret motive which brought the "hundreds of well-dressed American citizens" to look on at torture "without provocation, . . . standing by merely in cold dislike." The explanation is the passage of the address that begins: "As I read the newspaper accounts of the scene enacted here in Coatesville a year ago, I seemed to get a glimpse into the unconscious soul of this country . . . ," and which ends: "No theories about the race problem, no statistics, legislation, or mere educational endeavor, can quite meet the lack which that day revealed in the American people. For what we saw was death."

These few lines, from a man who had never heard of Freud and whose vocation since youth had been neither practical politics nor academic psychology but literature, are enough to show how inadequate is the tag of "belated Abolitionist" which Chapman's friend Owen Wister tried to fasten on him. There was nothing belated about Chapman, and his fanaticism is not abolitionist but creative. I say creative despite the degraded usage which permits writers of conventional short stories in a college course and compilers of copy in a public relations firm to call their work "creative." Chapman wrought no fictions like these; he created because he worked to bring into existence in the culture of his time something which no one before had conceived—a new American type which, while remaining native and natural, would differ in thought and feeling from the American, common or distinguished, of the post Civil War period.

What Chapman saw in the American soul at Coatesville was death, and what he struggled to substitute for it was life—life through the free activity of mind. His tragedy was that he himself was heavily burdened with death, with abolitionism, and that his entourage, far from fanning the spark of life in him, or bringing it fuel, isolated it and in the end all but extinguished it. Whether bent on life, as at Coatesville, or on death, as in the early episode leading to the self-mutilation of his left hand, he was known as "mad Jack Chapman," and his soberest, wisest thoughts reached little farther than the circle of friends who found him "fascinating."

No one using that word then or now seems to be aware that it implies the immobility and imminent end of a weak creature in the grip of a strong and strange one. But the fact remains that he who fascinates is bound to destroy, not create. And this suggests the

way in which the lack of a suitable environment eliminates genius
—by surrounding him, not with calculated antagonism and directed
force, but with weakness and passivity. It was this kind of environment, conformist by commercial tradition, that Chapman found
smothering American culture and thwarting the country's possible
destiny.

Chapman is obviously a forerunner, with Mencken and the
writers of *The Smart Set,* of the critical activity which gave its
character to the twenties. But though Chapman lived until 1933
he did not take part in the great postwar change or clearly grasp
its significance. To him "the war" and "the postwar mood" always
meant the events and attitudes of his formative years, the brassy,
resonant, hollow years from 1861 to 1914. The second aftermath of
blood held nothing for him. The First World War had wounded
him in his attachment to European civilization, had deprived him of
a much-loved son, and had left the death side of him uppermost. In
the twenties his balked energies burst forth spasmodically in utterances of the most deplorable sort against racial and religious groups,
contradictory explosions of anger which he soon forgot, but which
revealed in him the accumulation of guilt, the frenzy of impotence
seeking a scapegoat for its failure to achieve cultural regeneration.

It is the unmerited lot of those who, like Chapman, are born in
the wrong time and the wrong class and with the wrong income—
whether too large or too small—that they catch only occasional
glimpses of their actual role. At times Chapman knew perfectly
well what he would mean to succeeding generations: "I am saying
things which will some day be thought of, rather than trying to get
the attention of any one." Translate "getting the attention of anyone" into political or literary success and you begin to see why it
was necessary, beneficent, that Chapman should fail. No man of
reputation in politics or letters could have gone to Coatesville, even
if such a man had been as ready as Chapman was to risk his life.
The increased public importance of the act would most likely have
turned penance into riot, and would certainly have robbed the day
and the deed of their inward and symbolic meaning.

But Chapman also knew that in order to have the things he was
saying thought of in a later day, he would have to appear in his
fragmentary and not wholly satisfactory form:

I confess that I had rather stand out for posterity in a hideous silhouette, as having been wrong on every question of my time, than be erased into a cypher by my biographer. But biographers do not feel in this way toward their heroes. Each one feels that he has undertaken to do his best by his patron. Therefore they stand the man under a north light in a photographer's attic, suggest the attitude, and then take the picture;—whereas, in real life, the man was standing on the balcony of a burning building which the next moment collapsed, and in it he was crushed beyond the semblance of humanity.

One is struck by the recurrence of the image of burning in Chapman's life and works: it was by burning his hand deliberately that he tried to atone for thrashing a man with whom he later found he had no legitimate quarrel; and it is as by a kind of capricious flame that his genius gave life to the most miscellaneous of miscellaneous writings—two books on political reform, essays on Greek genius, on Emerson, Whitman, Balzac, Shakespeare; sketches of his contemporaries; translations and moral and religious speculations; a life of William Lloyd Garrison; and numerous attempts at original plays—for adults and for children—on such native themes as Benedict Arnold and John Brown. Much of Chapman's best work was published in periodicals and later gathered into volumes now very scarce; but much else remains, unknown even to scholarship, in the Houghton Library at Harvard.

### 3.

Yet as one looks today at this neglected but indispensable witness of an age in part destroyed, the first thing one notices is that though the burning building blotted him from view, his features were not crushed out of human semblance. Indeed, in his fiery incompleteness and buffeted integrity he looks like some of his predecessors from Poe to Melville and the elder Henry James, or like his contemporaries Adams and Mencken; he looks, in short, like the American as Critic.

But Chapman would be simply another specimen, of different stature and scope, if he did not possess two characteristics uniquely his—his humor and his style. To this day, and perhaps for all time, the fact that his work gives no earnest of solemnity will stand in the way of his acceptance by some readers: it is so hard, apparently, to believe words that one can readily make out, and so unnecessary to be grateful for thoughts that are given us fully, quickly, and agreeably. Some remnant of savage fear tells us that profundity has no business with the easy and the agreeable, so that in our atavistic moments we do not trust the man who writes as if improvising and who flouts professionalism. Listen to Chapman trying to de-contaminate literature, a premature advocate of the great books who appeals to the comic spirit rather than to philosophy:

> Literature is for our immediate happiness and for the awakening of more literature; and the life of it lies in the very seed and kernel of the grain. Footnotes and critical information attack the creative instinct. The spirit is daunted, the tongue tied by them. Many a lad has known less about Shakespeare after a college course on Shakespeare than he did when the only phrase he knew was 'Aroint thee, witch'—and he didn't know where that came from. Now he can write the etymology of the words on an examination paper; but the witch herself has vanished. Information is the enemy to poetry. If the old Greeks had known as much about Achilles as we do, the Iliad would never have been written. . . .
>
> The Nineteenth Century has left a hedge of critical literature about every great writer of antiquity. By the time a student has bored his way through the treatises, he is old, and he is dull. He cannot taste the honey, for he has exhausted himself in cutting down the tree. Let us climb and sip. Three generations of modern scholars have befogged and begoggled their wits over Aeschylus and Horace. Let us never read the learning of these investigators. Let us be ignorant, nimble, and enthusiastic. Let us never drink of that cup of delusion, critical knowledge. A scholar reads the books of other scholars, lest he shall say something that shows ignorance. Conscience and professional ambition keep him at it. He dare not miss a trick; just as the social climber dare not miss a party. Jaded and surfeited, both scholar and climber accept the servitude. They must know all these dull people, because these dull people are in the game that they are playing. Thus, one result of scholars and scholarship is to interpose a phalanx of inferior minds between the young intelligence and the great wits

of the past. Must the novice read those forty pages of Willamo-witz-Mollendorff which cover each dialogue of Plato like the grease on a Strasbourg paté? . . . Accurate scholarship, when it prevails, is the epilogue to literature.

It is easy to see why Chapman was not taken up by the profes-sionals—whether academic pundits or established critics. And in their understandable resentment against a man who breaks up their game and says that literature is an elemental fact rather than a genteel livelihood, they did not bother to find out what he was after. Too many of the attacks on scholarship and professionalism are a device for hiding imperfect knowledge or catching the ear of the groundlings—not worth scrutiny. It is time saved to dismiss the plaintiff.

What then was Chapman's intent throughout the variety of sub-jects and causes that he espoused? If he was a Critic, why is he not as much a parasite on genius as those he attacked? What did he criticize that puts him in a special category? Quite simply, it was the mind of America. Chapman, whose means enabled him to fol-low his unprofitable bent, made cultural criticism his sole vocation and he suffered the penalty. For it is obvious that the Republic has no use for critics of his sort. Partisan objectors, yes, since they satisfy party feelings. But a Socrates, no. Not only does such a man annoy, without furnishing a reasonable ulterior motive, but he is usually hard to interpret. What, for example, is Chapman's book on Garri-son? How do we classify it? Longer than an essay, it is not a biography, for it pays no heed to proportion or chronology; and though based on much reading and reflection, it does not exhibit that sashaying among monographs which we readily take as a guaranty of soundness.

American historians now treasure Chapman's *Garrison,* which is hard to come by, but its author made not the slightest attempt to have his readers either like it or approve it. Pretense of any kind was foreign to him, and he felt no shame in writing to his wife, about his projected *John Brown,* "You know I've never known the literature of the subjects I wrote on. I never knew the Emerson literature—except Emerson himself." But Chapman went to Har-pers Ferry, staying at the Hillton House, and noting that "the coffee is made of peanuts, but the eggs are very good." The remark is a clue to Chapman's criticism, as it is to that of all great critics, from Dryden and Hazlitt to Nietzsche and Shaw: their work is autobiography enlarged; their opinions are not gathered but felt; their truth is not a work of ratiocination but a secretion from experience. Chapman belongs to that company by his dedication and depth, and despite the fact that he was an American working on the native mind.

If we accept Tocqueville's conclusion that in their intellectual deportment democracies are heavy, stern, and pedantic, then we may expect Chapman's fame to increase slowly. Present-day readers who might want to like him because he is very much what they profess to admire—an individualist, a dissenter, an enemy to business mores as to all "other-directed" behavior—will have a hard time swallowing his aristocratic levity and Romantic passion. They will be alienated by his violence, not seeing that in being upset by what they rightly call aberrations, their judgment of the man is unbalanced in just the degree to which aberration upsets the balance in him. Having the gift of passion, Chapman necessarily erred more than once in his expression of it, especially in private life. But anyone who pretends to superior critical poise must show it by concentrating on a writer's *perfect* expressions of passion (as we do in a poet), and by taking in stride such things as onslaughts in letters that have come to light only because their writer had other claims to our regard. In other words, biography should be the servant, not the arbiter, of artistic judgment.

The reader may like to test his own feelings in this matter by glancing at passages from two letters of Chapman's to Dr. Drury, headmaster of St. Paul's School, the second illustrating Chapman's saving self-consciousness:

> Do you really think that if I *had* any ideas on the parent and child question I'd waste them on you? But just now I am taking a loaf and trying to forget the whole subject. Is the education of the young the whole of life? I hate the young—I'm worn out with them. They absorb you and suck you dry and are vampires and selfish brutes at best. Give me some good old rumsoaked club men—who *can't* be improved and make no moral claims. . . .
> Your school English is monstrous. I say "your" just to be dis-

agreeable—as one says "your" railways, "your" climate, etc. to foreigners—for I know you can't do anything about it.

One easily measures the distance from such a maladjusted tone and uncooperative epithets to the tone and epithets in favor today. I have in mind not only the public relations man and his "literature," but also the liberal, progressive educator and *his* characteristic prose. The sight of these contrasts brings us face to face with a paradox: intellectually isolated, Chapman inveighed against the genteel tradition which we think we disposed of in the years between *Main Street* and the New Deal; and yet the period of Chapman's clamoring in the desert was the one that produced just such passionate, self-assertive, inner-directed characters as he; whereas the emancipated twenties and thirties have produced chiefly organization men of various grades and compact little groups of habitual dissenters. It is as if an American tradition, begun with Jefferson and Cooper, had ended in Chapman's day with Mencken and himself.

However this may be, of Chapman's descent from this great tradition there can be no doubt; the link is at once spiritual and genealogical. Born in New York in the year after the outbreak of the Civil War, John Jay Chapman numbered Huguenot, Dutch, and English ancestors, including the revolutionary John Jay after whom he was named. The family motto was a form of predestination—*Crescit sub pondere virtus:* "Courage Increases Under a Burden." (Who today dares to have a motto?) Chapman went to Harvard, married into New England's Brahmin class, and shared with them the kind of connection with the intellect of Europe which disappeared with the depression and which has not been restored by Fulbright fellowships. The very phrase "exchange of persons" which describes our "programs" of understanding suggests the difference.

It also suggests in what realm we should look for the main cause of the break in the American tradition. It lies in politics, including the politics of education. Chapman's career is here a symptom. The desire of a young man of wealth and breeding to "do something" about political corruption had nothing uncommon about it in the year 1885. Chapman joined the City Reform Club, founded by Theodore Roosevelt, and gave up a dozen years to maneuvering, addressing crowds, pamphleteering, and quarreling with T. R. The happy result for us is the pair of descriptive and philosophical volumes, *Practical Agitation* and *Causes and Consequences.*

Wishing to remain honest rather than to gain power, Chapman gave up practical agitation and turned to cultural criticism which, when genuine, is always marked (as we can see today in the work of Trilling) by politics. But by the time that Chapman had matured his talent a properly political class of educated readers was disappearing. The application of cultural criticism from Tocqueville to Whitman had been too spasmodic, political power had been too frequently dispersed among successive new classes, to produce a continuing audience for such writings as Chapman's. These writings were "curious," "fascinating," even "amusing," but they could not affect minds that were either indifferent to or scornful of politics.

His thought was too sinewy, too concentrated, and too simple all at once. The cultural critic has to have an audience that knows what to make of his utterances—or else he must exhort them to do this or that in detail, which is not his business and spoils his art. The muckrakers, of course, were highly articulate in this way, but they never achieved a style nor condensed their indignation into a thought. Compare with theirs a gambit in Chapman's best manner: "It is the ambition of the agitator to use the machinery of government to make men more unselfish. Insofar as he succeeds in this, he is creating a living church, the only sort of state church that would be entirely at one with our system, because it would be merely a representation in the formal government of a spirit abroad among the people."

This flies too high if not met halfway by a concrete imagining, and what follows looks like paradox: "Misgovernment in the United States is an incident in the history of commerce. It is part of the triumph of industrial progress." As for the illustration, it is too ironic: "During the year, a very nice point of law arises as to the rights of the railroad to certain valuable land claimed by the town. The city attorney is an able man, and reasonable. In spite of his ability, he manages to state the city's case on an untenable ground. A decision follows in favor of the railroad." Finally, the critic being a man who can look within even when his passions are in play, portrays himself in exactly the ludicrous light in which he appeared to the solid citizen: "After canvassing the whole community, the stranger finds five persons who are willing to work to defeat the district attorney: a young doctor of good education and small practice, a young lawyer who thinks he can make use of the movement by betraying it, a retired anti-slavery preacher, a maiden lady, and a piano tuner."

To a true American this can never be entirely a joke, for as Chapman pointed out: "We have escaped an age of tyrants, because the eyes of the bosses and their masters were fixed on money. They were not ambitious."

The whole history of American intellectual life, as well as of American foreign policy since 1945, is written in that last sentence. We still go to work with money, not with political ambition. And this principle, once discovered, leads Chapman back to his main theme, the American mind: "Mere financial dishonesty is of very little importance in the history of civilization. Who cares whether Caesar stole or Caesar Borgia cheated? Their intellects stayed clear. The real evil that follows in the wake of a commercial dishonesty so general as ours is the intellectual dishonesty it generates. . . . This state of mind does not merely prevent a man having positive opinions. The American is incapable of taking a real interest in anything. The lack of passion in the American—noticeable in his books and in himself—comes from the same habitual mental distraction; for passion is concentration. . . . When a man takes a living interest in anything, we call him a 'crank.' There is an element of self-sacrifice in any honest intellectual work which we detect at once and score with contumely."

What Chapman was pointing to was not a native lack but a defect of nurture. The clear-eyed men of passion kept being born in this country as elsewhere, but they found no echoes; they spoke as if to a soundproofed generation. Emerson had long since made the same complaint: "To be great is to be misunderstood. . . . The virtue in most request is conformity. Self-reliance is its aversion. It loves not realities and creators, but names and customs." Whitman, too, for all his commitment to the democratic spirit, had warned of a "certain highly deceptive popular intellectuality" which is "an almost complete failure in its social aspects and aesthetic results." In Henry Adams the same insight turned civic passion into a toxic vinegar—to such a degree that we find Chapman relishing *The*

*Education* but also excoriating it as "an odious book . . . by an egoist who conceives himself to be an intellectual." How can the cultural critic afford to reject his culture—his material—in toto?

Having recognized the futility of shouting at men who refuse power because they are either frightened of it or more interested in money, Chapman—like his predecessors since Jefferson—turns to education, the source of present evil and of potential good in the national life. They all pray in aid teachers, scholars, and true universities. But they have in mind much more than the improvement of the curriculum and the "requirements." Chapman's intent was not in fact to reform education, but to make it work—for the first time on this continent—in the hope of giving it a national utility.

The first step was to break the popular association of intellect with programs and institutions, the bad habit of looking upon learning as properly quarantined in the schools. To this end Chapman worked in a manner that knew no limits of occasion or seemliness. From the epistolary rockets he discharged at the headmasters of his boys' schools to the vivid expositions of the intangible in *Learning and Other Essays,* he kept his eye on what might be in place of what was. A striking example of his farsightedness occurs in his severe but just portrait of President Eliot of Harvard, with its account of the "social idea" in education:

> This idea was vigorously carried out by the authorities . . . when they made the discovery that something was wrong at Harvard, that nobody loved anybody there, and that the thing to do was to give weekly teas at Brook's Hall, to ask everyone, to get ladies from Boston, bishops from anywhere, social people at any cost, social talent to bridge the gulf between instructors and instructed. Nobly they labored. It was shoulder-to-shoulder, never say die, love one love all, more tea, more ladies.

But President Eliot, then universally revered, "was the spiritual father of the glacial era theretofore in progress. . . . I have sometimes stopped to shake hands with him because I thought it was right—and also, I confess, because I thought it would cause him pain. Such is the silliness of the undergraduate mind. The trustees, the ladies, bishops and steerers of Harvard, having received new warmth themselves . . . got at President Eliot and thawed him out. . . . [He] responded to the treatment; he glowed, he beamed. He really did have a warm place in him and they moved this round in front where people could feel it; and by Jove, the new Legend was launched."

Under the mask of frivolous anecdote lies Chapman's thesis that intellect can be a social force. Chapman was one of the first critics of false specialization through the elective system, and one of the first advocates of general education. As things stood he saw no meaningful relation between the university and the *literacy* of the country it was supposedly serving. On the one hand were the few boys who are born with an insatiable desire for true culture, and on the other, the rest who "come up to college with broken sets of rudimentary reminiscence, and without knowing what they want or how to get it." Neither group received anything but mechanical attention; it was a travesty of learning (as it still is) to "set a man to making original researches in anthropology and Hindu metaphysics when he has had no experience of life and only a classroom knowledge of books."

4.

We should linger on that last phrase lest it be confused with the vulgar contrast of book knowledge with experience: Chapman refers to "a classroom knowledge *of books*" and calls for an experienced knowledge *of books*. The liberalization of the university since Chapman's day has broken down barriers until everyone proclaims that book knowledge must be applied to life. Government and industry are now filled with academic experts, and by imitation everyone babbles the language of scholarship. But hearing that language one may wonder whether its acceptance in the market place is not a Pyrrhic victory for learning. For it may well be that it is only a classroom knowledge of books that is being transferred to the already abstract and woolly operations of the business and the governmental minds. What is still needed, as it was when Chapman wrote, is the worldly knowledge of books, that ready application of intellect to society and of experience to written thought, which Chapman shows in all his studies: the market place re-entering the word and being transfigured by it.

In this view the contents of books are a necessity, not for relaxation (neurotic idea!), not for the cultivation of the genteel virtues, and even less for the acquiring of "valuable information," but for the extension of the sense of life, and especially the sense of the scale of life. In the superb piece on Balzac, Chapman shows how it happens that in the writings of the masters art and life are continuous, and consequently how a piece of art becomes, for the fit reader, a piece of life added to his personal stock. "The internal world of his fiction is the real world for Balzac, and he contrives to make it the real world for his readers . . . one sees it rather than reads of it; one experiences it rather than sees it. . . . Even when he bores us he interests us. There is a residuum in his thought."

To Chapman, art of this sort was a secret, a mystery. "We cannot hope to know what it is." Perhaps he should have had an inkling, for his own work partakes of this art, in essence and in expression. His thought finds images without poeticizing and leaps logical chasms surefootedly. Occasionally choppy for fear of academicism ("gamboge and style, with its however's and moreover's and semi-colons"), he seldom deviates from *his* style, which is that of perfect informality and vehement lucidity.

But the mystery of art, which is the mystery of spirit, throws into relief the tragedy of intellect, which is to discover that its clarity and its power can never work in harness. What intellect achieves is not what it intended and this failure, which it understands, it cannot control. Chapman perceived the fated gap when he said of a political decline: "like all organic change, it was unconscious." The idea of the unconscious is indeed almost as frequent in his writings as the image of fire, and this triangle—intellect, violence, and the power of the unconscious—marks the boundaries of his thought.

His being torn among these opposing forces is not to be wondered at. It results from the profound effect of the Civil War and Reconstruction upon his mind, and it may even represent an unchanging condition of cultural criticism in America. Here certainly the impulse to violence has been matched by the faith in education, which is at once a blurred version of the joy in intellect and a recognition of the desirability of unconscious change. What Chapman rightly finds unique in Garrison is that he combined a violent passion for pure doctrine with the arts of a moderator and the selflessness of a saint. Garrison prepared a revolution and he did it like a Lenin, but without a Red Army.

That the second American revolution ended in blood was not Garrison's choice, nor is it Chapman's when he summons us to the third revolution which shall free us from the tyranny of Business Behavior. The courage for a new mind, which he wants to create in us, calls for the difficult linking of Intellect with Unconscious, instead of with violence as mankind in extremity prefers. He would have us exert violence within, forcing old habits into the light, killing them off by intent, and forming new ones deliberately until they sink again into unconsciousness as part of our nature.

It is to inspire this upheaval that Chapman depicts, attacks, ridicules, and apologizes for his contemporaries. He knows, of course, that his words cannot be a sufficient cause of change, just as he knows that better educational methods will not remake American culture. He can only hope to say what "some day will be thought of." There is no other way for intellect to exert its undeniable power; but to be effective in time that power, like any other, requires quantity and concentration. And on this point, surely, we are still Chapman's contemporaries. Education, books, ideas, the courage of intellect have not kept pace with our need for them.

One sign of this is that we have not yet withdrawn Chapman from the shades. Another is that we have renamed rather than destroyed the cultural evils he fought with. A third is that we have allowed the divorce of education from intellect to become almost final. The pedantry against which Chapman warned is general while strength of mind is rare. It is not enough that we decry Conformity in the abstract. True intellect is always concrete and practical, using abstraction merely as a shorthand to define feeling and conduct. But to do this the creator of forms must find receivers. The coexistence of maker and taker is what constitutes a culture in the honorific sense, what approximates the symbol of a national mind.

In such a culture, as part of such a mind, the Chapmans could develop their gifts more harmoniously, and communicate them by a swifter contagion; though solitary in their study, they would find friends and adversaries close at hand to give resonance to their words; and if this did not—as it could not—prevent social crimes and moral catastrophes, it might at least insure that at critical moments there would be found more than one man in the nation to go to Coatesville.

*1947–1957*

## Bibliographical Note

I. The selections in the present volume were published in or as books by John Jay Chapman under the following titles and dates:

*William Lloyd Garrison,* Moffat, Yard and Company, New York, 1913; Second Revised Edition, Atlantic Monthly Press, Boston, 1921.

"Emerson" and "Walt Whitman," in *Emerson and Other Essays,* Scribners, New York, 1898; Second Edition, Moffat, Yard and Company, New York, 1909.

"William James," "Mr. Brimmer," "Mrs. Whitman," "President Eliot," and "Julia Ward Howe," in *Memories and Milestones,* Moffat, Yard and Company, New York, 1915.

"Coatesville" and "The Negro Question," in *Memories and Milestones,* Moffat, Yard and Company, New York, 1915.

"Society," in *Causes and Consequences* (opening of Ch. II), Scribners, New York, 1898.

"Shakespeare" in *Greek Genius and Other Essays,* Moffat, Yard and Company, 1915.

II. Other works by Chapman include:

*Learning and Other Essays,* Moffat, Yard and Company, New York, 1910.

*A Glance Toward Shakespeare,* Atlantic Monthly Press, Boston, 1922.

*Letters and Religion,* Atlantic Monthly Press, Boston, 1924.

*Dante,* Houghton Mifflin Company, Boston and New York, 1927.

*Lucian, Plato, and Greek Morals,* Houghton Mifflin Company, Boston and New York, 1931.

*New Horizons in American Life,* Columbia University Press, New York, 1932.

III. About Chapman:

Bernstein, Melvin, "John Jay Chapman and the Insurgent Individual," in *American Radicals: Some Problems and Personalities,* Monthly Review Press, New York, 1957.

Hovey, Richard B., *John Jay Chapman: the Early Years;* unpublished doctoral dissertation, Harvard University, Cambridge, 1950.

Howe, M. A. De Wolfe, *John Jay Chapman and His Letters,* Houghton Mifflin Company, Boston and New York, 1937.

Wilson, Edmund, "John Jay Chapman," in *The Triple Thinkers,* Harcourt, Brace and Company, New York, 1938.

Wister, Owen, *Two Appreciations;* privately printed, The Marchbanks Press, New York, 1934.

# Contents

# PART THREE

# PART FOUR

# PART ONE

PART ONE

# William Lloyd Garrison

## PREFACE FOR THE SECOND EDITION [1921]

I ONCE KNEW A MAN who wrote a brilliant biography of Abraham
Lincoln. He himself belonged to the Civil War epoch, and while
writing the book in about the year 1895, he became so absorbed and
excited by that war as he studied it, and lived it over again, that he
could not sleep at night. He paced the room, lost in thought, awed
by his subject. It was a contemporary of this biographer who told
me that, while the Civil War was in progress, the enthusiastic historian had taken no interest in it; it didn't seem to attract his
attention.

This anecdote shows how much easier it is to see a hero in the
past than in the present. The historian is a book-trained man; records and documents speak to him; dead things live again. But he
cannot get his mind into focus upon anything so near as the present.
He is distracted by the present, but supported by the past; for in the
past he is not alone. As he studies it, the whole literature of his
chosen period holds up his hands: hundreds of minds rush to his
aid, while all religion and philosophy stand at his elbow.

It is easy to explain why Garrison has never been adopted as a
popular hero in America. He gave a purge to his countrymen, and
the bitter taste of it remained in our mouths ever after. Moreover,
the odium of Slavery, which he branded on America's brow, seemed
to survive in the very name of Garrison, and we would willingly
have forgotten the man. After the Civil War there was not, appar-

ently, time for our scholars to think about him. Certain it is that the educated American has known little about him, and shies and mutters at his name. And yet equally certain is it that the history of the United States between 1800 and 1860 will some day be rewritten with this man as its central figure.

How soon will that day come, and what will be the signs of its dawning? The laws of mind and nature are not likely to be reversed to save the feelings and prejudices of the American people, a people who are not given to historic speculation and who have been mentally enfeebled by success. It is not for Garrison that I am concerned, but for a people that praises the prophets, builds altars to courage, enshrines the idea of the Individual Soul; but a people, it would seem, who cannot see a real man when he appears, because he makes them uncomfortable. Garrison made his compatriots uncomfortable; even to read about him made them uncomfortable but yesterday.

In reprinting this little book, the thought crosses my mind that perhaps the shock and anguish of the Great War, which so humanized our nation, may have left us with a keener, more religious, and more dramatic understanding of our Anti-slavery period than we possessed prior to 1914. Certainly when this book appeared in 1913, the average American seemed to hear the name of Garrison with distaste, and to regard a book about him as superfluous. While I was writing it, one of my best friends, and a very learned gentleman, said to me, "A book about William Lloyd Garrison? Heave a brick at him for me!"—and the popular feeling in America of that day seemed to support the remark. But the times have changed. The flames of the Great War have passed through us. The successive shocks of that experience struck upon our people till we resounded in unison like a great bell; and there is not a soul among us that has not been shaken to its depths.

The heroic echoes of the terrible struggle have died away and left all the nations dizzy and defocalized, worn out by effort and emotion, and, apparently, more cynical and bent on petty aims than they were before the ordeal. But this tidal revulsion is in the way of Nature. She acts by waves and inundations, by recessions, mudflats, and desolation. It appears just now as if all the tin cans and dead dogs of humanity were exposed to view. Nevertheless, the tides will surge in once more. The devastated regions will be reclaimed and reanimated—in spots, of course, and irregularly as is Nature's wont. The great, heroic impulse of that war is not really lost. It lies invisibly planted in our hearts, and especially in the hearts of the younger generation, who will never know from how many old shibboleths and cramping views they have been liberated by having taken part in something that was universal. Our own past will assume fresh aspects in our eyes. Americans will come to see their own history in a more normal perspective than they did formerly. The fog of self-consciousness that has hung above our Anti-slavery period will be dissipated in the minds of our historians, and we shall see Garrison as one of our greatest heroes—a man born to a task as large as his country's destiny, who turned the tide of his age, and left an imprint of his mind and character upon us, as certain and as visible as the imprint left upon us by Washington himself.

J. J. C.

## I. INTRODUCTION

THE PERIODS of history that are most interesting are those which have been lighted up by spiritual bonfires. As we read about such epochs we seem to feel the fires rekindling in our bosoms. Through the identity of those historic flames with our own, we become aware of our portion in the past, and of our mission in the present. The names of the actors, to be sure, are changed; the names of the forces at work vary continually. Yet the substance of the story is ever the same; the fable deals with ourselves. And therefore that fable stirs the intimate embers in us. Here, within us, are those smothered and banked furnaces which the stride of History has left behind it—the only now living part, the only real part and absolute remnant of the divine pageant.

There are some periods of great conflagration where a whole epoch is lighted up with one great flame of idea, which takes perhaps a few decades to arise, blaze, and fall; during which time it shows all men in its glare. Willy-nilly they can be and are seen by this light and by no other. Willy-nilly their chief interest for the future lies in their relation to this idea. In spite of themselves they are thrilling, illustrative figures, seen in lurid and logical distortion, —abstracts and epitomes of human life. Nay, they stand forever as creatures that have been caught and held, cracked open, thrown living upon a screen, burned alive perhaps by a searching and terrible bonfire and recorded in the act—as the citizens of Pompeii were recorded by the eruption of Mount Vesuvius.

It happened that a period of this kind passed over the United States between the years 1830 and 1865. There is nothing to be found in that epoch which does not draw its significance, its interest, its permanent power from the slavery question. There is no man whose life falls within that epoch whose character was not controlled by that question, or whose portrait can be seen by any other light than the light of that fire. Subtract that light and you have darkness; you cannot see the man at all. In the biographies of certain distinguished conservatives of that time you may often observe the softening of the portrait by the omission of unpleasant records, the omission by the biographers of those test judgments and test ordeals with which the times were well supplied. By these omissions the man vanishes from the page of his own book. The page grows suddenly blank. You check yourself and wonder who it was that you were reading about. Now the reason of this disappearance of the leading character from your mind is that the biographer has drawn someone who *could* not have existed. The man must have answered aye or nay to the question which the times were putting. And, in fact, he did so answer. By this answer he could have been seen. Without it he does not exist.

I confess that I had rather stand out for posterity in a hideous silhouette, as having been wrong on every question of my time, than be erased into a cipher by my biographer. But biographers do not feel in this way toward their heroes. Each one feels that he has undertaken to do his best by his patron. Therefore they stand the man under a north light in a photographer's attic, suggest his attitude, and thus take the picture;—whereas, in real life, the man was standing on the balcony of a burning building which the next moment collapsed, and in it he was crushed beyond the semblance of humanity. The Civil War,—that war with its years of interminable length, its battles of such successive and monstrous carnage, its dragged-out reiterations of horror and agony, and its even worse tortures of hope deferred,—hope all but extinct,—that war of which it is impossible to read even a summary without becoming so worn out by distress that you forget everything that went before in the country's history and emerge, as it were, a new man at the close of your perusal;—that war was no accident. It was involved in every syllable which every inhabitant of America uttered or neglected to utter in regard to the slavery question between 1830 and 1860. The gathering and coming on of that war, its vaporous distillation from the breath of every man, its slow, inevitable formation in the sky, its retreats and apparent dispersals, its renewed visibilities—all of them governed by some inscrutable logic—and its final descent in lightning and deluge;—these matters make the history of the interval between 1830 and 1865. That history is all one galvanic throb, one course of human passion, one Nemesis, one deliverance. And with the assassination of Lincoln in 1865 there falls from on high the great, unifying stroke that leaves the tragedy sublime. No poet ever invented such a scheme of curse, so all-involving, so remotely rising in an obscure past and holding an entire nation in its mysterious bondage—a scheme based on natural law, led forward and unfolded from mood to mood, from climax to climax, and plunging at the close into the depths of a fathomless pity. The action of the drama is upon such a scale that a quarter of the earth has to be devoted to it. Yet the argument is so trite that it will hardly bear statement. Perhaps the true way to view the whole matter is to regard it as the throwing off by healthy morality of a little piece of left-over wickedness—that bad heritage of antiquity, domestic slavery. The logical and awful steps by which the process went forward merely exhibit familiar, moral, and poetic truth. What else could they exhibit?

We are ungrateful to the intellects of the past; or rather, like children we take it for granted that somebody must supply us with our supper and our ideas; and, for the most part, it is difficult to discover the extent of our indebtedness, whether, for example, to Charlemagne or to the scholars who have revealed him. Yet everything we know and live by is due to the mind of someone in the past: its formulation, at any rate, was the act of a man.

These same illuminations of history that we have been speaking of were due to the enlightenment of individual minds. Our Revolution of 1776 was made interesting by its state papers, and to-day our knowledge of that time is a knowledge of the minds of Washington, Franklin, and the other patriots. Now the light by which we to-day see the Anti-slavery period was first shed on it by one man—William Lloyd Garrison. That slavery was wrong, everyone knew in his heart. The point seen by Garrison was the practical point that the slavery issue was the only thing worth thinking about, and that all else must be postponed till slavery was abolished. He saw this by a God-given act of vision in 1829; and it was true. The history of the spread of this idea of Garrison's is the history of the United States during the thirty years after it loomed in his mind. From the day Garrison established the *Liberator* he was the strongest man in America. He was affected in his thought by no one. What he was thinking, all men were destined to think. How had he found that clew and skeleton-key to his age, which put him in possession of such terrible power? What he hurled in the air went everywhere and smote all men. Tide and tempest served him. His power of arousing uncontrollable disgust was a gift, like magic; and he seems to sail upon it as a demon upon the wind. Not Andrew Jackson, nor John Quincy Adams, nor Webster, nor Clay, nor Benton, nor Calhoun,—who dance like shadows about his machine,—but William Lloyd Garrison becomes the central figure in American life.

If one could see a mystical presentation of the epoch, one would see Garrison as a Titan, turning a giant grindstone or electrical power-wheel, from which radiated vibrations in larger and in ever larger, more communicative circles and spheres of agitation, till there was not a man, woman, or child in America who was not a-tremble.

We know, of course, that the source of these radiations was not in Garrison. They came from the infinite and passed out into the infinite. Had there been no Garrison they would somehow have arrived and at some time would have prevailed. But historically speaking they did actually pass through Garrison: he vitalized and permanently changed this nation as much as one man ever did the same for any nation in the history of the world.

## II. THE BACKGROUND

LET US CONSIDER the first fifty years of our national history. There was never a moment during this time when the slavery issue was not a sleeping serpent. That issue lay coiled up under the table during the deliberations of the Constitutional Convention in 1787.

It was, owing to the invention of the cotton gin, more than half awake at the time of the Louisiana Purchase in 1803; and slavery was continued in the Louisiana Territory by the terms of the treaty. Thereafter slavery was always in everyone's *mind,* though not always on his tongue. A slave state and a free state were, as a matter of practice, always admitted in pairs. Thus, Vermont and Kentucky, Tennessee and Ohio, Louisiana and Indiana, Mississippi and Illinois, had each been offset against the other. This was to preserve the balance of power. The whole country, however, was in a state of unstable equilibrium and the era of good feeling oscillated upon the top of a craggy peak.

At last, in 1818-20, came two years of fierce, open struggle over slavery in the admission of Missouri, which state was formed from part of the Louisiana Purchase. Southern threats of disunion clashed with Northern taunts of defiance in the House of Representatives. In the outcome, the Missouri Compromise admitted Missouri *with slavery;* and prohibited slavery in that part of the Louisiana Purchase which lay north of the latitude of 36° 30', except in the portion included in Missouri. This compromise became, in the public mind, as sacred as the Constitution itself; so that when, in 1854, the Compromise was repealed, the whole North felt that the bottom had dropped out of their government. The North believed itself to be betrayed. The savage feeling which led up to war developed rapidly at the North after this time. The war came as the final outcome of a great malady. But we must return to 1820.

During the decade that followed the Missouri Compromise everyone in America fell sick. It was not a sickness that kept men in bed. They went about their business—the lawyer to court, the lady to pay calls, the merchant to his wharf. The amusements, and the religious, literary, and educational occupations of mankind went forward as usual. But they all went forward under the gradually descending fringe of a mist, an unwholesome-feeling cloud of oppression. No one could say why it was that his food did not nourish him quite as it used to do, nor his unspoken philosophy of life any longer cover the needs of his nature. This was especially strange, because everybody ought to have been perfectly happy. Had not the country emerged from the War of the Revolution in the shape of a new and glorious Birth of Time—a sample to all mankind? Had it not survived the dangers of the second war with

Great Britain? And what then remained for us except to go forward victoriously and become a splendid, successful, vigorous, and benevolent people? Everything was settled that concerned the stability of our form of government. The future could surely contain nothing except joyous progress.

The Americans of 1820–30 expounded the glorious nature of their own destiny. They challenged the casual visitor to deny it; and became quite noted for their insistence upon this claim, and for their determination to secure the acknowledgement of it by all men.

At the bottom of this nervous concern there was not, as is generally supposed, merely the bumptious pride and ignorance of a new nation. There was something more complex and more honorable; there was an inner knowledge that none of these things were true. This knowledge was forced upon our fathers by their familiarity with their own political literature and with the Declaration of Independence in particular. There was a chasm between the agreeable statement that all men are created free and equal, and the horrible fact of human slavery. The thought of this incongruity troubled every American. No recondite or difficult reasoning was required to produce the mental anguish that now began to oppress America. The only thing necessary was leisure for anguish, and this leisure first became possible at the close of the second war with Great Britain. The operation of the thought was almost entirely unconscious, and its issue in pain almost entirely unexpressed.

The articulate classes had not talked much about slavery since the days of the constitutional compromises, and it is the aged Jefferson who writes from Monticello apropos of the Missouri Compromise—"This momentous question, like a fire-bell in the night, awakened and filled me with terror. I considered it at once the knell of the Union."

Now there never was a moment in the history of the country when this fire-bell was quite silent. The educational policy of the articulate classes of society during the first fifty years of the Nation's life had been to hush the bell.

Ever since the Southern members in the Constitutional Convention had showed their teeth, and threatened to withdraw if slavery were disturbed, a policy of silence had been adopted. The questions covered by the Constitution were to be regarded as conclusively settled. The bandages must never be taken off them. Any person who reviews the history of the American Revolution can sympathize with this timidity; for it seems like a miracle that the Colonies should ever come together—so antagonistic were their interests, and their ideals. The Colonists feared some new breach, and there ensued a non-intellectual determination that certain questions should not be re-examined: this determination gradually grew into our great stupefying dogma which says to the private citizen, "This is our way of doing things: you-be-damned: intellect has nothing to do with the matter: it is American." This dogma, which arose out of the needs of our early days, has become the most widespread form of metaphysical faith among us. No doubt all nations harbor similar prejudices as to their own institutions; but the nations of Europe have been jostled into liberalism by their contiguity one with another; and the jostling is now being extended to us. During our early history, however, we were isolated, and our intellectual classes took their American history a little too seriously. The state of mind of our statesmen and scholars in that epoch is well summed up in Webster's reply to Hayne. That speech closes an epoch. It is the great paving-stone of conclusive demonstration, placed upon the mouth of a natural spring.

All this while something had been left out in all the nation's political and social philosophy—something which policy forbade men to search for, and this something was beginning to move in the pit of the stomach of Americans, and to make them feel exceedingly and vaguely ill. In order to bind the Colonies into a more lasting union, a certain suppression of truth, a certain trampling upon instinct had been resorted to in the Constitution. All the parties to that instrument thoroughly understood the iniquity of slavery and deplored it. All the parties were ashamed of slavery and yet felt obliged to perpetuate it. They wrapped up a twenty years' protection of the African slave trade in a colorless phrase.

"The migration or importation of such persons as any of the states now existing shall think proper to admit, shall not be prohibited by the Congress prior to the year one thousand eight hundred and eight, but a tax or duty may be imposed on such importations, not exceeding ten dollars for each person."

Now the slave trade meant the purchase upon African coasts of Negroes and Negresses, their branding, herding, manacling, and transportation between decks across tropical seas. The African slave trade is probably the most brutal organized crime in history. Our fathers did not dare to name it. So of the fugitive-slave law;—the Constitution deals with it in the cruel, quiet way in which monstrous tyranny deals with the fictions of administrative law. "No person held to service or labor in one state under the laws thereof, escaping into another, shall, in consequence of any law or regulation therein, be discharged from such service or labor; but shall be delivered up on claim of the party to whom such service or labor may be due."

In an age in which the Inquisition is absolutely dominant, its officials are almost kind. The leaden touch of hypocrisy was thus in the heart of our Constitution. Cold-heartedness radiated from the Ark of our Covenant. We condone this because we know that many of these fathers really did believe that slavery was probably going to diminish and die out in the country. Even while protecting it they hoped for the best, and knew not what they did. But as slavery became more important instead of less important, and as the cruelty of it became more visible, the bond of the document pressed upon the conscience of the people. We had undertaken more than we could perform. The suppression of truth, the trampling upon instinct, which we had accepted as a duty, was stifling us. For the first fifty years of our national life no reaction was visible. And then there ensued a fermentation, a tumult in the heart which nothing could quell. This tumult began long before it showed itself. Its dialectic and logic were developed and ready for use, like the wings of the locust in the shell. The natures of men were beginning to heave and to swell—and at last, when Garrison speaks out, behold, he is in electrical communication with an age over-charged with passion. His thought is understood immediately. Every implication, every consequence, every remote contingency has been anticipated in the public consciousness, and there ensues explosion after explosion: crash generates crash: storm-routes of continuous passion plow the heavens across the continent from sea to sea. In truth our whole civilization, our social life, our religious feelings, our political ideas, had all become accommodated to cruelty, representative of tyranny. The gigantic backbone of business-interest was a slavery backbone. We were a slave republic. For a generation, may, for two hundred years, we had tolerated slavery; and for a generation it had been a sacred thing—a man must suppress his feelings in speaking of it.

Now there is nothing more injurious to the character and to the intellect than the suppression of generous emotion. It means death: —sickness to the individual, blight to the race. Compassion shining through the heart wears the very name and face of Divine Life. It makes the limbs strong and the mind capable; it strengthens the stomach and supports the intestines. Cramp this emotion, and you will have a half-dead man, whose children will be less well-nourished than himself.

It is hard to imagine the falsetto condition of life in the Northern States in 1829;—the lack of spontaneity and naturalness about everybody, so far as externals went, and the presence of extreme solicitude in the bottom of everybody's heart. Emerson speaks in his journal (1834) of the fine manners of the young Southerners, brought up amidst slavery, and of the deference which Northerners, both old and young, habitually paid to the people of the South. It seems to have been regarded as a social duty at the North to shield the feelings of the Southerners, and, as it were, to apologize for not owning slaves. The feelings of the Northern philanthropist, however, were never regarded with delicacy. On the contrary it was thought to be his duty to suppress his feelings. Any exhibition of humane sentiment where slavery was concerned—and it was always concerned—was punished immediately. The most natural impulses, the most simple acts of human piety could be indulged in only through an initiation of fierce pain, generally followed by social ostracism. The right to draw one's breath involved a struggle with Apollyon.

"Only a few days before one of our meetings," writes Henry I. Bowditch, one of Garrison's early recruits from the social world of Boston, "a young lady had hoped that I 'would never become an Abolitionist,' and about the same time Frederick Douglass appeared as a runaway slave. He was at the meeting in Marlboro' Chapel. Of course I was introduced to him, and, as I would have invited a white friend, I asked him home to dine with me in my small abode in Bedford Street. It is useless to deny that I did not like the thought of walking with him in open midday up Washington Street. I *hoped* I would not meet any of my acquaintances. I had, however, hardly turned into the street before I met the young lady who had expressed her wish as above stated. I am glad now to say that I *did not skulk*. I looked at her straight and bowed in 'my most gracious manner' as if I were 'all right,' while I saw by her look of regret that she thought me 'all wrong.' It was, however, something like a cold sponge-bath,—that Washington Street walk by the side of a black man,—rather terrible at the outset, but wonderfully warming and refreshing afterwards! I had literally jumped 'in medias res.' But I did not hear until years afterwards, and a long time after Douglass had held office in Washington under Federal Government, and the slavery of his own race had been washed out in blood, what I was doing for him at the moment that as a friend I asked him to walk home with me to dinner. How little do we appreciate acts that seem trivial or something worse to us, but which to others, affected by such acts, are of indispensable importance! Beautiful to me seems now the act, inasmuch as it helped to raise a poor, down-trodden soul into a proper self-appreciation. And how much I thank God that He led me by giving me a love of freedom, and something like a conscience to act as I did then." *

The strain of that walk upon Bowditch is felt forty years later in his account of it. The profound political instinct which led him to take the walk is as noticeable as the religious nature of his impulse. It is wonderful to reflect how little the significance of the act could have been understood by any casual observer of the scene. Here is a man who turns down one street rather than another, upon meeting an acquaintance. He looks like a gentleman doing an act of politeness; while he is, in fact, a saint going through the fire for his faith, and a hero saving the republic. So banal are externals, so deep is reality. But our present interest in the incident lies in this— that it measures the separation of Massachusetts from the ordinary standards of Europe. Frederick Douglass was almost a man of genius and he *looked* like a man of genius. His photograph at the time of his escape from slavery might be the photograph of a musician or a painter. He was the kind of man who, in a Paris or London salon, would excite anyone's passing notice, as perhaps a South American diplomat or artist.

---

* Many years afterwards, when an assemblage of anti-slavery veterans and hosts of young colored men were honoring Frederick Douglass in a public hall in Boston, he alluded to this incident with the remarks, "Dr. Bowditch I greet joyfully here, for he first treated me *as if I were a man*."

An intelligent foreign observer might have told Bowditch that the sufferings which both Bowditch and Douglass were enduring betrayed the fact that a social revolution was under way. They were the sign of an approaching homogeneity. This universal disturbance, this universal throe is the first thing that all the people of the United States ever experienced together. Their former unions had been political and external: this was spiritual and internal.

We are familiar with the Northern form of the uneasiness, because the Northerner could speak. He cried out; and through his utterance came the cure. But of the pain of the Southerner, to whom all expression of feeling was denied, we know nothing. With the rise of Abolition, perished every vestige of free speech at the South. Events now converged to crush the manhood out of the slave-holding classes. A Southerner could not be gentle, unselfish, quick to speak his thought, or genuinely interested in anything. His opinions were prepared for him before he was born; and they were light-killing illusions—the precursors of mania. The enactment of very stringent and inhuman slave codes, and the prohibition of all education to the slaves followed in the wake of the Abolition outbreaks. The maturing of a sort of philosophy of slavery, according to which slavery was seen as the cornerstone of religion and progress, was the work of the following decade, and the task of Calhoun. The corollaries to this philososphy which involved an abandonment of popular education, and the cutting-off of the South from every intellectual contact with the civilization of Europe, were duly worked out during the next thirty years. By the time the war came there existed a sort of Religion of Slavedom. The Pro-slavery Northern Democrats of Buchanan's time held opinions which would have shocked the most pronounced slaveholders of 1820.

During all this time Virginia and the Carolinas—which constituted the Holy Land of the Slave Dispensation—endured a silent exodus and migration on the part of the more liberal spirits. Men even went to New Orleans to escape the tyranny of slave opinion at Charleston. Thus were the souls of Americans squeezed and their tempers made acid. A slightly *too ready responsiveness* to stimulus of any kind came to be the mark of the American, whether at the North or at the South; the difference being that the too ready response at the South was apt to be an insult, at the North an apology.

This hair-trigger nervousness on the part of everybody was the result of poison in the system. What could the manly Southern youth do? Leave all and follow Abolition? He knew of Abolition only that it was a villainous attack on his father's character and property. He was in the grip of a relentless, moving hurricane of distorted views, false feelings, erroneous philosophy; and he knew nothing clearly, understood nothing clearly, until he perished upon the battlefields of the Civil War, fighting like a hero.

It is impossible in describing the course of the Slave Power between 1832–65 to avoid harsh language. If ever wickedness came upward in the counsels of men, it did so here. Yet there are elements in all these matters which elude our analysis. The virtues glimmer and seem to go out; but they are never really extinguished. How much idealism, how much latent heroism must have existed in the South during all these years before the war, was seen when the war came. Villains do not choose for themselves Commanders like Robert E. Lee and Stonewall Jackson. It is lost, that old society, and it died almost speechless—died justly and inevitably. Yet we do well to remember with what a flame of sacrifice it perished, to remember with what force, what devotion, what heroism, Humanity showed herself to be still adorned in that hour of an all-devouring atonement.

The great fever came to an end with Appomattox. The delirium stopped: the plague had been expelled. The nation was not dead: the nation was at the beginning of a long convalescence. It is, however, about the earlier symptoms of the disorder that I would speak here, about the presentiments of headache and nausea, and about that dreadfullest moment in all sickness (as it seems to me), the moment when we admit that something serious is coming on.

The struggle between the North and the South began over free speech about the Negro, and especially about the right of benevolent people at the North to extend their benevolence to the Negro, as, for instance, in their schools, Sunday-schools, hospitals, etc. Now the South sincerely believed that the Missouri Compromise of 1820 had morally bound the North not to talk about slavery in private conversation, and not to treat the Negro as a human being. The

South had succeeded in imposing this conviction upon the whole North.

"The patriotism of all classes," wrote Edward Everett, Governor of Massachusetts, in a message to his Legislature, "the patriotism of all classes must be invoked to abstain from discussion, which by exasperating the master, can have no other effect than to render more oppressive the condition of the slave."

This paralysis of dumbness and of fear touched everyone. It was not exactly fear, either, but a sort of subtle freemasonry, a secret belief that nothing must be disturbed. The Southerners lived in sincere terror of slave uprisings—and they managed to convey a mysterious tremor to the North upon the subject.

Dr. Channing was that age's figure-head. He was the most eminent man in the country; the moral sciences were his province. He was, therefore, constantly appealed to by all persons and parties upon the slavery question. His responses and his conduct upon such occasions give the best key to that age which we have; and his character will be discussed as long as posterity takes an interest in the epoch. This must be my excuse for recurring to Dr. Channing from time to time and for using him, at this point, to illustrate the flatness and tameness of good men in that age; yes, to illustrate the spiritual domination of evil at the time when Garrison began his crusade. The drawing-rooms of our grandfathers' times contained automata; ghosts clustered about the dinner tables. The people had forgotten what the sound of a mans' voice was like. That is why they were so startled by Garrison.

Even Channing, who was a true saint, and, when time was given him, a courageous man, is an injured being—like a beautiful plant which has grown to maturity in a dungeon. Under the pressure of his own conscience and of certain hammering Abolitionists who were his friends, he wrote an analysis of slavery, and stood shoulder to shoulder with the Abolitionists on the question of free speech. It is to his everlasting honor that he did this: for he sincerely deplored the methods of the Abolitionists and was incapable of understanding their mission. By his writings on slavery and by his act in standing by the Abolitionists on the question of free speech, Channing became a broken idol to all of the South and to half of his Boston admirers. We must never confound him, as the Abolitionists were prone to do, with the contemporary flock of time-serving parsons. Channing was a man who could, and did, go through the fire for principle. But he was a man lacking in instinct, a sad man, too reasonable to understand this crisis or know how to meet it. He was trampled upon by his congregation, and knew not how to save himself.

Dr. Channing's coldness toward Abolition might be shown by his words to Daniel Webster in 1828, deprecating any agitation of the slavery question; by his studied avoidance of Garrison in social life; by his inability, even in the Essay on Slavery, to see the importance of the Abolition movement;—or in a hundred other ways. On the other hand, Dr. Channing's services to the Anti-slavery cause could be illustrated by this same essay, and by the esteem and love which many leading Anti-slavery people always bore him. Let us, however, go to the bottom of the whole matter.

On January 13th, 1840, Dr. Charles Follen, a German enthusiast and one of the few highly educated men among the Abolitionists, was burned alive in the ill-fated steamer *Lexington,* while on a journey from New York to Boston. Follen was a young doctor of laws and a teacher at the University of Jena, who had been prosecuted for his liberal opinions by the reactionary governments of Prussia and Austria in 1824. He had fled to Switzerland and thence to the United States. His friends in this country secured him a post as lecturer, and afterwards as professor, at Harvard College; which post he lost through expressing his opinions on slavery. He afterwards took a pastorate in the Unitarian Church and lost it through the same cause.

Follen was what Goethe used to call a "Schoene Seele,"—beloved of all. He was an especial friend of Channing's. His tragic death was at the time considered by the Abolitionists as the severest blow which they had yet received. They sought a place to hold a commemorative meeting in his honor, and they applied to Channing for permission to use his church; which Channing accorded. The standing committee of the church, however, cancelled this permission. Channing's biographer speaks as follows:

"Nothing in all his (Channing's) intercourse with his people, nothing in his whole Anti-slavery experience, caused him so much pain as a refusal of the use of the church to the Massachusetts Anti-Slavery Society, on the sad occasion when all true-hearted persons were called to mourn the awful death of Charles Follen, and when the Rev. S. J. May had prepared a discourse in commemoration of the rare virtues of that heroic and honored man. It was not only the insult to the memory of a beloved friend that grieved him —though this could not but shock his quick and delicate feelings; still less was it the disregard, under such touching circumstances, of his well-known wishes, that wounded him most deeply; but this manifestation of a want of high sentiment in the congregation to which, for so many years, he had officiated as pastor, made him question the usefulness of his whole ministry. To what end had he poured out his soul, if such conduct was a practical embodiment of the principles and precepts which he had so earnestly inculcated? This event brought home to his heart the conviction that the need was very urgent of a thorough application of the Christian law of love to all existing social relations."

It is evident to the common mind that Channing should have resigned his post rather than accept this affront from his flock. Nay, Channing should have resigned twenty years earlier, and upon the first occasion when any such subjection of his own impulses was required of him. The anecdote shows the skeleton that lurked in all the vestry rooms of that period. It shows also how partial are the *philosophic* illuminations of men. Dr. Channing disbelieved in the principle of association. It was one of the points in his disapproval of the Anti-slavery people that they worked through associations; for he had a philosophic disbelief in the theory of association. I share this disbelief with Dr. Channing; the miserable squabbles between Anti-slavery associations in which the reformers wasted their force and impaired their tempers, show very clearly the dangers inherent in association, which dangers Channing very clearly saw. Yet Channing was himself the servant of an association; and every fault in his relation to the great moral question of his time may be traced to that fact.

Association,—business or social, literary or artistic, religious or scientific,—all association is opposed to any disrupting idea. The merchants and lawyers of Boston fled Abolition as a plague; they regarded Abolition as an enemy to be fought with all weapons. Garrison was once taken to hear Dr. Channing by an acquaintance of both parties, and he sat in a pew which belonged to a conservative family, but which that family had been in the habit of throwing open to others. On the Tuesday following this apparition of Garrison in the sacred pew, the future use of it was withdrawn by a stiff note from the conservative family. The reason for this excess of caution was that the South disciplined Northern merchants by a withdrawal of business; and the South kept its eyes open. A rumor that Garrison had been seen in a particular pew might make the pew-owner a marked man for commercial punishment. "Mr. May," said a New York merchant of the first rank to the reformer, whom he summoned to an interview during the progress of an Anti-slavery meeting, "Mr. May, we are not such fools as not to know that slavery is a great evil; a great wrong. But it was consented to by the founders of our Republic. It was provided for in the Constitution of our Union. A great portion of the property of the Southerners is invested under its sanction; and the business of the North, as well as the South, has become adjusted to it. There are millions upon millions of dollars due from Southerners to the merchants and mechanics of this city alone, the payment of which would be jeopardized by any rupture between the North and the South. We cannot afford, sir, to let you and your associates succeed in your endeavor to overthrow slavery. It is not a matter of principle with us. It is a matter of business necessity. We cannot afford to let you succeed. And I have called you out to let you know, and to let your fellow laborers know, that we do not mean to allow you to succeed. We mean, sir," said he, with increased emphasis,— "we mean, sir, to put you Abolitionists down,—by fair means if we can, by foul means if we must."

Truly the world was not very different then from what it is to-day. If a man takes a stand against any business interest, however iniquitous, that interest will strike at him on the following day.


### III. THE FIGURE

THE ESSENTIAL QUALITY of all this old society was that it was *cold*. In the last analysis,—after the historical and constitutional questions have been patiently analyzed, after economics and sociology have had their say,—the trouble with the American of 1830 was that he had a cold heart. Cruelty, lust, business interest, remoteness from European influence had led to the establishment of an unfeeling civilization. The essential quality of Garrison is that he is hot. This must be borne in mind at every moment as the chief and real quality of Garrison. Disregard the arguments; sink every intellectual conception, every bit of logic and of analysis, and look upon the age:—you see a cold age. Look upon Garrison:—you see a hot coal of fire. He plunges through the icy atmosphere like a burning meteorite from another planet.

There is a second contrast. The age was conciliatory: Garrison is aggressive. These two forms of the contrast between Garrison and his age lie close together and merge into each other: yet they are not entirely identical: the first concerns the emotions, the second, the intellect. Conciliation was the sin of that age. Now this anti-type, this personified enemy of his age,—Garrison,—must in his nature be self-reliant, self-assertive, self-sufficient. He relates himself to no precedent. He strikes out from his inner thought. He is even swords-drawn with his own thought of yesterday. When he changes his mind he asks God to forgive him for ever having thought otherwise. His instinct is so thoroughly opposed to any authority except the inner light of conscience, that he makes that conscience—his local, momentary conscience—into a column of smoke sent by the Lord. Not Bunyan, not Luther is greater than Garrison on this side of his nature. He is not an intellectual person. He is not a highly educated man. But he is a Will of the first magnitude, a will made perfect, because almost entirely unconscious, almost entirely dedicated and subdued to its mission.

I quote here the whole of the first editorial of the *Liberator* (January 1st, 1831), because the whole of Garrison is in it. In reading it let us remember the shattering, repulsive power which self-assertion exercises over smooth, cold people of good taste, whose worldly fortunes and sincere spiritual beliefs are bound up for all eternity with smoothness, coldness, and good taste. The punctuation and typesetting of the article, and the verses (not his own) at the end of it, may also be noted as indicating Garrison's taste and education:

"In the month of August, I issued proposals for publishing the *Liberator* in Washington City; but the enterprise, though hailed in different sections of the country, was palsied by public indifference. Since that time, the removal of the *Genius of Universal Emancipation* to the Seat of Government has rendered less imperious the establishment of a similar periodical in that quarter.

"During my recent tour for the purpose of exciting the minds of the people by a series of discourses on the subject of slavery, every place that I visited gave fresh evidence of the fact that a greater revolution in public sentiment was to be effected in the free States —*and particularly in New England*—than at the South. I found contempt more bitter, opposition more active, detraction more relentless, prejudice more stubborn, and apathy more frozen, than among slave-owners themselves. Of course, there were individual exceptions to the contrary. This state of things afflicted, but did not dishearten me. I determined at every hazard to lift up the standard of emancipation in the eyes of the nation, *within sight of Bunker Hill and in the birthplace of liberty*. That standard is now unfurled; and long may it float, unhurt by the spoliations of time or the missiles of a desperate foe—yea, till every chain be broken, and every bondman set free! Let Southern oppressors tremble—let their secret abettors tremble—let their Northern apologists tremble —let all the enemies of the persecuted blacks tremble.

"I deem the publication of my original Prospectus unnecessary, as it has obtained a wide circulation. The principles therein inculcated will be steadily pursued in this paper, excepting that I shall not array myself as the political partisan of any man. In defending the great cause of human rights, I wish to derive the assistance of all religions and of all parties."

Thus began Garrison in his first editorial in the *Liberator*. Does this seem egotism, this almost pompous deliberation, this taking off his coat and laying it across a chair as he makes his bow to the public? Yes, it is egotism. It is gigantic egotism—but not the egotism of vanity or self-seeking. It is the selfless egotism of a supreme self-assertion, put forth unconsciously by human nature; and as such it is in itself a sample of what that age needed, the sample of a spirit of independence without which slavery never could and never would have been abolished. Let us proceed with the editorial. . . . "Assenting to the 'self-evident truth' maintained in the American Declaration of Independence, 'that all men are created equal, and endowed by their Creator with certain inalienable rights—among which are life, liberty, and the pursuit of happiness,' I shall strenuously contend for the immediate enfranchisement of our slave population. In Park Street Church, on the Fourth of July, 1829, in an address on slavery, I unreflectingly assented to the popular but pernicious doctrine of *gradual* abolition. I seize this opportunity to make a full and unequivocal recantation, and thus publicly to ask pardon of my God, of my country, and of my brethren, the poor slaves, for having uttered a sentiment so full of timidity, injustice, and absurdity. A similar recantation, from my pen, was published in the *Genius of Universal Emancipation* at Baltimore, in September, 1829. My conscience is now satisfied.

"I am aware that many object to the severity of my language; but is there not cause for severity? I *will be* as harsh as truth, and as uncompromising as justice. On this subject, I do not wish to think, or speak, or write, with moderation. No! no! Tell a man whose house is on fire to give a moderate alarm; tell him to moderately rescue his wife from the hands of the ravisher; tell the mother to gradually extricate her babe from the fire into which it has fallen;—but urge me not to use moderation in a cause like the present. I am in earnest—I will not equivocate—I will not excuse—I will not retreat a single inch—AND I WILL BE HEARD. The apathy of the people is enough to make every statue leap from its pedestal, and to hasten the resurrection of the dead.

"It is pretended that I am retarding the cause of emancipation by the coarseness of my invective and the precipitancy of my measures. *The charge is not true.* On this question my influence—humble as it is—is felt at this moment to a considerable extent, and shall be felt in coming years—not perniciously, but beneficially—not as a curse, but as a blessing; and posterity will bear testimony that I was right. I desire to thank God that He enables me to disregard 'the fear of man which bringeth a snare,' and to speak his truth in its simplicity and power. . . .

. . . "And here I close with this fresh dedication:

"Oppression! I have seen thee, face to face,
And met thy cruel eye and cloudy brow;
But thy soul-withering glance I fear not now—
For dread to prouder feelings doth give place
Of deep abhorrence! Scouring the disgrace
Of slavish knees that at thy footstool bow,
I also kneel—but with far other vow
Do hail thee and thy herd of hirelings base:—

I swear, while life-blood warms my throbbing veins,
Still to oppose and thwart, with heart and hand,
Thy brutalizing sway—till Afric's chains
Are burst, and Freedom rules the rescued land,—
Trampling Oppression and his iron rod:
*Such is the vow I take*—SO HELP ME GOD!"

Garrison's early history is the familiar tale of poverty, and reminds one of Benjamin Franklin's boyhood. His mother, a person of education and refinement, was, during Garrison's babyhood, plunged into bitter destitution. He was born in Newburyport, Massachusetts, in 1805. At the age of nine, in order to help pay for his board, he was working for Deacon Bartlett in Newburyport. Later, he learned shoemaking at Lynn, cabinet-making at Haverhill, and in 1818, at the age of thirteen, was apprenticed to a printer and newspaper publisher. Now began his true education. He read Scott, Byron, Moore, Pope, and Campbell; and at the age of seventeen, was writing newspaper articles in the style of the day. By the time he was twenty, Garrison was a thoroughgoing printer and journalist; and during the last three years of his apprenticeship he had entire charge of his master's paper. During the next four years, he edited four newspapers, and embraced various reforms besides Anti-slavery, e.g., Temperance, Education, Peace, Sabbatarianism, etc. He seems at this period to be like a hound on a scent, as he takes up and abandons one newspaper after another. He is already a reformer, already a boiling enthusiast, already an insuppressible Volubility, already one-ideaed upon any subject that he treats. If his theme be Temperance, then moderate drinking is the worst enemy of man. He joins most heartily in the anathema against tobacco either in chewing, smoking, or snuffing. He is against capital punishment and imprisonment for debt, and it is safe to say that he would, at a moment's notice, have delivered a violent judgment upon any subject that aroused his compassion.

Whatever else he was, he was a full-grown being at the age of twenty-four, when Benjamin Lundy persuaded him to devote his life to the cause of the slave. Benjamin Lundy, the quiet Quaker, had been editing the *Genius of Universal Emancipation* since 1821, and was at this time (1828) established in Baltimore, where he had recently been assaulted and almost killed in the streets by Austin

Woolfolk, a slave trader. Lundy's practice was to walk from town to town throughout the country, founding Anti-slavery societies, and introducing his newspaper. He first met Garrison while he was on a visit to Boston, and at a later date he walked from Baltimore to Bennington, Vermont, where Garrison was editing a journal, in order to convert Garrison. He succeeded. Garrison left Vermont and became co-editor of the *Genius* in Baltimore. Before he migrated to Baltimore, however, he visited Boston and there on July 4th, 1829, he delivered an address in the Park Street Church which is really the beginning of his mission. The Reverend John Pierpont (the grandfather of Pierpont Morgan) was present and wrote a hymn for the occasion. Whittier, a stripling, was also present. The tone and substance of this address are strikingly like those of Emerson's Phi Beta Kappa address (delivered six years later), in which Emerson made his manly salutatory to his age. Garrison's words are as follows:—

"I speak not as a partisan or an opponent of any man or measures, when I say that our politics are rotten to the core. We boast of our freedom, who go shackled to the polls, year after year, by tens, and hundreds, and thousands! We talk of free agency, who are the veriest machines—the merest automata—in the hands of unprincipled jugglers! We prate of integrity, and virtue, and independence, who sell our birthright for office, and who, nine times in ten, do not get Esau's bargain—no, not even a mess of pottage! Is it republicanism to say that the majority can do no wrong? Then I am not a republican. Is it aristocracy to say that the people sometimes shamefully abuse their high trust? Then I am an aristocrat. . . .

"Before God, I must say, that such a glaring contradiction as exists between our creed and practice, the annals of six thousand years cannot parallel. In view of it, I am ashamed of my country. I am sick of our unmeaning declamation in praise of liberty and equality; of our hypocritical cant about the unalienable rights of man. I could not, for my right hand, stand up before a European assembly, and exult that I am an American citizen, and denounce the usurpations of a kingly government as wicked and unjust; or, should I make the attempt, the recollection of my country's barbarity and despotism would blister my lips, and cover my cheeks with burning blushes of shame."

Let us now take a few sentences from Emerson's Phi Beta Kappa address:

"The spirit of the American freeman is already suspected to be timid, imitative, tame. Public and private avarice make the air we breathe thick and fat. The scholar is decent, indolent, complaisant. See already the tragic consequence. The mind of this country, taught to aim at low objects, eats upon itself. . . . Young men of the fairest promise, who begin life upon our shores, inflated by the mountain winds, shined upon by all the stars of God, find the earth below not in unison with these, but are hindered from action by the disgust which the principles on which business is managed inspire, and turn drudges, or die of disgust, some of them suicides. What is the remedy? They did not yet see, and thousands of young men as hopeful now crowding to the barriers for the career do not yet see, that if the single man plant himself indomitably on his instincts, and there abide, the huge world will come round to him."

The difference between Emerson and Garrison is that Emerson is interested in æsthetic, Garrison in social matters. The one represents the world of intellect, the other, the world of feeling. Both speak the same idea, each according to his own idiom. Both are, in essence, affronting the same evil—the Dominion of Slavery. The difference is that Garrison has seen the evil plainly, and has laid his hand upon it; Emerson was to live in ignorance of its specific nature for many years to come. I shall revert again to the relation between these two young men, both so noble, both of such immense consequence to the country, each of them, in a sense, the father of all of us—whose spirits were raised up by God to shed new life upon America.

We must return to Garrison as the co-editor with Lundy of the *Genius of Universal Emancipation* in Baltimore. Inasmuch as Garrison had already received his revelation as to *immediate* emancipation, and Lundy favored slower methods, the two partners agreed to sign their articles separately. Baltimore was, at that time, the most northern port in the coastwise slave trade: and Garrison constantly saw the slaves being shipped south in New England bottoms. It was not long before Garrison was thrown into jail in Baltimore as the result of a suit for criminal libel, brought by a New England slave trader whom he had denounced. The Mr. Todd whom he "libeled," and about whom he spoke only the truth, was a fellow townsman of Garrison's, being a native of Newburyport, Mass., and was thus a natural target for Garrison's invective. Garrison remained in jail seven weeks, during which time he conducted a most telling campaign of pamphlets, private letters and public cards, sonnets, letters to editors, etc., with the result that the whole of America heard of the incident. Mr. Arthur Tappan of New York became interested in the case, and secured Garrison's release by paying the fine of one hundred dollars. This was in the spring of 1830.

Thus it may be seen that at the time that Garrison returned to Boston and established his *Liberator* (1830–31) he was twenty-five years old, a consummate controversialist, and the apostle of a new theory—Immediate Emancipation, for which he had already suffered imprisonment. The world has no terrors for a man like this.

Anti-slavery action did not begin with Garrison. There had been Anti-slavery societies for fifty years before him; there existed in 1830 perhaps a hundred and fifty of them, many of them being in the slave states. But the new movement did not spring from these old societies. It was militant as they were not: it was dissatified with their mild methods and inactivity: in fact, it denounced them. The new movement came bursting up like a subterranean torrent.

I have no doubt that Garrison and his mission were somehow fundamentally connected with the labors of the Anti-slavery men who kept the name of mercy alive between 1776 and 1820. Yet these old agencies were upheaved from beneath. Abolition appeared at the North and overslaughed them; the Slave Power developed new heat at the South and burned out the roots of them. Any single anecdote of those times will be apt to illustrate both sides of the question, i.e., the new vulture quality of slavery at the South, and the new bulldog quality of Abolition at the North. For instance, when the Southern statesmen recognized the existence of Abolition, they began passing laws against the introduction of Abolition literature into the South, and they began to correspond with Northern statesmen and officials with the aim of suppressing Garrison. The Legislature of Georgia, in 1831, offered a reward of $5000 for the arrest and conviction of Garrison under the laws of Georgia. The Southern press went into paroxysms of clamorous rage. On the other hand, Garrison is by no means deficient in vigor of feeling. The following is his comment on the reward:

"A price set upon the head of a citizen of Massachusetts—for what? For daring to give his opinions of the moral aspect of slavery! Where is the liberty of the press and of speech? Where the spirit of our fathers? Where the immunities secured to us by our Bill of Right? Are we the slaves of Southern taskmasters? Is it treason to maintain the principles of the Declaration of Independence? Must we say that slavery is a sacred and benovolent institution, or be silent? Know this, ye senatorial patrons of kidnappers! that we despise your threats as much as we deplore your infatuation: nay, more—know that a hundred men stand ready to fill our place as soon as it is made vacant by violence. The *Liberator* shall yet live—live to warn you of your danger and guilt—live to plead for the perishing slaves—live to hail the day of universal emancipation!"

Now we can see at a glance that this new Abolition is much more than Abolition: it is Courage. Garrison's tone here takes us back a generation to James Otis, to John Adams, and to the other Revolutionary heroes; and he is really standing for constitutional liberty quite as distinctly, and at as crucial a moment, as those gentlemen had done. Garrison's language is harsh; but he is almost the only out-and-out masculine person in the North. No: there was one other—the aged John Quincy Adams; and Adams was as harsh, and as unmeasured, as Garrison. Nay, Adams was personally bitter, which Garrison never was. Adams was, in reality, a survivor of 1776, an untamed aristocrat—and he bore a vase of the old fire in his bosom. This was permitted to Adams—because no one could stop him; but men vaguely imagined that Garrison's fire could be put out.

In 1831, Garrison was indicted in North Carolina. The South was not wrong in thinking that the official classes at the North would lend aid in suppressing the new movement. Judge Thatcher of the Municipal Court in Boston made a charge to the Grand Jury (1832) in which he laid the foundation for the criminal prosecution of Abolitionists. No one could tell just how far subserviency might go. The Mayor of Boston, Harrison Gray Otis, was naturally appealed to by the Southern statesmen to protect them against the circulation of Abolition literature. It was in 1829 that Otis was first called on to do something about "Walker's appeal," a fierce, Biblical pamphlet, full of power, written by a colored man in Boston and urging the slaves to rise. Otis replied that the author had not made himself amenable to the laws of Massachusetts, and that the book had caused no excitement in Boston. Garrison had had nothing to do with Walker's pamphlet, and had publicly condemned its doctrines. None the less, Walker's appeal was an outcrop of the same subterranean fire that coursed through Garrison,—and when Nat Turner's Slave Rebellion broke out (1831) and a dozen white families were murdered in Virginia, the whole South was thrown into a panic, and attributed the insurrection to the teachings of the Abolitionists.

This puny rebellion was easily put down. Turner was hanged, his followers were burnt with hot irons, their faces were mutilated, their jaws broken asunder, their hamstrings cut, their bodies stuck like hogs, their heads spiked to the whipping-post. No connection was ever discovered between Nat Turner's Rebellion and the Abolitionists, who never at any time sent their papers to slaves. The illiteracy of the blacks made it improbable that they had been influenced by any sort of writings. And yet one cannot help feeling that the existence of a militant propaganda in their behalf had reached the consciousness of the slaves, and that this rising was the outcome of the new age. Angels' wings were beating upon the air, and charging it with both life and death, till even dumb slaves felt the impulsion. Various Southern governors, statesmen, and newspapers renewed the campaign against the *Liberator,* and Otis was again appealed to.

"To be more specific in our object," says the *National Intelligencer* which was published in Washington, and was one of the most influential journals of the epoch, "we now appeal to the worthy Mayor of the City of Boston, whether no law can be found to prevent the publication, in the city over which he presides, of such diabolical papers (copies of the *Liberator*) as we have seen a sample of here in the hands of slaves, and of which there are many in circulation to the south of us. We have no doubt whatever of the feelings of Mr. Otis on this subject, or those of his respectable constituents. We know they would prompt him and them to arrest the instigator of human butchery in his mad career. We know the difficulty which surrounds the subject, because the nuisance is not a nuisance, technically speaking, within the limits of Massachusetts. But, surely, if the courts of law have no power, public opinion has to interfere, until the intelligent Legislature of Massachusetts can provide a durable remedy for this most appalling grievance. . . ."

Robert Y. Hayne of Columbia, S. C., begged Otis to find out whether Garrison had mailed him (Hayne) a copy of the *Liberator*. Otis obsequiously sent a deputy to question Garrison. This was something very like a prostitution of his office on the part of Mayor Otis; because what Hayne wanted was to obtain *evidence* to be used in a criminal prosecution of Garrison. Garrison at once becomes the able constitutional lawyer.

"The Hon. Robert Y. Hayne of Columbia, S. C.," says the *Liberator* of October 29th, 1831, "(through the medium of a letter), wishes to know of the Mayor of Boston, who sent a number of the *Liberator* to him, a few weeks ago. The Mayor of Boston (through the medium of a deputy) wishes to know of Mr. Garrison whether he sent the aforesaid number to the aforesaid individual. Mr. Garrison (through the medium of his paper) wishes to know of the Hon. Robert Y. Hayne of Columbia, S. C., and the Mayor of Boston, what authority they have to put such questions?"

We can see in this, as in all the rest of Garrison's activity, the tactician of genius. We can see also the inner relation between morality and constitutional law, which exists in all ages. The Reformer is always struggling against arbitrary power. He invokes the protection of some law or custom which exists, or ought to exist. In cases where this law or custom has a historic basis, the struggle goes on in the form of constitutional law. The picture of the Reformer is always the picture of Courage and of Mercy: the courageous man who is, by his conduct, protecting the weak. It is this vision of courage and mercy in operation, that melts the heart and inspires new courage and mercy in the beholder. Here is the great question which stands behind all the details; for courage and mercy are of eternal importance. That is why we hear so much of Pym, Hampden, etc. Their conduct has a direct relation to present conditions. No day passes in which every man is not put to the test many times over, as to his personal relation towards the cowardices and cruelties of his own age.

Mayor Otis saw nothing important in the episode which has given him a Dantesque immortality. He had never heard of the *Liberator*. He therefore, procured a copy of it.

"I am told," he said, "that it is supported chiefly by the free colored people; that the number of subscribers in Baltimore and Washington exceeds that of *those in this city,* and that it is gratuitously left at one or two of the reading-rooms in this place. It is edited by an individual who formerly lived at Baltimore, where his feelings have been exasperated by some occurrences consequent to his publications there, on topics connected with the condition of slaves in this country. . . ."

At a later period Otis wrote:

"Some time afterward, it was reported to me by the city officers that they had ferreted out the paper and its editor; that his office was an obscure hole, his only visible auxiliary a negro boy, and his supporters a very few insignificant persons of all colors. This information, with the consent of the aldermen, I communicated to the above-named governors, with an assurance of my belief that the new fanaticism had not made, nor was likely to make, proselytes among the respectable classes of our people. In this, however, I was mistaken."

History has left us, in this anecdote, a silhouette of Harrison Gray Otis, one of Boston's most eminent personages at that time, —the representative of the old Puritan blood, of the education, wealth, good looks, social prominence, and political power of Boston's leaders. In how short a time, and with how easy a transformation does patriot turn tyrant. Here is the nephew of James Otis, hand in glove with the iniquity of his age. He who was rocked in the cradle of liberty, is now the agent of the Inquisition. And he is perfectly innocent. He is a mere toy and creature of his time. A new issue has arisen that neither he nor his generation understand, and behold, they have become oppressors.

The Hercules that is to save mankind from these monsters is in the meanwhile working fourteen hours a day, setting type. The *Liberator* was begun without a dollar of capital and without a single subscriber. Garrison and his partner, Isaac Knapp, a young white man equally poor and equally able to bear privation, composed, set, and printed the paper themselves. They lived chiefly upon bread and milk, a few cakes and a little fruit, obtained from the baker's shop opposite and from a petty cake and fruit shop in the basement. "I was often at the office of the *Liberator,*" wrote the Rev. James C. White. "I knew of his (Garrison's) self-denials. I knew he slept in the office with a table for a bed, a book for a pillow, and a self-prepared scanty meal for his rations in the office, while he set up his articles in the *Liberator* with his own hand, and without previous committal to paper."

"It was a pretty large room," says Josiah Copley, who visited it in the winter of 1832–33, "but there was nothing in it to relieve its dreariness but two or three very common chairs and a pine desk in the corner, at which a pale, delicate, and apparently over-tasked gentleman was sitting. . . . I never was more astonished. All my preconceptions were at fault. My ideal of the man was that of a stout, rugged, dark-visaged desperado—something like we picture a pirate. He was a quiet, gentle, and I might say handsome man— a gentleman indeed, in every sense of the word."

"The dingy walls; the small windows, bespattered with printer's ink; the press standing in one corner; the composing-stands opposite; the long editorial and mailing table, covered with newspapers; the bed of the editor and publisher on the floor—all these," says Oliver Johnson, "make a picture never to be forgotten."

## IV. PICTURES OF THE STRUGGLE

THERE ARE PAGES in the memoirs of Anti-slavery that shine with a light which sanctifies this continent, and which will be undiminished a thousand years hence. Nay, it will shine more clearly then than now; for we are still living in the valley of the shadow of death.

The war followed so quickly upon the true awakening of the nation as to the nature of slavery that those early watchers, whose cries had aroused us, were still in coventry; they were still held to be odious, although their piercing appeal had put life and religion into all. The North died for the slave, with condemnation of the Abolitionist upon its lips. This paradoxical outcome was due to the rapidity with which events moved during the final crisis. A revolution may be studied in its origins, and may be comprehended through its results; but during the actual cascade that leads from the one epoch to the other, scene succeeds scene with such fury that history becomes unintelligible. In the years that intervened between the Kansas troubles and the outbreak of the war, so many things happened at once that all issues and all feelings were telescoped together. There followed the picturesque horrors and scenes of war-time; there followed the new patriotism, the new heroes, the New Legend—all of it so vivid, so drenched in grief, so glorified by honor, so informed with the meaning of a new heaven and a new earth, that the immediate past was belittled. The Abolitionists thus passed straight from the odium of people preaching unpleasant truth to the odium of people proclaiming what everybody knows. They have never had a heyday. Their cause triumphed but not they themselves. They still remain under a cloud in America, and are regarded with some distrust by the historian and by the common man. I can scarcely find a man who sees in these early Abolitionists, as I do, the lamp and light of the whole after-coming epoch. Perhaps our age is still too near to theirs to do it justice; and the mere flight of time may bring men to a truer perspective of the whole matter.

Religious animosities do not die out in a moment. Many of us still feel a lambent and rising heat course through our veins in reading the history of the religious wars of three centuries ago. This is because those wars have come down in family life, and are thus a part of the intimate personal history of men. So of this just-buried cause, Abolition. Consider how the American of to-day reads the Constitutional History of the years before the war. Nullification, the Texas scheme, the Mexican War, the Repeal of the Missouri Compromise, the Kansas troubles—all these things and every subsidiary foreign or domestic issue in our annals, are interesting to us because we feel so intimately the hot place in each one of them. Part of this heat comes from prejudice and accident, part of it from the central focus of truth; and we cannot always be sure which kind it is that burns in us. But there is a species of glow that can be trusted. It comes to us when we read accounts of heroism. Tales of noble self-sacrifice never remain mere adjuncts to a creed, or portions of a partisan tradition. They contain in themselves the whole of salvation. Posterity will recur to the age of the Anti-slavery movement in order to find there those little digests of human nature which are true to all time. Here are the gems in the treasury of a nation's life; and it matters not to later ages whether the geological strata in which they lie embedded be Catholic or Protestant, Christian or pagan, political or religious.

Whenever a reform movement is started in this world and is

making headway, the evils which it threatens instinctively strive to gain control over it. We see this every day in our local citizens' movements, which always begin by sincere activity, and almost always grow effete through capture by the politicians. Our civil service associations tend to become absorbed by the political parties, who man them with paid officials, and run up the expenses till the cure has become a part of the disease. This oscillation between reform and absorption goes on ceaselessly; and the young prophet always finds himself obliged to attack and destroy some sham reform association, bearing a fine name, before he can get at the real evil. Let us note this also; that a somnolent and inactive reform association, with a fine name, and an aroma of original benevolence about it, and perhaps even a superficially good record, is the very sort of association to attract respectable, rich, lazy, and conservative people.

The Colonization Society in 1830 presented an extreme case of sham reform. It had been started in 1816 in Virginia, with the avowed object of transporting free Negroes to Africa. It had been pushed with diligence and paraded as the cure for the evils of slavery, and its benevolence was assumed on all hands. Everybody of consequence belonged to it. Garrison, himself, joined it in good faith. This Colonization Society had, by an invisible process, half conscious, half unconscious, been transformed into a serviceable organ and member of the Slave Power. In order to investigate the real functions of this society, Garrison, in 1831, obtained from its headquarters at Washington, the files of its documents and of its newspaper, the *African Repository*.

"The result of his labors," says Oliver Johnson, "was seen in a bulky pamphlet, that came from the press in the spring, entitled 'Thoughts on African Colonization; or, an impartial Exhibition of the Doctrines, Principles and Purposes of the American Colonization Society; together with the Resolutions, Addresses and Remonstrances of the Free People of Color.' As a compilation of facts and authorities it was unanswerable and overwhelming. It condemned the Colonization Society out of its own mouth, and by a weight of evidence that was irresistible. There was just enough of comment to elucidate the testimony from official sources and bring it within the comprehension of the simplest reader. His indictment contained ten averments, viz.: 1. The American Colonization Society is pledged not to oppose the system of slavery; 2. It apologizes for slavery and slave-holders; 3. It recognizes slaves as property; 4. It increases the value of slaves; 5. It is the enemy of immediate abolition; 6. It is nourished by fear and selfishness; 7. It aims at the utter expulsion of the blacks; 8. It is the disparager of the free blacks; 9. It denies the possibility of elevating the blacks in this country; 10. It deceives and misleads the Nation. Each of these averments was supported by pages of citations from the annual reports of the society, from the pages of its official organ, the *African Repository,* and from the speeches of its leading champions in all parts of the country. It was impossible to set this evidence aside, and equally so to resist the conclusions drawn therefrom. The work could not be, and therefore was not answered."

The book made a tremendous sensation and became the arsenal of the Abolitionists in this country and of their exponents abroad. "It was early in 1852, I think," says Elizur Wright, "that Mr. Garrison struck the greatest blow of his life—or any man's life—by publishing in a thick pamphlet, with all the emphasis that a printer knows how to give to types, his *Thoughts on Colonization.*" The Colonization Society was an embodiment of the public consciousness. It was prevalent, it was a part of the people's daily life. All the great divines belonged to it, all the academic bigwigs, social figureheads and moneyed men. And yet, in fact, Colonization was a sort of obscene dragon that lay before the Palace of Slavery to devour or corrupt all assailants. Garrison attacked it like Perseus, with a ferocity which to this day is thrilling. His eyes, his words, and his sword flash and glitter. And he slew it. He cut off its supplies, he destroyed its reputation in Europe; and he thereby opened the path between the Abolition movement and the conscience of America. Nothing he ever did was more able. Nothing that Frederick the Great, Washington or Napoleon ever did in the field of war was more brilliant than this political foray of Garrison, then at the age of twenty-seven, upon the key-position and jugular vein of slavery.

Among the immediate consequences of Garrison's pamphlet on colonization was the contest over Lane Seminary at Cincinnati, a contest which became the storm center of Abolition influence for a year, and qualified public opinion ever after. I quote part of the account given by Oliver Johnson from his well-known volume on Garrison and his time—from which many of these illustrations are taken. Johnson was a right-hand man of Garrison's and at times was editor and co-editor of the *Liberator*. He gave up his life to Anti-slavery, and is a fair example of the sort of man who came into existence, as if by miracle, when Garrison stamped his foot in 1830.

"The founding of Lane Seminary, at the gateway of the great West, was a part of this plan, to extend the influence of Orthodoxy, and Dr. Beecher,* being generally recognized as the leader of New England Revivalism, and the strongest representative of the advanced school of Orthodoxy at that day, Mr. Tappan thought that he of all others was the man best fitted to train a body of ministers for the new field. The Doctor, after considerable delay, and to the great grief of his Boston church, accepted the appointment. Such was his fame that a large class of students, of unusual maturity of judgment and ripeness of Christian experience, was at once attracted to the Seminary. In the literary and theological departments together, they numbered about one hundred and ten. Eleven of these were from different slave States; seven were sons of slaveholders; one was himself a slaveholder, and one had purchased his freedom from cruel bondage by the payment of a large sum of money, which he had earned by extra labor. Besides these there were ten others who had resided for longer or shorter periods in the slave States, and made careful observation of the character and workings of slavery. The youngest of these students was nineteen years of age; most of those in the theological department were more than twenty-six, and several were over thirty. Most if not all of them had been converted in the revivals of that period, and were filled with the revival spirit in which Dr. Beecher so much delighted. A more earnest and devoted band of students was probably never gathered in any theological seminary. The Doctor had great pride as well as confidence in them."

The students in this Seminary at Cincinnati were planning to form a Colonization Society, and Garrison's pamphlet being in the air, its arguments were being used to oppose the plan. The students therefore organized a nine days' solemn debate upon the whole matter, with the result that Garrison and Immediate Emancipation carried the day. In the meantime the country at large took an interest in the affair, and the press assailed the Seminary as a hotbed of

* Rev. Lyman Beecher, father of Henry Ward Beecher and of Harriet Beecher Stowe.

Abolition. Dr. Lyman Beecher and the trustees were harried and threatened. The hearts of the Abolitionists were stirred to the depths.

"In every part of the free States," says Oliver Johnson, "there were Christian men and godly women not a few, who prayed to God night and day that Lyman Beecher might be imbued with strength and courage to stand up nobly in the face of the storm that raged around him, and maintain the right of his pupils, as candidates for the Christian ministry, to investigate and discuss the subject of slavery, and to bear their testimony against it as a sin, and a mighty hindrance to the spread of the Gospel."

At last, the trustees of the Seminary, thinking to avoid the danger, forbade the students to discuss slavery at all—even in private. The outcome was that seventy or eighty students resigned in a body. The institution was disgraced and wrecked; it never recovered from the experience. The greatest result of the episode, however, was this, that the young men who resigned became, by force of circumstances, something like public characters. Their first step was a public one—into the arena. They issued an appeal to the Christian public, and many of them went out into the world as protagonists of Abolition.

Here was a miraculous draught indeed; for, of course, among them were men of mark; and Theodore D. Weld, the ringleader, was, as Johnson says, the peer of Beecher himself in native ability. Thus burst a seed-pod of Abolition. This propagative influence had been in Garrison's pamphlet. That pamphlet evoked, it elicited, it agitated. When we come later to review Garrison's writings, let us remember what these writings accomplished. Let us remember that, however tedious this pamphlet on Colonization may seem to us, however dead it may fall, under criticism, to-day, it had this life-giving quality in its own time.

Another of the early picturesque episodes of Anti-slavery history was the case of Prudence Crandall. It set the world ringing, and caused new champions to step forward, fully armed, out of that mystical wood which ever fringes the open lawns where heroes are at combat.

I again quote from Oliver Johnson:

"In 1832, Prudence Crandall, a Quaker young woman of high character, established in Canterbury, Windham County, Conn., a school for young ladies. Now there was in that town a respectable colored farmer named Harris, who had a daughter, a bright girl of seventeen, who, having passed creditably through one of the district schools, desired to qualify herself to be a teacher of colored children. She was a girl of pleasing appearance and manners, a member of the Congregational church, and of a hue not darker than that of some persons who pass for white. Miss Crandall, good Quaker that she was, admitted this girl to her school. The pupils, some of whom had been associated with her in the district school, made no objection; but some of the parents were offended, and demanded the removal of the dark-skinned pupil. Miss Crandall made a strong appeal in behalf of the girl, and did her best to overcome the prejudices of the objectors, but in vain. After reflection she came to the conclusion, from a sense of duty, to open her school to other girls of a dark complexion. The announcement of her purpose threw the whole town into a ferment. A town-meeting was held in the Congregational church, and so fierce was the excitement that the Rev. Samuel J. May and Mr. Arnold Buffum, the Quaker President of the New England Anti-Slavery Society, who had been deputed by Miss Crandall to speak for her, were denied a hearing."

Why has this woman no tablet? Will the annals of Canterbury, Connecticut, show a more heroic figure during the next thousand years—that the hamlet waits to celebrate its patron saint? Had Prudence Crandall lived in the time of Diocletian, or in the time of Savonarola, or in the time of Garibaldi, she would have had a shrine to which Americans would have flocked to-day. Not without immense influence was the stand she made. It cost two years of struggle, during which the Slave Power, as we have seen, passed such bills to suppress her as, in the rebound, weakened its hold on the people of the North. We now find it hard to imagine that, in 1834, it should have been a crime in Connecticut to give primary education to colored girls. Yet such was the case. Prudence Crandall was indicted.

At her first trial there was a disagreement of the jury. Upon the second she was convicted. An appeal was thereupon taken and was followed by a disagreement among the judges. Thereafter the matter was allowed to drop, through the finding of a flaw in the indictment. All this, however, was not done in a corner, nor without the indignation of all warm-hearted people, nor without the exhibition of splendid legal ability on both sides of the contest. Important law-suits were the bull-fights of America before the war. This one called into being a new local newspaper, supported by Arthur Tappan, because the existing papers would publish only the Pro-slavery side of the contest. It called into activity also several new propagandists of the first order, including C. C. Burleigh, who was turned from the career of a brilliant advocate and was transformed for life into an evangelist of liberty, through the courage of this woman. Her story showed the lengths to which the Slave Power not only would but *could* go at the North, and gave a glance into the burning pit, which even casual and callous persons could not forget.

It was while this long contest was in progress that the National Anti-Slavery Society was formed by a meeting at Philadelphia of about sixty Abolitionists, from eleven states. How young these men were may be judged by the fact that forty-five of them survived to witness the emancipation of the slaves thirty years later. I quote a few paragraphs from Samuel J. May's reminiscences, which picture the state of mind of these men as their deliberations of several days drew to a close. The men had, for the most part, never seen each other before this meeting. A declaration of principles had been prepared.

"Between twelve and one o'clock," says Mr. May, "we repaired with the *Declaration* to the hall. Edwin P. Atlee, the chairman, read it to the Convention. Never in my life have I seen a deeper impression made by words than was made by that admirable document upon all who were there present. . . .

"At the suggestion of an Orthodox brother, and without a vote of the Convention, our President himself, then an Orthodox minister, readily condescended to the scruples of our Quaker brethren, so far as not to *call upon* any individual to offer prayer; but at the opening of our sessions each day he gave notice that a portion of time would be spent in prayer. Any one prayed aloud who was moved to do so. It was at the suggestion also of an Orthodox member that we agreed to dispense with all titles, civil or ecclesiastical. Accordingly, you will not find in the published minutes of the Convention appendages to any names,—neither D. D., nor Rev., nor Hon., nor Esq.,—no, not even plain Mr. We met as fellow men, in the cause of suffering fellow men. . . .

"I cannot describe the holy enthusiasm which lighted up every face as we gathered around the table on which the Declaration lay, to put our names to that sacred instrument. It seemed to me that every man's heart was in his hand—as if every one felt that he was about to offer himself a living sacrifice in the cause of *freedom,* and to do it cheerfully. There are moments when heart touches heart, and souls flow into one another. That was such a moment. I was in them and they in me; we were all one. There was no need that each should tell the other how he felt and what he thought, for we were in each other's bosoms. I am sure there was not, in all our hearts, the thought of ever making violent, much less mortal, defense of the liberty of speech, or the freedom of the press, or of our own persons, though we foresaw that they all would be grievously outraged. Our President, Beriah Green, in his admirable closing speech, gave utterance to what we all felt and intended should be our course of conduct. He distinctly foretold the obloquy, the despiteful treatment, the bitter persecution, perhaps even the cruel deaths we were going to encounter in the prosecution of the undertaking to which we had bound ourselves."

The age played its part quite handsomely in apportioning persecution to the new preachers of the Gospel. The case of Amos Dresser may be cited as a sample from Oliver Johnson:

"Amos Dresser, a young theological student (a native of Berkshire County, Mass.), went to Nashville, Tenn., in the summer of 1835, to sell the 'Cottage Bible.' His crime was that he was a member of an anti-slavery society, and that he had some anti-slavery tracts in his trunk. *For this he was flogged in the public square of the city,* under the direction of a Vigilance Committee, composed of the most distinguished citizens, some of them prominent members of churches. He received twenty lashes on the bare back from a cowskin. On the previous Sunday he had received the bread and wine of the communion from the hands of one of the members of that Vigilance Committee! Another member of the Committee was a prominent Methodist, whose house was the resort of the preachers and bishops of his denomination."

Now Dresser was a Massachusetts man. One wonders how the slaveholders would have behaved if a Southerner had, for any cause whatever, been treated in Massachusetts as Dresser was treated in Tennesee. But the North made no complaints. It is incredible—and this is the difficulty which the whole epoch presents to us—it is incredible that the earth should ever have nurtured such a race of cowards as the dominant classes in our Northern States seem to have been. And yet we know they were no worse, nor very different from other persons recorded in history; they furnish merely an acute, recent example of how self-interest can corrupt character, of how tyranny can delude intellect. The sufferings of such persons as Dresser are never lost. It required just such exhibitions as this to make the North see to what depths it had sunk. For many years, however, the North could draw no inference from such cases, except this:—that persons like Dresser were misguided fools, who interfered with matters best left alone.

The next picture must be of another kind. It shall be of the young Puritan divine, Samuel J. May, a descendant of the Sewalls and Quincys and of all that Eighteenth Century New England aristocracy of learning and virtue, which seems to have dwindled and withered in a single generation, and left—except for one or two bright spirits—nothing but shadow-characters, and feeble-natured persons on the stage. The occasion of May's conversion was Garrison's first Boston address, which was given in 1830 in Julien Hall, the hall being lent for the purpose by an association of avowed infidels. Garrison had but recently denounced the principles of these men; for at this time he was intensely orthodox. The lesson in charity he thus received from opponents must have been salutary, even to him. The whole incident, including May's conversion, shows how closely knitted together are all the liberal impulses in a community. At this time May was thirty-three. His family besought him to shun the new fanaticism; but he put their counsels gently aside. May is the angel of Anti-slavery. He gives the following account of his conversion:

"Presently the young man (Garrison) arose, modestly, but with an air of calm determination, and delivered such a lecture as he only, I believe, at that time, could have written; for he only had had his eyes so anointed that he could see that outrages perpetrated upon Africans were wrongs done to our common humanity; he only, I believe, had had his ears so completely unstopped of 'prejudice against color' that the cries of enslaved black men and black women sounded to him as if they came from brothers and sisters.

"He began with expressing deep regret and shame for the zeal he had lately manifested in the Colonization cause. It was, he confessed, a zeal without knowledge. He had been deceived by the misrepresentations so diligently given, throughout the free States by Southern agents, of the design and tendency of the Colonization scheme. During his few months' residence in Maryland he had been completely undeceived. He had there found out that the design of those who originated, and the especial intentions of those in the Southern States that engaged in the plan, were to remove from the country, as 'a disturbing element' in slaveholding communities, all the free colored people, so that the bondmen might the more easily be held in subjection. He exhibited in graphic sketches and glowing colors the suffering of the enslaved, and denounced the plan of Colonization as devised and adapted to perpetuate the system, and intensify the wrongs of American slavery, and therefore utterly undeserving of the patronage of lovers of liberty and friends of humanity.

"Never before was I so affected by the speech of man. When he had ceased speaking I said to those around me: 'That is a providential man; he is a prophet; he will shake our nation to its center, but he will shake slavery out of it. We ought to know him, we ought to help him. Come, let us go and give him our hands.' Mr. Sewall and Mr. Alcott went up with me, and we introduced each other. I said to him: 'Mr. Garrison, I am not sure that I can indorse all you have said this evening. Much of it requires careful consideration. But I am prepared to embrace you. I am sure you are called to a great work and I mean to help you.'"

With a mind as acute as a lawyer's, and a spirit as unselfish as a seraph's, May plunged into the cause. It is he who appeared upon the scene to protect and to represent Prudence Crandall at the meeting of her townsfolk which it was not safe for her to attend. It is he who has left us the best short book on the early years of the movement, from which book many of these illustrations are taken. He was of milder speech than Garrison. "O my friend," cried May at the close of an expostulation with Garrison, "do try to moderate your indignation, and keep more cool; why, you are all on fire." Garrison stopped, laid his hand on May's shoulder with a kind but emphatic pressure, and said slowly: "Brother May, I have need to be *all on fire,* for I have mountains of ice about me to melt." "From that time to this," adds Mr. May, "I have never said a word

to Mr. Garrison in complaint of his style. I am more than half satisfied that he was right then, and we who objected were mistaken."

May was not so political-minded as Garrison; he had not Garrison's strategic understanding of the fight, nor Garrison's gift of
becoming the central whirlpool of idea and of persecution. But he
was the diviner spirit of the two. I do not think Garrison could
have made the following appeal. It moves in a region of humility
which is foreign to Garrison's nature, to his tactics and to his
genius. Dr. Channing had been a family friend of the Mays, and
had been particularly kind to Samuel when the latter was a small
boy. This affectionate relationship had never been shaken. The
story must be told by May himself.

"Late in the year 1834," says Mr. May, "being on a visit in Boston, I spent several hours with Dr. Channing in earnest conversation upon Abolitionism and Abolitionists. My habitual reverence
for him was such that I had always been apt to defer perhaps too
readily to his opinions, or not to make a very stout defense of my
own when they differed from his. But at the time to which I refer
I had become so thoroughly convinced of the truth of the essential
doctrines of the American Anti-Slavery Society, and so earnestly
engaged in the dissemination of them that our conversation assumed, more than it had ever done, the character of a debate. He
acknowledged the inestimable importance of the object we had in
view. The evils of Slavery, he assented, could not be overstated. He
allowed that removal to Africa ought not to be made a condition of
the liberation of the enslaved. But he hesitated still to accept the
doctrine of immediate emancipation. His principal objections, however, were alleged against the severity of our denunciations, the
harshness of our epithets, the vehemence, heat, and excitement
caused by the harangues at our meetings, and still more by Mr.
Garrison's *Liberator*. The Doctor dwelt upon these objections,
which, if they were as well founded as he assumed them to be, lay
against what was only incidental, not an essential part of our
movement. He dwelt upon them until I became impatient, and,
forgetting for the moment my wonted deference, I broke out with
not a little warmth of expression and manner:

" 'Dr. Channing,' I said, 'I am tired of these complaints. The
cause of suffering humanity, the cause of our oppressed, crushed
colored countrymen, has called as loudly upon others as upon us

Abolitionists. It was just as incumbent upon others as upon us to espouse it. *We* are not to blame that wiser and better men did not espouse it long ago. The cry of millions, suffering the cruel bondage in our land, had been heard for half a century and disregarded. "The wise and prudent" saw the terrible wrong, but thought it not wise and prudent to lift a finger for its correction. The priests and Levites beheld their robbed and wounded countrymen, but passed by on the other side. The children of Abraham held their peace, and at last "the very stones have cried out" in abhorrence of this tremendous iniquity; and you must expect them to cry out like "the stones." You must not wonder if many of those who have been left to take up this great cause, do not plead it in all that seemliness of phrase which the scholars and practiced rhetoricians of our country might use. You must not expect them to manage with all the calmness and discretion that clergymen and statesmen might exhibit. But the scholars, the statesmen, the clergy had done nothing,—did not seem about to do anything; and for my part I thank God that at last any persons, be they who they may, have earnestly engaged in this cause; for no *movement* can be in vain. We Abolitionists are what we are—babes, sucklings, obscure men, silly women, publicans, sinners, and we shall manage this matter just as might be expected of such persons as we are. It is unbecoming in abler men who stood by and would do nothing to complain of us because we do no better.

"'Dr. Channing,' I continued with increased earnestness, 'it is not *our fault* that those who might have conducted this great reform more prudently have left it to us to manage as we may. It is not *our fault* that those who might have pleaded for the enslaved so much more wisely and eloquently, both with the pen and the living voice, than we can, have been silent. We are not to blame, sir, that you, who, more perhaps than any other man, might have so raised the voice of remonstrance that it should have been heard throughout the length and breadth of the land—we are not to blame, sir, that you have not so spoken. And now that inferior men have been compelled to speak and act against what you acknowledge to be an awful system of iniquity, it is not becoming in you to complain of us because we do it in an inferior style. Why, sir, have you not taken this matter in hand yourself? Why have you not spoken to the nation long ago, as you, better than any other one, could have spoken?'

"At this point I bethought me to whom I was administering this rebuke,—the man who stood among the highest of the great and good in our land,—the man whose reputation for wisdom and sanctity had become world-wide,—the man, too, who had ever treated me with the kindness of a father, and whom, from my childhood, I had been accustomed to revere more than any one living. I was almost overwhelmed with a sense of my temerity. His countenance showed that he was much moved. I could not suppose he would receive all I had said very graciously. I waited his reply in painful expectation. The minutes seemed very long that elapsed before the silence was broken. Then in a very subdued manner and in the kindliest tones of his voice he said, 'Brother May, I acknowledge the justice of your reproof. I have been silent too long.' Never shall I forget his words, look and whole appearance. I then and there saw the beauty, the magnanimity, the humility of a truly great Christian soul. He was exalted in my esteem more even than before."

Surely this is as moving an appeal as one man ever made to another; and the figures of May and Channing seem to stand as in a bas-relief symbolizing the old and the new generation. Are the caverns of Anti-slavery controversy strewn with fragments of such marble as this? I know that Emerson used to say that eloquence was dog-cheap at Anti-slavery meetings; but I did not expect to find gestures so sublime or episodes so moving. The figures of Hebrew history—of Jacob and Joseph, of Nathan and David, of Hagar and Ishmael—rise before us in their solemn, soul-subduing reality; and are one in spirit with these Anti-slavery scenes.

My shelves are lined with books about Saint Francis of Assisi; my walls are papered with photographs of men of genius in Florence, and of saints in Siena. I desire also to remember the saints of New England. We Americans are digging for art and for intellect in Troy, in Sardis and in Egypt. Let us sometimes also dig in the old records of our own towns; and, while doing so, let us pray that mind be given us to understand what we bring to light.

In the year following his interview with May (1836), Dr. Channing published his famous pamphlet on Slavery, which was of enormous value to the Anti-slavery cause, though it did not coincide with Abolition opinion. It condemned Slavery to heart's content, but did not advocate immediate action. The engines of rationalism and the fountains of morality were by Channing turned upon the entire subject. This was no half-work: it was thorough. Channing's name carried the book into houses, both at the North and in the South where no Abolition literature could penetrate; and made it a mile-stone in the progress of Anti-slavery. Its most lasting importance to posterity, however, is that it proves Channing's courage, and shows that his occasional subserviency toward his Trustees was not due to a defect in his nature, but to a defect in his education, a defect in his vision. Could the matter have been explained to his mind through the elaborate machinery of his own philosophy, he would have broken his chains. There are plenty of people to whom the crucial problems of their own lives never get presented in terms that they can understand.

Abolitionists were, of course, not satisfied with Channing's pamphlet; for he could not sanction their views; and indeed he repeated many of the commonplace charges against them,—e. g., "that the Abolitionists exaggerated the importance of their cause; that they sent their literature to the slave; that their language was too violent,"—etc. Most of these charges appear to-day to contradict the main thesis of the book, and to record merely the nervous petulance of that age.

The Slave Barons and their Boston friends were cut to the heart by Channing's essay. They denounced him as an even more dangerous enemy than Garrison. If, at times, we feel dissatisfied with Channing's caution, we should remember that he was a middle-aged man when these problems arose. Channing was born in 1780; and Anti-slavery was an agony in the blood of young men, in 1829.

I have referred to John Quincy Adams' detestation of slavery. He was, however, never an Abolitionist, and he did not even favor the abolition of slavery in the District of Columbia. For this latter opinion he had the most fantastic reason; namely that, although the residents of the District had no votes, and were governed by Congress, nevertheless he felt himself to be all the more bound in honor to act during his term in Congress as if he were the representative chosen by the people of that District; that is, to act according to what he knew to be the will of his *quasi* constituents. But, for his *real* constituents he held no such reverence, and in his dealings with them he was governed by his own conscience. Such are the vagaries of men.

The romantic, extravagant nature of this man was, at an early age, put in irons to law, diplomacy, politics, and administrative duty. He was a born agitator, who appeared at a time when his peculiar talents were not demanded by the age. In John Quincy Adams' boyhood all the talents and energies of this country were required for the assembling, setting in motion, and keeping together of the machineries of our new Government. There was no demand for an agitator, whose function is always to displace, to disperse, and to pull apart. And thus it happened with John Quincy Adams that he was never young till he was old. The opportunity to exercise his extraordinary talents for agitation came when he took his seat in Congress toward the close of his long, brilliant career. He proceeded to focus the entire attention of the country upon one or two points of parliamentary procedure.

Now an agitator is a man who is willing to make use of the members of government, not only for the various purposes for which they are framed,—as, e. g., the Legislature to legislate, the Judiciary to adjudicate, the Executive to administer, etc.,—but this man makes use of any or all of them as a machine to spread an idea. He uses the forms of government as an educational apparatus. The branch of the Anti-slavery cause which it became Adams' fate to develop, was the conflict between Slavery and the right to petition. The policy of the Slave Power was to smother all petitions upon the subject of Slavery which came before Congress, by laying them upon the table unread. During half a dozen years Adams fought this fight practically alone. If we picture to ourselves a man who had grown up with the country, who had the most intimate recondite, passionate knowledge of its constitutional law, dedicating himself to the plainest proposition regarding free speech, and proclaiming it in the face of a howling but comparatively unlettered majority, who seethed, and raged, and raved about him like the waves about a light-house—we have John Quincy Adams at an age of over seventy, presenting the Abolition petitions in Congress. His figure is part of the Anti-slavery struggle. It is clear to our instinct that if Adams did not have Abolition in his veins, he had something almost as good; he had the thing that Abolition was the sign of, namely, courage. His peculiar kind of courage was, in one sense,

not as good as Abolition; for it was not an elixir. It would never
have abolished slavery: it was not self-perpetuating. It would have
died with him. Yet the passion within him, which he cloaked under
the name of Free Speech, was in reality the Will to Pity, the Will
to Love, the Will to express freely that emotional side of man's
nature with which he himself was so richly endowed. This is why
the last page of this man's life lifts him into a new kind of greatness. It makes no difference what he did before this era. His service
to the Abolition cause was proportionate to his position. His conduct showed the country what slavery pointed to, and demonstrated
also the conservative nature of Abolition. It showed that Abolition
was at one with the foundations of society. The aristocracy of Boston, during these years, regarded John Quincy Adams as an *enfant
terrible;* but the people of Massachusetts stood by him and, in the
end, rallied to congratulate him at a monster meeting. Human
nature could not withhold its tribute of admiration.

George Thompson, an Englishman, whose life had been devoted
to the cause of Anti-slavery in the British colonies, and who was
one of the greatest popular orators of that day, had done more than
any one man to abolish West Indian Slavery; and it was natural
that Garrison, who went to England in 1833 for conference with
the victorious British Abolitionists, should enlist Thompson in the
American cause and bring him to America. Upon the passage of
the Act abolishing Slavery in the West Indies, Lord Brougham had
risen in the House of Lords and said: "I rise to take the crown of
this most glorious victory from every other head, and place it upon
George Thompson's. He has done more than any other man to
achieve it."

One can imagine how the Americans of 1833, who set a price on
the heads of their own compatriots when they were Abolitionists,
would welcome the most powerful, the most popular living advocate of the hated cause—a stranger and an Englishman. Thompson
was mobbed and hounded, threatened, insulted, and would have
been killed if fate had assisted ever so little by lending the opportunity. I shall content myself with giving Mr. May's description of
Thompson's eloquence.

"Mr. Thompson then went on to give us a graphic, glowing account of the long and fierce conflict they had had in England for
the abolition of slavery in the British West Indies. His eloquence

rose to a still higher order. His narrative became *a continuous metaphor,* admirably sustained. He represented the Anti-slavery enterprise in which he had been so long engaged as a stout, well-built ship, manned by a noble-hearted crew, launched upon a stormy ocean, bound to carry inestimable relief to 800,000 sufferers in a far-distant land. He clothed all kinds of opposition they had met, all the difficulties they had contended with, in imagery suggested by the observation and experience of the voyager across the Atlantic in the most tempestuous season of the year. In the height of his descriptions, my attention was withdrawn from the emotions enkindled in my own bosom sufficiently to observe the effect of his eloquence upon half a dozen boys, of twelve or fourteen years of age, sitting together not far from the platform. They were completely possessed by it. When the ship reeled or plunged or staggered in the storms, they unconsciously went through the same motions. When the enemy attacked her, the boys took the liveliest part in battle—manning the guns, or handing shot and shell, or pressing forward to repulse the boarders. When the ship struck upon an iceberg, the boys almost fell from their seats in the recoil. When the sails and topmasts were well-nigh carried away by the gale, they seemed to be straining themselves to prevent the damage; and when at length the ship triumphantly sailed into her destined port with colors flying and signals of glad tidings floating from her topmast, and the shout of welcome rose from thousands of expectant freedmen on the shore, the boys gave three loud cheers, 'Hurrah! Hurrah! Hurrah!' This irrepressible explosion of their feelings brought them at once to themselves. They blushed, covered their faces, sank down on their seats, one of them upon the floor."

It was one thing for the American to thrill for the liberty of Greece, Poland, or Hungary; and another to allow foreign enthusiasts to thrill over American Anti-slavery. Thompson was marked for assassination and kidnapping; and a gibbet was erected for him in Boston. It was Thompson whom the mob were in search of when they caught Garrison at the meeting of the Female Anti-slavery Society, soon to be described. The impertinence of Thompson consisted in his being a foreigner, and this fact played upon the peculiar American weakness—our sensitiveness to foreign opinion. "He comes here from the dark corrupt institutions of Europe," said Mr. Sprague in Faneuil Hall, "to enlighten *us* upon the rights of man and the moral duties of our own condition. Received by our hospitality, he stands here upon our soil, protected by our laws, and hurls 'firebrands, arrows and death' into the habitations of our neighbors, and friends, and brothers; and when he shall have kindled a conflagration which is sweeping in desolation over the land, he has only to embark for his own country, and there look serenely back with indifference or exultation upon the widespread ruin by which *our* cities are wrapt in flames, and *our* garments rolled in blood. . . . If the storm comes, *we* must abide its pelting; if convulsions come, *we* must be in the midst of them. To *us,* then, it belongs to judge of the exigencies of our own condition, to provide for our own safety, and perform our own duties without the audacious interference of foreign emissaries."

I am grateful to this man, George Thompson. He stood for courage in 1835 in Massachusetts. He typified courage also at a later time during the Civil War when he stood with John Bright and W. E. Forster as the expounders of the cause of the North before the people of Great Britain. He was one of the friends of the United States to whom it is due that England's governing classes did not assist the South openly, and thereby give rise to an age-long, never-dying antagonism between England and America. I am glad that George Thompson lived to be thanked by Lincoln and his Cabinet, and to be ceremoniously received in a House of Representatives thronged with the best intellects and hearts in America.

## V. THE CRISIS

I HAVE GIVEN the foregoing sketches almost at random, and, where possible, in the words of others, in order to call up the decade between 1830 and 1840 without myself feeling the responsibility of a historian, and without asking the reader to give a chronological attention. Facts often speak for themselves more truly, the less we explain them; and the philosophy of history is perhaps a delusion.

It was between 1830 and 1840 that the real work of Garrison was done. At the beginning of that decade Abolition was a cry in the wilderness; at the end of it, Abolition was a part of the American mind. Garrison's occupation throughout the epoch was to tend his engine—his *Liberator*—and to assist in the formation of Anti-slavery societies. Every breath of the movement was chronicled in the

*Liberator,* every new convert wrote to Garrison for help. Garrison was the focus, the exchange, the center and heart of Anti-slavery activity. He was the channel into which the new streams flowed. If a drop of Abolition fell from the sky anywhere in America, it was found in the *Liberator* upon the following morning. This drawing of the new men into a knowledge of each other made magical heat. Every Abolition act or thought went immediately into the general Abolition consciousness. It was Garrison who caused the heat-lightning of 1825 to turn into the thunderbolts of 1835. His gift of doing this was his greatness.

We must imagine Garrison then, as always, behind and underneath the machinery and in touch with all the forces at work, writing away at his terrible *Liberator*—fomenting, rebuking, retorting, supporting, expounding, thundering, scolding. The continuousness of Garrison is appalling, and fatigues even the retrospective imagination of posterity: he is like an all-night hotel: he is possessed: he is like something let loose. I dread the din of him. I cover my head and fix my mind on other things; but there is Garrison hammering away, till he catches my eye and forces me to attend to him. If Garrison can do this to me, who am protected from dread of him by eighty years of intervening time, think how his lash must have fallen upon the thin skins of our ancestors!

Garrison, then, and his propaganda went forward; the South under its resentment swelled and fretted, and every phase of the matter was day by day recorded in the *Liberator,* which remains as the inexhaustible coal-bed and historical deposit of these things. Every leaf and twig, every letter, every quarrel, every prayer, is here preserved in the immortality of petrifaction. To be in himself the focalization and to leave behind him the fossilization of that wonderful epoch was Garrison's function.

The crisis in the struggle came in 1835-6, when a great attempt was seriously made by the whole organized force of the Slave Power to put down the Abolitionists. This suppression was to be done in the ordinary, historic way—through laws to be made against them, and through violence, where law fell short. It will be seen in an instant that law was, throughout, on the side of the Abolitionists; and this is the reason why the violence was so great. The South could not get at Garrison through sheriffs and jailers. Therefore it was tempted to resort to riots and extra-legal terrorism.

It was lured into the fabrication of myths—as for instance, the myth that the constitution protected slavery against adverse opinion, the myth that the Abolitionists favored slave-insurrection, the myth that the language of the Abolitionists was so extreme as to make them the enemies of society, the exceedingly absurd myth that to send Anti-slavery publications through the United States mails directed to adult white men in the South was, somehow, an atrocious outrage.

The truth is that between 1830 and 1835, the element of passion was rising past the danger point, and running into something like insanity in the Southern mind. A madman believes his own logic, and ever drives it further. The failure of law to protect the South left no accurate demarcation as to their demands. At the beginning, the slaveholders protested that Garrison should be silenced, because he was a fanatic; but before long they were demanding that the Abolitionists should be hanged, and were mingling the name of Channing in their execrations. In the beginning they demanded only to be let alone; but before long they were swearing that the South should buy and sell slaves underneath Bunker Hill monument.

This tidal fury could not be conciliated. Anything that threatened the existence of Slavery stimulated the fury—and the time had come when all nature began to threaten Slavery. Slavery began, in fact, to stalk abroad and horrify the world: Slavery came out of its lair. At first there were meetings in the South, destruction of Abolition literature in the mails; then white Vigilance Committees, and State Legislatures called, in chorus, upon the North to stop the plague of Abolition by the enactment of stringent laws against the reformers. A giant demonstration was planned by the friends of the South to take place at Faneuil Hall in Boston—1500 names being appended to the call for the meeting. This meeting was to demonstrate the good faith of the North towards the slaveholders, and to give public opinion a set towards the enactment of criminal statutes against Anti-slavery. The meeting was a tremendous success and proved to be a sort of "view-halloo" for Slavery. It was naturally followed by an increase of riots and mob violence against the Abolitionists. The most important of the new ebullitions was the so called Boston mob (October 21, 1835), which led Garrison about with a rope round him—and might easily have ended in his death.

General Jackson, the President of the United States, referred to the recent Pro-slavery demonstration at the North in his Message to Congress, in December, 1835.

"It is fortunate for the country," he says, "that the good sense, the generous feeling, and the deep-rooted attachment of the people of the non-slaveholding States to the Union, and to their fellow citizens of the same blood in the South, have given so strong and impressive a tone to the sentiments entertained against the proceedings of the misguided persons who have engaged in these unconstitutional and wicked attempts ['to circulate through the mails inflammatory appeals addressed to the passions of the slaves']."

Here was support from high quarters. It was not till January, 1836, that the time came for Edward Everett, Governor of Massachusetts, to take notice of the entreaties of the Southern States. In his Message to the Massachusetts Legislature he intimated that the Abolitionists could be punished under the law as it stood: because "whatever by direct and necessary operation is calculated to excite insurrection among slaves may be prosecuted as a misdemeanor at common law." This part of his Message was referred to a joint Committee of Five of the Legislature, together with the Southern entreaties. It was in the hearings before this committee, that the work was done which put an end to Southern hopes of enslaving Massachusetts. The great attempt was foiled. The South had done its utmost to suppress Abolition, and had failed. After this time, Abolition is in the field as an accepted fact. Within eight years thereafter, in 1844, Birney was nominated for the Presidency as the candidate of a third party.

We must think of this whole Southern movement as a big, mountainous wave, involving multitudinous lesser waves and eddies, which, as it rolled forward and surged back, created complex disturbances, all interlocked with one another. The power of the South was exerted over the President at Washington and over the ruffian on the street corner, and it was all one power, one pull together, one control. Let us take a rapid but clear glance over certain stages of the movement which have already been mentioned. The popular feeling at the South, which was the motive power of the whole affair, may be illustrated in a paragraph from the *Richmond Whig*:

"Let the hell-hounds of the North beware. Let them not feel too much security in their homes, or imagine that they who throw fire-brands, although from, as they think, so safe a distance, will be permitted to escape with impunity. There are thousands now animated with a spirit to brave every danger to bring these felons to justice on the soil of the Southern States, whose women and children they have dared to endanger by their hell-concocted plots. We have *feared* that Southern exasperation would seize some of the prime conspirators in their very beds, and drag them to meet the punishment due their offenses. We fear it no longer. We hope it may be so, and our applause as one man shall follow the successful enterprise."

This then is the outer ring of fiery feeling which dreamed of moving Northward and doing, it knew not what, to put down Abolition. The spirit of violence, as shown, for instance, in the breaking into of the United States Post-office at Charleston, S. C., and the seizing of Abolition newspapers for a bonfire, was redoubled by the attitude of the Federal authorities. The United States Postmaster-General, Amos Kendall, a Massachusetts man, approved the deed. Now, the only reason why riots do not occur every day, accompanied by destruction of property and injury to unoffending persons, is that the strong arm of law and order is against the ubiquitous loafer and ruffian. Once let this gentleman see a chance of rioting with impunity, and he instantly appears and riots. How easily then did disturbances follow when State and National officials, as well as the rich and respectable classes, gave the cue. The average man at the time we are chronicling really believed that the Abolitionist was a criminal in essence, and ought to be proclaimed as such by law.

The Anti-slavery writers, in describing this period, use the terminology of fiercer times. Harriet Martineau calls it a "Martyr Age," and we constantly hear of the "reign of terror" in 1835. Now the term "persecution" is apt to call up in our minds the fiercest images of history, scenes of bloodshed and tyranny, combats with wild beasts in the amphitheater, executions in the market-place, men driven to hide in caves in the rocks, etc. The unpleasantnesses and injustices to which the Abolitionists were subjected never justified a literal application of the terms "martyr," "reign of terror," etc.; but the word "persecution" is most aptly used to describe their sufferings, if we reflect that there are persecutions which do not result in death. Prudence Crandall was certainly persecuted; the Abolitionist was harassed and his life was made as uncomfortable as the law would permit. The outrages, both legal and extra-legal, which fell upon Anti-slavery people, may be studied at leisure in the press of the time. They lie upon any page of the history of that day. The following are severe cases. They are mentioned in the large life of Garrison:

"Dr. Reuben Crandall, a perfectly innocent man and younger brother of Prudence Crandall, was thrown into a noisome jail in Georgetown, in the District of Columbia, on a charge of 'circulating Tappan, Garrison & Company's papers, encouraging the Negroes to insurrection,' for which a mob would fain have lynched him. . . . It was nearly a year before he was brought to trial, and meantime his health had been ruined."

"Five thousand dollars were offered on the Exchange in New York for the head of Arthur Tappan on Friday last," writes Henry Benson to Garrison. "Elizur Wright is barricading his house with shutters, bars and bolts."

"How imminent is the danger that hovers about the persons of our friends, George Thompson and Arthur Tappan!" writes Garrison to George Benson. "Rewards for the seizure of the latter are multiplying—in one place they offer three thousand dollars *for his ears*—a purse has been made up, publicly, of $20,000, in New Orleans for his person. I, too,—I desire to bless God,—am involved in almost equal peril. I have just received a letter written evidently by a friendly hand, in which I am apprised that 'my life is sought after, and a reward of $20,000 has been offered for my head by six Mississippians.' He says—'Beware of the assassin! May God protect you!' and signs himself 'A Marylander, and a resident of Philadelphia.' "

"Typical cases were the town-meeting appointment of a vigilance committee to prevent Anti-slavery meetings in Canaan, N. H.; the arrest of the Rev. George Storrs, at Northfield, in the same State, in a friendly pulpit, at the close of a discourse on slavery, as a 'common brawler,' and his subsequent sentence by a 'justice of the peace' to hard labor in the House of Correction for three months (not sustained on appeal); and the repeated destruction of Birney's *Philanthropist* printing-office by the 'gentlemen of property and standing' in Cincinnati—an outrage bearing a close resemblance to that engendered by the Faneuil Hall meeting, and ending in a midnight raid upon the colored homes of the city, with the connivance of the mayor."

As for mere social ostracism,—the refusal on the part of Beacon Street to ask Wendell Phillips to dinner, the black-balling at the Clubs in New York of distinguished Abolitionists,—the Muse of History cannot record these things among her tragedies. We have seen, in the case of Henry I. Bowditch and his walk with Douglass, upon what plane the drama moved. It was a drama of character, rather than a drama of blood. The Anti-slavery people are, however, not inexcusable in calling this epoch "the reign of terror." It was, at any rate, a reign of brickbats and anathema, which developed here and there into tarring and feathering and murder. The reason why it did not turn into a veritable reign of terror, a time of proscription and execution, is that the middle classes at the North awoke out of their lethargy, and protected the reformers instead of oppressing them. The passions were there; the introverted enthusiasm of the South and the martyr spirit of the Abolitionist were there. There also was the pliant tool between them— the Northern business man. This tool, however, broke.

The great meeting in Faneuil Hall, already spoken of, a meeting attended by numerous Southerners who made the journey to Boston on purpose, represents the apogee of the Sun of Liberty in America. In considering this meeting we are again baffled by the strangeness of its historic atmosphere; the low pulse of the Northerner is a puzzle to us. It is easy to understand and sympathize with the Southern tiger bereft of his prey, and with the Northern lamb who lifts up his voice for justice before being devoured. The first is the typical tyrant, and the second the typical saint. The conduct, however, of the Massachusetts Philistine, who looks like an educated gentleman and acts the part of a terrified servant, is a difficult thing to understand. We can get a sidelong glimpse into the mystery by remembering how people behave in moments of panic —with what meanness, with what irrational thoughtlessness, with what denial of their true selves. Now the Massachusetts statesmen, business men, and persons of distinction and wealth, had lived for years in a state of *continuous panic*. This had shredded them into spectres. It is quite true that there was a spiritual "reign of terror" at this epoch, a terror which intimately affected all classes, and the Abolitionists' phrase is thus truer than it seemed.

Peleg Sprague, one of Massachusetts' most distinguished men, a United States Senator and former Congressman, and a thoroughly representative mouthpiece of the Conservative classes at the North, spoke as follows at the memorable Pro-slavery meeting in Faneuil Hall:

"Time was, when . . . the generous and gallant Southrons came to our aid, and our fathers refused not to hold communion with slaveholders. . . . When *He,* that slaveholder (pointing to the full-length portrait of Washington), who from this canvas smiles upon you—his children—with paternal benignity, came with other slaveholders to drive the British myrmidons from this city and this hall, our fathers did not refuse to hold communion with him or them. With slaveholders they formed the Confederation, neither asking nor receiving any right to interfere in their domestic relations; with them they made the Declaration of Independence, coming from the pen of that other slaveholder, Thomas Jefferson, a name dear to every friend of human rights. And in the original draft of that Declaration was contained a most eloquent passage upon this very topic of negro slavery, which was stricken out in deference to the wishes of members from the South."

There is something about this language so far removed from good sense that it gives us pause. That *something* is the influence of terror. Mr. Harrison Gray Otis, who moved on a still higher social plane than Sprague, nay, who stood very near the gods in the imagination of Bostonians, spoke as follows:

"I deny that any body of men can lawfully associate for the purpose of undermining, more than for overthrowing, the government of our sister States. There may be no statute to make such combinations penal, because the offense is of a new complexion."

Mr. Otis found an even stronger objection to the Society in "its evident direction towards becoming a political association, whose object it will be, and whose tendency now is, to bear directly upon the ballot-boxes and to influence the elections," as in the recent case of Abbott Lawrence. "How soon might you see a majority in Congress returned under the influence of (Anti-slavery) associations?"

Otis' reasoning here is the chattering of teeth. "The ballot-box and election!"—why not? The slavery issue to come into politics—

who can prevent it? Where are we? Who is talking? Have I read that sentence aright? Such questions go through one's mind no matter how often one re-reads these speeches. It must be confessed that a city is not far from chaos when so much passion and so faint a rationality can go forth as the voice of her powerful classes, and of her educated men. The situation was greatly alleviated by the good sense and calmness of the Abolitionists; for although Garrison's language was generally blatant, his conduct was invariably exemplary; and the reformers' course of action in legal and legislative maneuvering was often brilliant in the extreme.

The Boston Abolitionists behaved during this trying season with circumspection. After the Faneuil Hall demonstration, Mayor Lyman, who had presided at that meeting, had, in a courteous if not friendly manner, privately counseled them to discontinue their meetings while the public mind was so heated, at the same time assuring them that he would protect them in their rights if they chose to exercise them. They therefore held only their constitutional meetings; and it was one of these which fell due on Wednesday, October 14, the anniversary of the formation of the Boston Female Anti-Slavery Society. This meeting was postponed and duly advertised for October 21, 1835. On that day a Pro-slavery mob, organized by newspaper men and business men, and composed of from two to five thousand particularly respectable persons, was got together for the purpose of tarring and feathering George Thompson, who was believed to be at the meeting. As Thompson was not to be found, the mob cried out for Garrison. It surged into the women's meeting where Garrison was. For some time the thirty women went forward with their prayers and proceedings while the mob howled upon them. Garrison left the meeting in order to protect it, but could not escape from the building on account of the crowd. He therefore retreated across the hall to the Anti-slavery office which happened to be in the same building. Thither the crowd followed him.

"An assault," according to Garrison's account of the matter, "was now made upon the door of the office, the lower panel of which was instantly dashed to pieces. Stooping down and glaring upon me as I sat at the desk, writing an account of the riot to a distant friend, the ruffians cried out—'There he is! That's Garrison! Out with the scoundrel!' etc., etc. Turning to Mr. Burleigh, I said—

'You may as well open the door, and let them come in and do their worst.' But he, with great presence of mind, went out, locked the door, put the key in his pocket, and by his admirable firmness succeeded in keeping the office safe."

Mayor Lyman now appeared upon the scene, and prevailed upon the women to adjourn. They passed down the staircase "amid manifestations of revengeful brutality" and so, in a close column, to the house of Francis Jackson, a new and powerful recruit to their cause. Mayor Lyman now had to deal with the mob. Their attention had been attracted to the Antislavery sign board and Mayor Lyman permitted its demolition by the crowd, a betrayal of his trust as custodian of property and of the peace which Garrison never forgave. The Mayor thereupon devoted his energies to helping Garrison to make good his escape from the mob. Garrison was induced to get out of a rear window, and one of the sheriffs, in order to persuade the crowd to disperse, announced that Garrison had escaped. The crowd, however, got on his track and followed after him. It came up with him in a carpenter's shop. The crowd was made up of both friends and foes.

"On seeing me," continues Garrison, "three or four of the rioters, uttering a yell, furiously dragged me to the window, with the intention of hurling me from that height to the ground; but one of them relented and said—'Don't let us kill him outright.' So they drew me back, and coiled a rope about my body—probably to drag me through the streets. I bowed to the mob, and requesting them to wait patiently until I could descend, went down upon a ladder that was raised for that purpose. I fortunately extricated myself from the rope, and was seized by two or three powerful men, to whose firmness, policy, and muscular energy I am probably indebted for my preservation. They led me along bareheaded (for I had lost my hat), through a mighty crowd, ever and anon shouting, 'He shan't be hurt! You shan't hurt him! Don't hurt him! He is an American,' etc., etc. This seemed to excite sympathy among many in the crowd, and they reiterated the cry, 'He shan't be hurt!'"

At this point we will turn to Charles Burleigh's tale: "Going to the Post-office, I saw the crowd pouring out from Wilson's Lane into State Street with a deal of clamor and shouting, and heard the exulting cry, 'They've got him—they've got him.' And so, sure enough, they had. The tide set toward the south door of the City Hall, and in a few minutes I saw Garrison between two men who held him and led him along, while the throng pressed on every side, as if eager to devour him alive. His head was bare, his face a little more highly colored than in his most tranquil moments, as if flushed by moderate exercise, and his countenance composed." In the upshot, Mayor Lyman's efforts to save him were successful; and Garrison was forthwith jailed for the night as a disturber of the peace.

Throughout this episode Garrison acted with wisdom and courage. Had he behaved in any different manner, had he shown fight, as Lovejoy did at Alton, had his followers become exasperated, bloodshed would probably have followed and the whole controversy in Boston would thenceforth have been overcast by the spirit of civil war. The thing to be noted is that Garrison's conduct during this mob was an exemplification of the whole Anti-slavery policy, which had been fully set out in the documents and literature of the movement during the preceding five years. Moral agitation with no resort to force, no resistance to force, was the Abolition watchword.

When a whole age is completely insane upon some subject, sane views upon that subject will seem like madness to the age. It was thus perfectly normal that the assembly of moderate and holy persons who met in Philadelphia to form the national Anti-Slavery Society in 1833, and parted, as we have seen, with tears and prayers, —should have been both watched and guarded by the police. These men seemed to that age like dangerous malefactors. So also was it accordant with spiritual law that Garrison should have been shut up as a rioter on the night following the Boston mob. He was a man of little humor where his principles were at stake, and could see nothing in the arrest but a ghastly paradox; whereas in reality that arrest is a charming epitome of the times.

How much danger was Garrison in while being dragged and hustled through the streets of Boston? Was there a pot of hot tar and a bath of feathers waiting at some convenient corner, which would have been produced and set in operation on the Common, but for Mayor Lyman's timely interference? Very likely there was. There seems to have been a plan to maltreat Thompson, which plan was divulged to the public through broadsides and to Garrison through anonymous letters, one of the letters being friendly. We see the Garrison mob to-day as the sticking-point of violence in Boston. We know that this mob was not followed by a series of mobs. We see that it did no damage to speak of; and therefore we cannot help thinking of it as a harmless affair. But a mob has always something devilish and incalculable in its action, and a mob led by gentlemen, a mob in which the ruffian saw that he was supported by the Bank President, and that no prosecution could possibly follow in the wake of the day, might be the most dangerous of all mobs. The experience of Birney and his press in Ohio, of Lovejoy and his press in Illinois, the burning of Pennsylvania Hall in Philadelphia and countless other acts of violence show that the Abolitionists did right to be alarmed.

As a matter of fact they were seriously frightened. Though Garrison and the ladies put on as bold a front as they could, they did not feel like shaking hands with their old friend Mayor Lyman and regarding that mob as a joke. There was, after all, a real and terrific force at the back of the mob. It was the mob of the *Richmond Whig,* of the Faneuil Hall Pro-Slavery meeting. The Southern fire had moved North, and seemed to encircle the Anti-slavery agitators. The "gentlemen of property and standing"—to use the pompous newspaper phrase of the day—who led the mob, were actuated by one of the major passions of humanity—defense of property.

For in a big sense, in a metaphorical sense, the South was right; and all this Abolition movement was a servile uprising. The slave heart and soul had somehow come into communion with the Anti-slavery heart and soul, and together they were generating an earthquake beneath the slaver's feet. This whole religious message is mirrored in "Uncle Tom's Cabin," a book which it took twenty years of Abolition to make the soil for. "Uncle Tom's Cabin" appeared in 1852 and is to-day our key to that whole epoch: but the vision of that book was in the heart of the Anti-slavery people long before. They gave that vision to the world; they gave it to Harriet Beecher. The pictures and thoughts of "Uncle Tom's Cabin" were sown into the mind of Harriet Beecher as a child; the emotion of it was generated in 1829. And so the early instinct to put down this whole movement as a servile insurrection had justification in fact.

As a general rule servile insurrections are put down by officials;

by judges, sheriffs and troops. Historic reasons made this course not feasible at the North. Therefore the deluded upper classes of Boston, who had thrown in their fortunes with slavery, did what all determined men do when law fails them—they took the field personally. The women who marched through the rioters trembled with antagonism, if not with fear. One of them wrote afterwards:

"When we emerged into the open daylight, there went up a roar of rage and contempt, which increased when they saw that we did not intend to separate, but walked in regular procession. They slowly gave way as we came out. As far as we could look either way the crowd extended—evidently of the so-called 'wealthy and respectable,' 'the moral worth,' 'the influence and standing.' We saw the faces of those we had, till now, thought friends; men whom we never before met without giving the hand in friendly salutation; men whom till now we should have called upon for condemnation of ruffianism, with confidence that the appeal would be answered."

There is something old-world, something more like the Eighteenth Century than the Nineteenth in this scene; I would not miss it out of our history. But the people who took part in it could never think of it lightly. It was too real, too fierce, too dangerous. The mob was too near, and its genteel character was unpleasant. I have at times thought that the Anti-slavery people were almost ungrateful to Theodore Lyman. To them he was a man who had not done his duty; he should have protected their sign. He should have defied and dispersed the rioters, instead of conciliating the mob and dispersing the ladies' meeting. He should have jailed the ringleaders in the riot and conducted Garrison in safety to his home. And yet, for an official during a great mania, and for a man by nature timid during a riot, he seems to me to have done fairly well. He appeared upon the scene of conflict, and in the end saved Garrison from the clutches of the mob. The Abolitionists, like lawyers in a jury case, never missed a point; and the points against Lyman were obvious. He was a pawn in their demonstration. It was their function to throw up a clear silhouette of the times, and to show just how far Theodore Lyman had fallen short of efficient courage, and Boston, of liberty. We cannot hold them to the historic perspective, nor expect them to display a judicial temper upon the matter.

I myself, however, feel grateful to Lyman for saving Garrison;

though I also respect Garrison for not altering his criticism by an iota because of the personal question. He could not step aside for a moment and play the part of philosophic spectator. As well expect a point which is moving in a curve in obedience to an algebraical formula to change its course for reasons of politeness. Let us not forget that all these people were wound up, and that each man and each group of men in the struggle was following a track like one of the heavenly bodies; being governed by a logic, unseen, mighty, and terrible, leading to greater things.

The Boston mob gives a barometrical record of conditions in the North in 1835. Every village had its Garrison, its Mayor Lyman, its Francis Jackson. Moved by the spectacle of Garrison's persecution, Charles Sumner, Henry I. Bowditch, and Wendell Phillips became converts to the cause. Every village in the North after October 21, produced its Bowditch, its Sumner, its Phillips. There were now six State and three hundred auxiliary Anti-slavery societies, all formed since 1831. "So then," comments Garrison, "we derive from our opponents these instructive but paradoxical facts—that without numbers, we are multitudinous; that without power, we are sapping the foundations of the Confederacy; that without a plan, we are hastening the abolition of slavery; and without reason or talent we are rapidly converting the nation."

For the second time within three months it became wise for Garrison to leave Boston. His landlord, quite naturally, feared for the safety of his house. The printing-office of the *Liberator* was closed, and the work was done clandestinely elsewhere. During this winter the Abolitionists kept rather quiet; but they emerged in the spring to attend the Lunt Committee—that Committee appointed by Governor Everett to consider the requests from Southern legislatures that Massachusetts should do something to suppress Anti-slavery. The first hearing in the matter was held on March 4th, 1836, at the State House. The audience was so large that the Hall of the House of Representatives had to be used. Many women, including Harriet Martineau, were there, and the social, political and mercantile classes of Boston were represented. When the meeting came to order Samuel J. May set forth the history of Abolition and showed the mildness of its methods. Ellis Gray Loring, one of the earliest aristocrats to join the cause, reviewed the perfect legality of the ideals and conduct of the Anti-slavery societies. The gentle

Charles Follen, a learned and saintly man, began to expound the rights of man and to explain to the Committee the natural sequence of cause and effect which existed between the Faneuil Hall Pro-slavery meeting in August and the treatment of Garrison by the mob in October. Chairman Lunt, who seems to have been a narrow partisan who little understood the issue under discussion, and who thought it his duty towards his constituents to browbeat the reformers, declined to allow Follen to pursue this line of argument. The Abolitionists, upon this rebuff, brought the hearing promptly to a close, asserting that they must be allowed to make their own arguments or none. They immediately petitioned the Legislature for permission to argue their own case in their own way before the Committee. This militant front assumed by the little body of Protestants was a very able piece of tactics. Their real appeal was, of course, directed to the grand public—not to the public of the city of Boston, but to the people of the State of Massachusetts who were watching the whole proceeding with passionate interest. Would the Legislature dare to refuse the Abolitionists permission to present their own arguments in their own way? The permission was granted.

The second hearing before the Lunt Committee was a stormy one. It was naturally crowded, because of the issues raised by the first. Mr. Lunt behaved, strange to say, with the same singular stupidity as at the first meeting. Let us remember that this hearing was for the moment the center of the great storm of passion that had moved up from the South during the preceding year and by which it was hoped that the Abolition cause would be engulfed and obliterated. The center of the storm, however, is perfectly calm. The voice that comes from it is not a still small voice, but a very calm voice. It is the voice of Samuel J. May. "It seemed," said Mr. May, addressing the chairman, "it seemed on the 4th instant that the chairman considered that we came here by his grace to exculpate ourselves from the charges alleged against us by the legislatures of several of the Southern States; and that we were not to be permitted to express our anxious apprehensions of the effects of any acts by our Legislature intended to gratify the wishes of those States. In order, therefore, that we might appear before you in the *exercise of our right as free citizens,* we have appealed to the Senate and House of Representatives, and have their permission to do so. Dr. Follen was setting before you what we deem the most serious evil to be apprehended from any condemnatory resolutions which the Legislature might be induced to pass; and if he is not permitted to press this upon your consideration our interview with the Committee must end here."

Mr. Follen was allowed by the chairman to proceed, but the following speaker, Rev. William Goodell, was compelled to sit down by the chairman. He was at the moment in the midst of a most telling quotation from Gov. McDuffie, of South Carolina, who had said that "the laboring population of no nation on earth are entitled to liberty or capable of enjoying it." "Sit down," said Mr. Lunt, "the Committee will hear no more of it." The Abolitionists immediately and meekly showed their compliance by beginning to leave the Hall.

This is magnificent agitation: it is impossible for reformers to be more able than this. Such conduct sends out an appeal to common sense, to justice, to fair play, to the mind of the average man and of the courageous person everywhere. And lo, before the Hall had emptied itself, there came a response to that appeal, a response from one whose mere name was a summary of the traditions he spoke for. "The audience here began to leave the Hall," continues Mr. May, "but were arrested by a voice in their midst. It was the voice of Gamaliel Bradford, not a member of the Anti-Slavery Society, who had come there only as a spectator, but had been so moved by what he had witnessed that he pronounced an eloquent, thrilling, impassioned, but respectful appeal in favor of free discussion." When Bradford sat down Mr. George Bond, one of the most prominent merchants and estimable gentlemen of Boston, made a speech to the same effect.

Abolition thus began to penetrate the stalwart and sensible classes. It could no longer be regarded as merely the infatuation of foolish persons. There were still to be years of struggle, but the loneliness was at an end. The great shattering climax of all this period was the murder of Elijah P. Lovejoy, a young Presbyterian minister and native of Maine, on November 7th, 1837, at Alton, Ill. He was shot down as he emerged from the burning building in which the last of four Anti-slavery printing-presses perished at the hands of infuriated Pro-slavery rioters. Lovejoy, though a clergyman, had determined to protect his rights of free speech under the Constitutional forms of self-defense. He and his friends had armed themselves according to law, and were under the protection of the Mayor of the town. They thus stood like the embattled farmer at Lexington—nay, more strongly, for these men were not Revolutionists, but peaceful citizens resisting illegal violence. Lovejoy was ruthlessly shot down by a shower of bullets from the street. Here was something that the average American could understand. It was not expressed in Biblical language, nor did it come from a saint; but it spoke to the fighting instinct in the common man.

Nothing except John Brown's Raid ever sent such a shock across the continent, or so stirred the North to understand and to resist the advance of slavery as Lovejoy's murder. The Abolitionists of Boston immediately sought Faneuil Hall, which was at first refused. Dr. Channing, heading the free-speech movement, joined with the Abolitionists in claiming the right to use the Hall. It was felt that the great public was behind this claim: the use of the Hall was granted. There followed that meeting to which the dazzling eloquence of Wendell Phillips has given immortality. It was a free-speech, not an Abolition meeting, its object being to protest against Lovejoy's murder as a crime against the statutory right of free speech.

We see here a very different situation from the state of things at the Faneuil Hall Pro-slavery meeting of 1835, when slavery had hired the Hall and held the floor. At the Lovejoy meeting freedom had hired the Hall and held the floor. Nevertheless the meeting was to some extent packed by the Pro-slavery element who hoped to stampede it in favor of the South. Phillips was an unknown young lawyer, the scion of a very distinguished family, and he had gone to the meeting without any intention of taking part in its proceedings. He was drawn into the fray by the extraordinary speech of James T. Austin, attorney-general of Massachusetts and leader of the conservatives. Austin declared that Lovejoy was not only presumptuous and imprudent while he lived, but that he "died as the fool dieth." He compared the murderers of Lovejoy with the men who destroyed the tea in Boston harbor, and said that wherever the Abolition fever raged there were mobs and murders. Austin was vociferously applauded and there was some prospect that the whole meeting would break up in a riot. Phillips had great difficulty in getting the attention of the audience. "Mr. Chairman," he said, "we have met for the freest discussion of these resolutions and the events which gave rise to them." (Cries of "question," "hear him," "go on," "no gagging"—etc.) "I hope I shall be permitted to express my surprise at the sentiments of the last speaker—surprise not only at such sentiments from such a man, but at the applause they have received within these walls. A comparison has been drawn between the events of the Revolution and the tragedy at Alton. We have heard it asserted here, in Faneuil Hall, that Great Britain had a right to tax the Colonies; and we have heard the mob at Alton, the drunken murderers of Lovejoy, compared to those patriot fathers who threw the tea overboard! (Great applause.) Fellow-citizens, is this Faneuil Hall doctrine?" ("No, no.") After giving a clear exposition of the difference between the riot at Alton and the Boston Tea Party, Phillips continued: "Sir, when I heard the gentleman lay down principles which place the murderers of Alton side by side with Otis and Hancock, with Quincy and Adams, I thought those pictured lips (pointing to the portraits in the Hall) would have broken into voice to rebuke the recreant American—the slanderer of the dead. (Great applause and counter-applause.) The gentleman said that he should sink into insignificance if he dared not gainsay the principles of these resolutions. Sir, for the sentiments he has uttered, on soil consecreated by the prayers of Puritans, and the blood of patriots, the earth should have yawned and swallowed him up." (Applause and hisses, with cries of "Take that back!") The uproar became so great that for a time no one could be heard. At length the Hon. William Sturgis came to Mr. Phillips's side at the front of the platform. He was met with cries of "Phillips or nobody," "Make him take back *recreant;* he shan't go on till he takes it back." When it was understood that Mr. Sturgis meant to sustain, not to interrupt Mr. Phillips, he was listened to and said, "I did not come here to take part in this discussion, nor do I intend to; but I do entreat you, fellow citizens, by everything you hold sacred, —I conjure you by every association connected with this Hall, consecrated by our Fathers to freedom of discussion,—that you listen to every man who addresses you in a decorous manner." Phillips resumed his speech and made in this, his début, one of the best remembered triumphs in a life of oratory. His speech, though imperfectly reported, is one of those historic speeches which carry their eloquence to the reader, even through the disguise of print. When Phillips was asked afterwards what his thoughts were during the delivery of it, he said he was thinking of nothing except the carrying of resolutions. This he accomplished and the vote of the meeting was cast for freedom: the murderers of Lovejoy were denounced.

The practical importance of this outcome to the Abolitionists is brought home to us in a letter written by one of them, a woman, to a friend in England. "Stout men, my husband for instance, came home that day and lifted up their voices and wept. Dr. Channing did not know how dangerous an experiment, as people count danger, he adventured. We knew that we must send our children out of town and sleep in our day garments that night, unless free discussion prevailed."

The burning of Pennsylvania Hall, in Philadelphia, in May, 1838, was among the last of the outrages committed during this epoch of persecution. There seems after this to have been a simmering down of the antagonism of the public to the Abolitionists, and it was not until 1850 that another great attempt, the last attempt, was made by the united South to control the destinies of the North.

## VI. RETROSPECT AND PROSPECT

It seems to be always the case in human affairs that conditions grow better and worse at the same time. An evil reaches its climax at the very moment that the corrective reform is making a hidden march upon it from an unexpected quarter. And so this epoch of crisis in mob violence against Abolition must be recorded as the epoch during which Abolition passed from the stage of moral agitation into the arena of practical politics. The Anti-slavery men had begun by heckling the clergy; they divided up the country into districts and sent their dreaded emissaries with lists of questions which the parsons had to answer. This process rent the churches, or rather it revealed the fact that the churches were Pro-slavery. In like manner the questioning of all candidates for office was taken up by the Abolitionists. In the year 1840 there were two thousand Anti-slavery societies with a membership of two hundred thousand. It is apparent that the political parties at the North were about to feel the same disruptive power run through their vitals that the churches had felt.

If you take up a history of the United States, or the biography of a statesman of this time, you will find that the author only begins to deal with Abolition in about the year 1840, that is, after it has reached the political stage. He writes perhaps a few pages, as Mr. Rhodes does, about the rise of the movement, taking for granted that the reader knows how Abolition got started, and why it was able so soon to overshadow all other questions. The same thing occurs in the history of the rise of Christianity; with this difference—that the early stages of Christianity are involved in obscurity; whereas the activities of the early years of Abolition are recorded in accessible and thrilling books. The historian, as a general rule, gives us only the history of politics. He seems not to be interested in the beginnings of things. And yet, those beginnings are the seed. The beginnings of any movement,—the epoch when it is in the stage of idea, of agitation, of moral impulse, and before it has assumed a shape that can be termed political,—these beginnings show its nature. In them you find the explanation of the later political stages.

The history of the Anti-slavery struggle after 1840—that is to say, the history of political Anti-slavery—has been well analyzed and understood, and can be traced in the biographies of our statesmen. I am not going to retrace it in this essay; for I believe that Garrison's distinctive work was accomplished before 1840. I shall content myself with a few observations which apply to the whole period between 1830 and 1860, and which are equally true of the agitational era and of the political era of the struggle.

The spread of Anti-slavery sentiment was brought about through the doings of the Slave Power. From the time when the State of Georgia in 1830 offered a reward for the arrest of Garrison, till South Carolina seceded in 1860, the education of the North was due to the activity of the South. While North and South were in ignorance of this fact, the form of the reaction and inter-action between Northern and Southern elements was the inevitable form through which such a drama must pass. The Slave Power believed that Garrison, with some almost superhuman agency, was moving upon it to devour it. Slavery, during the whole course of its long suicide, was, in its own view, striving to save itself from destruction. The Abolitionists brought into the conflict the element of Fate. The South knew that no form of compromise could bind Garrison. It felt this with the instinct of the hunted animal. It aimed a blow at the enemy, Abolition; and it struck free speech, it struck the right of petition, trial by jury, education, benevolence, common sense. Slavery began its death agony in 1830, and was driven from one step to another merely as a consequence of the nature of man. If the South could have smiled at Abolition, if it could have kept its temper and lent no hand in assisting the Abolitionists to bring forward their cause, then the way of the reformers would have been hard. This would have happened, perhaps, if Anti-slavery in America had been a pioneer cause, a new light leading the world. But our Anti-slavery cause was a mere means of catching up with Europe. The moral power of humanity at large prevented South Carolina from smiling at Abolition. The slave-owners trembled because they were a part of the thing which criticized them. Massachusetts and South Carolina were parts of that modern world in which their heart-strings met. This solidarity between the North and the South was the cause of the anguish, and the means of the cure.

In the early days of any movement it is only the expert who can read the times correctly. The lean prophet, in whose bosom the turmoil of a new age begins, sees proofs of that age everywhere. He thinks of nothing else, he cares for nothing else. Thus the Abolitionists could see in 1830 what the average man could not understand till 1845—that the Slave Power was a Moloch which controlled the politics of the North and which, in the nature of things, could stick at nothing while engaged in perpetuating that control. Garrison or May could perceive this in 1828 by taking an observation of Edward Everett or of Daniel Webster. But the average citizen could not see it; he lacked the detachment. His obfuscation was a part of the problem, a part of the evil in the period. In 1845 it required the Annexation of Texas to show to the man in the street those same truths which the Abolitionists had seen so plainly fifteen years before. The Annexation of Texas was the most educational of all the convulsive demonstrations of the South.

Where did the motive power reside from which all these changes proceeded? Was this motive power the conscience of the Abolitionists? I do not think so. The Abolitionists stand nearer to a sense of justice, nearer to rational modern life than the rest of our compatriots of that time. But the Abolitionists were not the motive power; they were merely the point of entrance of new life into the community. Every stroke of his pulse that told an Abolitionist that something must be done about slavery, could perform its functions only by flashing down to Georgia, and coming back in the form of anger and of grief. Every argument that split a vestry, or left a mind ruined, was necessary. It was essential that these things should come.

The metaphysical question was always the same, namely: "How far legal argument is valid when it contravenes human feelings?" The question assumed various forms while the fire was eating its way through society towards the powder magazine; but the substance of it never varied. The whole age-long contest in all its Protean forms is summarized in a well-known legal anecdote. Judge Harrington of Vermont is said to have told the attorney for a Southern owner who was seeking to recover a fugitive slave in 1808, that his "evidence of ownership" was insufficient. "What evidence does your Honor require?" "Nothing less than a bill of sale from God Almighty." This story gives the two elements, pity and business interest, expressed in terms of constitutional argument. It summarizes the labors of our statesmen,—Webster, Calhoun, Sumner, Taney, Douglas, Lincoln,—each of whom had his bout with the problem. The unfortunate American statesmen who were obliged to formulate a philosophy upon the matter seem to me like that procession of hypocrites in Dante's Purgatory, robed in mantles of lead. They emerge, each bent down with his weight of logic, blinded by his view of the inherited curse—nursing his critique of the constitution; they file across the pages of our history from Jefferson to Lincoln—sad, perplexed men.

The solution given by Garrison to the puzzle was that the law must give way, that the Constitution was of no importance, after all. This is what any American would have answered had the question concerned the Constitution of Switzerland or of Patagonia. But, for some reason, our own Constitution was regarded differently. I suppose that the politics, theology, and formal organization of the whole world are never so important as they pretend to be. The element of material interest in these matters gives them their awful weight to contemporaries. When we are dealing with a past age this element evaporates, and we see clearly that most of the importances of the world have no claim to our reverence. Now when a man has felt in this way about his own age, we call him a great man; because we agree with him. For this is the test, and the only conceivable test of greatness—that a man shall look upon his own age, and see it in the same light as that in which posterity sees it. We must concede greatness to Garrison. His early editorials upon the question of disunion show that he viewed our Constitution in true historical perspective as early as 1832.

Let us now remember some of the phases of the nightmare which, like a continuous Dreyfus case, perplexed all honest men, all thinking men in America for two generations. The Constitution was so inwoven with our social life that the conflict between the letter and the spirit was ubiquitous. The restless probings went forward at the fireside, in the club, in the shop; no pillow was free from them. Slavery covered every sentiment with a cloak. Slavery was in literature, in religion, in custom. This social, daily, domestic, discussion and heartburn was the true means of regeneration. The political history of slavery was to be the outcome of this fireside discussion. The constitutional theory which any man held was, in this epoch, the outcome of his personal struggle with evil. In other words the slavery question had become the symbol of the relation between good and evil in practical life. We notice in all this the tardiness of the political world in absorbing new ideas. The world of politics is always twenty years behind the world of thought. The world of politics lives and works in ideals which are twenty years old.

The result of all the upturnings of conscience, which went forward in millions of private breasts, was at length seen in the formation of the Republican Party. By the time that party was formed one could distinguish (as Mr. Rhodes points out), two classes of men among its members:—the men actuated by pity for the slave, of whom Sumner was the type; and the men actuated by resentment at being ruled from the South, of whom Seward was the type. It was, however, the Abolition tom-tom that had called both classes from the deep; and the Seward class was but an imperfect, half-awakened example of the true thing. The Seward class could never stand fire. Its courage,—for the infusion of courage was the sole function of that tom-tom,—its courage was in the head and not, as yet, in the vitals. This class was subject to splendid visitations of new idea; and yet it was also subject to the occasional panic-stricken discovery that the bottom had dropped out after all, and that one must go softly, because life could not be trusted.

The abstract, inscrutable nature of the contest between Freedom and Slavery first began to be revealed to the politicians in about 1850; and men then began to feel that the whole historic sequence of things was a fate-drama. Even then, everybody *in politics* was afraid to speak plainly about slavery. It required for instance, notable insight as well as great political courage for Lincoln to state what was known to everyone. In 1858 he took his political life in his hands, and spoke of "the house divided against itself." His associates were scandalized by his rashness, and begged him to omit the phrase. Merciful heavens! Had not this house been divided against itself for three-quarters of a century? Yes, truly, this whole matter was a fate-drama, and in a deeper sense than Seward imagined or than even Lincoln could guess. Seward with his perception of the "irrepressible conflict between opposing and enduring forces," and Lincoln with his vision of the blood of white men, drawn by the sword, which should repay the blood of slaves that had been drawn by the lash—saw only the main crash of the drama. The reality of it was profounder, and the trailing consequences of it were to be more terrible than they suspected.

The intellectual and moral heritages of slavery are with us still. The timidity of our public life and of our private conversation is a tradition from those times, which fifty years of freedom have not sufficed to efface. The morbid sensitiveness of the American to new political ideas has been a mystery to Europe. We cannot bear to hear a proposition plainly put;—or let me say, we are only recently beginning to cast off our hothouse condition, and to bear the sun and wind of the natural world. I do not know anything which measures the timidity of the American nation better than the moderation of Lincoln's speeches, a moderation which he was obliged to adopt in order to be listened to. He was always in danger of showing his heart; he must avoid the taint of Abolition, the suspicion of any attack upon the Constitution. He must step gingerly and remember what part of the State of Illinois he is in at the moment. Even when the war breaks out Lincoln is obliged to invent a way of looking at that war which shall place the Union cause in a popular light. He is obliged to pretend that the war is not primarily about slavery at all. He is obliged to speak about the war in such a way as would be incomprehensible to any one who is not a close student of our conditions. He must remember the Border States.

Here was a war over slavery which had been visibly brewing for more than a lifetime. The Anti-slavery party comes into power; the Slave States revolt and the question is whether the Government shall prosecute a war and extinguish slavery—or not. This is the way in which the educated foreigner viewed the matter, and he was right. There were, however, in the Northern and Border States, many educated Americans who had from their cradles been taught to regard slavery as a thing almost sacred—a thing which could not rightfully become a cause of war between the States. Therefore great caution had to be used in making any popular statement of the matter. This war must be looked upon as a war, not about Slavery but about Union. Lincoln was thus obliged to befog his State papers with such careful statements as to his being *for the Union* without slavery, or *for the Union* with slavery, that the outsider really began to doubt whether, perhaps, Lincoln meant that slavery might be retained in the end. Even in this crisis no one in political life was allowed to speak in plain terms. To do so was regarded as most unwise. The misguided and half-minded man of America had been trained to believe that Slavery was sacred; but *for the Union* he will die. So long as you call it Union he is ready to die for humanity.

Lincoln, then, during the years of his leadership was obliged to stoop to the complex, peculiar, and inferior character of the contemporary mind. He was one of the greatest political geniuses and one of the most beautiful characters that ever lived; and he managed somehow to be intellectually honest and very nearly frank while fulfilling his mission. Yet I can never read his debates with Douglas or consider his Border-State policy without being struck by the technical nature of all our history. One of Lincoln's chief interests in life, from early manhood onward, lay in emancipation. This he could not say and remain in politics; nay, he could not think it and remain in politics. He could not quite know himself and yet remain in politics. The awful weight of a creed that was never quite true—the creed of the Constitution—pressed down upon the intellects of our public men. This was the dower and curse of slavery.

The value of the epoch during which the curse was cast off is that, in reading about it, we can see thought move, and can find ourselves in sympathy with all shades of reform. Let us take an example at random, as one might take a drop of water for a sample of the ocean. In the dawn of the Abolition movement its adherents in New York State, who were responsible, educated and propertied persons, were a little afraid of the Garrisonians of Boston. The principles of the New York group are well stated by William Jay in the first number of the *Emancipator,* and are in striking contrast to the declarations of Garrison in the first number of the *Liberator,* which I have quoted on a previous page. Jay writes:

"The duty and policy of immediate emancipation, although clear to us, are not so to multitudes of people who abhor slavery and sincerely wish its removal. They take it for granted, no matter why or wherefore, that if the slaves were now liberated they would instantly cut the throats and fire the dwellings of their benefactors. Hence these good people look upon the advocates of emancipation as a set of dangerous fanatics, who are jeopardizing the peace of the Southern States and riveting the fetters of the slaves by the very attempt to break them. In their opinion the slaves are not fit for freedom, and therefore it is necessary to wait patiently till they are. Now, unless these patient waiters can be brought over to our side, emancipation is hopeless; for, first, they are an immense majority of all among us who are hostile to slavery; and, secondly, they are as conscientious in their opinions as we are in ours, and unless converted will oppose and defeat all our efforts. But how are they to be converted? Only by the exhibition of Truth. The moral, social, and political evils of slavery are but imperfectly known and considered. These should be portrayed in strong but true colors, and it would not be difficult to prove that, however inconvenient and dangerous emancipation may be, the continuance of slavery must be infinitely more inconvenient and dangerous.

"Constitutional restrictions, independent of other considerations, forbid all other than moral interference with slavery in the Southern States. But we have as good and perfect a right to exhort slaveholders to liberate their slaves as we have to exhort them to practice any virtue or avoid any vice. Nay, we have not only the right, but under certain circumstances it may be our duty to give such advice; and while we confine ourselves within the boundaries of right and duty, we may and ought to disregard the threats and denunciations by which we may be assailed.

"The question of slavery in the District of Columbia is totally distinct, as far as we are concerned, from that of slavery in the Southern States.

"As a member of Congress, I should think myself no more authorized to legislate for the slaves in Virginia than for the serfs of Russia. But Congress has full authority to abolish slavery in the District, and I think it to be its duty to do so. The public need information respecting the abominations committed at Washington with the sanction of their Representatives—abominations which will cease whenever those Representatives please. If this subject is fully and ably pressed upon the attention of our electors, they may perhaps be induced to require pledges from candidates for Congress for their votes for the removal of this foul stain from our National Government. As to the Colonization Society, it is neither a wicked conspiracy upon the one hand nor a panacea for slavery on the other. Many good and wise men belong to it and believe in its efficacy."

These New York men are in a more rational state of mind than Garrison was. When in 1833 Samuel J. May begged William Jay to join in forming a national Anti-Slavery Society, Jay paused. I suppose he had been reading the *Liberator*. He declined to join, on the ground that the local Societies could do the work as well for the time being, and that the great objection to Anti-slavery societies was that they aimed at unconstitutional interference with slavery. He suggested that if a National Society was to be formed, it should show, by its constitution, that the objects were *legal,* that is to say, it should acknowledge the exclusive rights of the Southern States to settle the matter of slavery within their own boundaries, and claim only the right to urge Congress to abolish slavery in the District of Columbia, and the territories.

The new Society did, in fact, adopt carefully drawn provisions expressive of Jay's idea, and Mr. Tuckerman, in his memoir of Jay, comments upon the circumstance as follows: "Looked at by the light of subsequent events, the importance of placing Anti-slavery upon a Constitutional basis cannot be over-rated. Upon the principles thus distinctly avowed rested the moral and political strength of the movement during the struggle of thirty years." It is impossible not to feel the truth of this reflection. The average American mind could only deal with the slavery matter when presented in legal form. Mr. Garrison, in spite of his denunciation of the Union, felt the force of this appeal to law and order. He actually signed the declarations of the new Society, which put the movement on a conservative basis, and he wrote editorially in the *Liberator* as follows "Abolitionists as clearly understand and as sacredly regard the Constitutional powers of Congress as do their traducers, and they know and have again and again asserted that Congress has no more rightful authority to sit in judgment upon Southern slavery than it has to legislate upon the abolition of slavery in the French colonies." This editorial is entirely out of key with Mr. Garrison's fundamental beliefs, as we shall see later. We have to remember, in reviewing any convulsive epoch in history, how frequently men, even great men, have been jolted forward and back between conflicting points of view. Garrison was subject to these revulsions, and was totally unconscious of his inconsistencies.

The point I would here make is that all these various and contradictory dogmas were necessary. Each one was an inevitable progression, going on in somebody's mind, and each helped to move the argument along. It is easy to see that the attitude of Jay in recommending legal action only, and the attitude of Garrison in denouncing the Constitution, as he did most of the time, were both of them necessary to the working-out of the problem.

There was another element of complication which assisted in disintegrating the Anti-slavery cause. As time went on Garrison kept confiding his new developments and changes in opinion to the columns of the *Liberator*. His views upon Peace, No-government, Woman's Rights, Non-resistance, as they formed themselves within him, were advocated with an incredible volubility which disquieted many other Abolitionists. After one or two attempts at schism, the more conservative Abolitionists formed a new Society which went by the name of the New Organization. With whom shall we sympathize among all these contending sects? Manifestly with them all. Let us examine the case of Woman's Rights. Women had been working in the Massachusetts Society and in the National Society from the beginning. Women were among the ablest, the most effective, the most saintly, the most distinguished, of the workers in the Abolition cause. Should they be admitted to equal fellowship or not? Manifestly they must be so admitted. Yet to do this identified the cause of Abolition with the theory of Woman's Rights, a conclusion most repugnant to many excellent Anti-slavery people. There must follow, then, a multiplication of sects; this was one of the logical necessities of the situation.

Now there was no person in the Abolition camp who understood these matters from a philosophic point of view. The New Organizationists were struggling to keep the cause pure, to keep it from being mixed up with other causes and ideas, such as Woman's Rights, Non-resistance, etc. Garrison was also struggling to keep the cause pure; to prevent it from being diluted, and from falling into the hands of sectarians, Presbyterians, Methodists, etc. In 1840 we find the Garrisonians chartering a steamboat, and taking several hundred men and women from Massachusetts, in order to "carry" the annual meeting in New York City for his ideas. Jay seems to have understood that the confusion was past cure, though he did not quite perceive that it was inevitable. His personal course was to resign from the Anti-slavery organizations when they veered away from Constitutional methods. He again became a free lance. In 1846 he writes: "Our Anti-slavery societies are for the most part virtually defunct. Anti-slavery conventions are whatever the leaders present happen to be; sometimes disgustingly irreligious, and very often Jacobinical and disorganizing; and frequently proscriptive of such of their brethren who will not consent to render Abolition a mere instrument for effecting certain political changes having no relation whatever to slavery."

Now let us take one step further and note this:—that at the time of the Annexation of Texas, Jay had arrived at Garrison's views as to the necessity of breaking up the Union. "Should the slaveholders succeed," says Jay, "in their design of annexing Texas, then indeed would I not merely discuss, but with all my powers would I advocate an immediate dissolution. I love my children, my friends, my country too well to leave them the prey to the accursed Government which would be sure to follow." And again: "A separation will be more easily effected *now* than when the relative strength of the South shall have been greatly augmented. Hereafter we shall be as serfs rebelling against their bonds. *Now,* if the North pleases, we may dissolve the Union without spilling a drop of blood."

It is impossible not to sympathize with the state of mind revealed in these last sentences—a state of mind to which Jay has been brought by the march of events. The truth is that the whole vast problem was constantly moving forward. Not only Garrison and Jay, but every soul who lived in America during these years held fluctuating views about the matter of slavery; and the complex controversy moved forward like a glacier, cracking and bending and groaning, and marking the everlasting rocks as it progressed. In the end, we come to see that the whole struggle was a solid struggle, an ever-changing Unity, an orchestra in which all the various instruments were interdependent and responsive to one another. We see also that each individual then living was somehow a little microcosm which reflected and had relations with the whole moving miracle; and that every element of the great universe was represented in him. We can perceive plainly, to-day, how necessary it was that each error should be made; that Garrison should issue his inconsecutive fulminations of dogma, and that Jay should retire in gloom, when the cause entered politics. We see how inevitable it was that the cause should be betrayed and polluted, soiled and kneaded into the mire of the world, woven into the web of American life. Gradually the leaven was invading and qualifying the whole lump.

## VII. THE MAN OF ACTION

IN CALLING UP THE SPIRIT of Garrison out of the irrecoverable past we must never forget that he was but a *part* of something;—we must call up the whole epoch. Garrison was as much an outcome of slavery as was "Uncle Tom's Cabin" or John C. Calhoun. He is a spiritual product; he is that suppressed part of man's nature, which could not co-exist with slavery. He is like a fiery salamander, who should emerge during a glacial epoch—crawling out from a volcano that was all the time hidden beneath the ice-crust. It is through the hot breath of this salamander that verdure is to be brought back to the earth, and the benign climate of modern life restored to America. To the conservative minds of his own time he appeared to be a monster; and he was a monster—a monster of virtue, a monster of love, a monster of power.

Let us not judge but only examine him. Fortunately the materials are abundant, the record is complete. His life in four enormous volumes has been written by his children; and the children of Garrison suppress nothing. We are brought into absolute contact with all of Garrison's singularities. This biography is not a critical work: it is, one might say, a work of idolatry. Every little battle is fought over again, and every word or gesture of the protagonist is deemed sacred. The reader feels oppressed by the one-sidedness of this procedure. One becomes sorry for the other actors in the great drama: for after all, these men could not help it that they were not Garrison; they seem to live out their lives under the pitiful inferiority of not being Garrison. For instance, Cassius M. Clay of Kentucky went to Yale College, and was, as a youth, converted to Anti-slavery by a lecture of Garrison's at New Haven. Clay returned to Kentucky, emancipated his slaves, and thereafter made relentless war on slavery, thus furnishing, say Garrison's biographers, "an example without parallel both of heroism *and of the folly of attempting to undermine the slave power from within.*" The italics are mine. But why do Garrison's children think it folly for a Southerner to agitate against slavery in Kentucky? It seems to me that to do so was right. I believe that the agitation of Clay in Kentucky somehow went to a spot in the slavery question that nothing else could have reached. It affected Garrison himself as nothing else ever affected him: it softened him. It was the conduct of Clay and Rankin (another Southerner) which caused Garrison to offer a resolution at the Cincinnati convention in 1853, in which he stated that the Abolitionists of the country were as much interested in the welfare of the slaveholders as they were in the elevation of the slaves. His habitual attitude towards the slaveholders had always been, "We do not acknowledge them to be within the pale of Christianity, of Republicanism, of humanity. This we say dispassionately, and not for the sake of using strong language."

Garrison, then, was touched by the almost miraculous courage of Clay. If there had been a few more such Southern Abolitionists, the bitterness of this whole epoch might have been qualified. It was, however, one of the stock taunts made against Garrison that he did not go South to agitate; and, therefore, these biographers reason that any agitation of slavery in the South must be "folly." The four great volumes contain frequent little hacks and side-cuts out of old controversies which are wearying to the modern reader. Nevertheless, the volumes contain also such mountains of precious ore, such a painstaking recovery of everything germane to the subject, such an angel-minded presentation of the blind side of Garrison, with the record of things said against him—that the reader is left with nothing but gratitude to these children who are so like the father that their very deficiencies, rightly taken, illuminate their subject. The children of Garrison have not written a philosophic history.* But there are other things in the world besides criticism, and some things more rare and more beautiful than the critical intellect. There is praise and worship; there is reverence and love; there is the girasole that turns towards the sun and follows him from the orient to his setting, ever in a dream, ever without knowing that he has changed his position, because *for her* he has not moved or changed; to her he is only himself.

Garrison was a man of action, that is to say, a man to whom ideas were revealed in relation to passing events, and who saw in ideas the levers and weapons with which he might act upon the world. A seer on the other hand is a man who views passing events by the light of ideas, and who counts upon his vision, not upon his action, for influence. The seer feels that the mere utterance of his thought, nay the mere vision of it, fulfills his function. Garrison was not a man of this kind. His mission was more lowly, more popular, more visible; and his intellectual grasp was restricted and uncertain. Garrison was a man of the market-place. Language to him was not the mere means of stating truth, but a mace to break open a jail. He was to be the instrument of great and rapid changes in public opinion during an epoch of terrible and fluctuating excitement. The thing which he is to see, to say, and to proclaim, from moment to moment, is as freshly given to him by prodigal nature, is as truly spontaneous, as the song of the thrush. He never calculates, he acts upon inspiration; he is always ingenuous, innocent, self-poised, and, as it were, inside of some self-acting machinery which controls his course, and rolls out the carpet of his life for him to walk on. We must remember this; for it is almost impossible not to use words which imply the contrary in describing the

---

* "Writing not without bias, surely, but in a spirit emulous of the absolute fairness which distinguished our father, we have done little more than coördinate *materials to serve* posterity in forming that judgment of him which we have no desire to forestall. In a literary point of view, we have aimed at nothing more than clearness, sequence and proportion."—Life of Garrison. Preface, p. xii.

acts of the practical man—the man who utters sharp sayings in order to gain attention, the man who gives no quarter when in the ring.

In reviewing the life of such a man we must take the logic of it as a whole; we must feel the unity of it as an organic process and torrent of force. It will contain many breaks in metaphysical unity; yet through these breaks may be seen the gushing stream of the spirit. I believe that Garrison shifted his ground and changed his mind less often than most men of that kaleidoscopic epoch. But we must not try to make him out more consistent than he was. All politics, including reform agitation, proceeds from day to day and from year to year under the illusion that the thing in hand is more important than it really is. All the actors are at every moment somewhat deceived; and to each of them the thing in hand ever a little blots out the sky. The agitator lives in a realm of exaggeration, of broadsides and italic types, of stampings of the foot and clenchings of the hand. He uses the terms and phrases of immortal truth to clamp together his leaky raft. The "belle réponse" of the martyr, the deep apothegm of the sage, and the words of Christ, are ever on his lips. Such things pass muster in politics without exciting comment. And yet, these statements of ideal truth, like the axioms of arithmetic, never quite square with the material world. They can only be felt and believed in mentally. You can never find or measure out an exact pound of anything or lay off a true mile; nor can you assign any accurate value to the influence of a good deed. Nevertheless, the inaccuracy which is permissible in the market-place is very much greater than the inaccuracy permissible to the historian who sits in his closet endeavoring to think clearly upon the matter.

The source of Garrison's power was the Bible. From his earliest days he read the Bible constantly, and prayed constantly. It was with this fire that he started his conflagration. Now the Bible is many things. It is a key to metaphysical truth, it is a compendium of large human wisdom, it is a code of ethics, it is the history of a race, and many other things beside. To Garrison, the Bible was the many-piped organ to which he sang the song of his life, and the arsenal from which he drew the weapons of his warfare. I doubt if any man ever knew the Bible so well, or could produce a text to fit a political emergency with such startling felicity as Garrison.

Take for example, the text provided by him for Wendell Phillips's speech on the Sunday morning following Lincoln's call for troops in 1861. "Therefore thus saith the Lord; Ye have not hearkened unto me in proclaiming liberty everyone to his brother, and every man to his neighbor: behold, I proclaim a liberty for you, saith the Lord, to the sword, to the pestilence, and to the famine."

I doubt whether Cromwell or Milton could have rivaled Garrison in this field of quotation; and the power of quotation is as dreadful a weapon as any which the human intellect can forge. From his boyhood upward Garrison's mind was soaked in the Bible and in no other book. His "Causes" are all drawn from the Bible, and most of them may be traced to the phrases and thoughts of Christ, as for instance Peace (Peace I give unto you), Perfectionism (Be ye therefore perfect), Non-resistance (Resist not evil), Anti-sabbatarianism (The Lord is Lord of the Sabbath). So also, a prejudice against all fixed forms of worship, against the authority of human government, against every binding of the spirit into conformity with human law—all these things grew up in Garrison's mind out of his Bible reading; as they have done in the minds of so many other men before and after him. He, himself, was not going to be bound, and never was bound, by any declaration nor by any document. He even arrived at distrusting the Bible itself, perceiving that the Bible itself was often a tyrant—much as Christ saw the tyranny of the law of Moses. All this part of Garrison's mental activity is his true vocation. Here he rages like a lion of Judah. By these onslaughts he is freeing people from their mental bonds: he is shaking down the palaces of Babylon.

His age was the age of social experiments, and he was ever ready to take on a new one. This hospitality to new dogmas annoyed his associates, and led, as we have seen, to revolts, schisms, and heresies in the Anti-slavery ranks. Garrison seems to have been assailed by such multitudinous revelations from on high that he was obliged to publish one dispensation in order to clear the wires for the next. There is one of these manifestoes which reveals the impromptu character of them all. "Despite its length," say the biographers, "the greater part of this important document must be given here." There follow several pages of fine print, concerning the causes uppermost in Garrison's mind, which evidently had filled up all the space in the *Liberator,* or used up all the ink in the office; and yet it appears at the close, that Garrison has forgotten to say anything about woman's rights. And so he calls out, like a man upon a departing stage-coach: "As our object is *universal emancipation,* to redeem women as well as men from a servile to an equal condition —we shall go for the RIGHTS OF WOMEN to their utmost extent."

In those days societies were founded for everything. No one ever paused to consider what things could or could not be accomplished through organization, nor how far the sayings of Christ were parts of one another, nor whether at the bottom of all these questions there lay some truth which enveloped them all. Every one rushed to utterance, and Garrison more than all men put together. So long as we consider his utterances in the large, as part of the upturning of that age, as the *sine qua non* of a new epoch, we love and value them. It is only when we collocate them, analyze them, and try to find something for our own souls in them, that they turn out to be emergency cries. They were designed towards local ends, they were practical politics, they do not always cohere with one another.

The great thesis to which he devoted his life, however, was unquestionably sound. He thus announced it in the *Liberator* in 1832:

"There is much declamation about the sacredness of the compact which was formed between the free and slave States, on the adoption of the Constitution. A sacred compact, forsooth! We pronounce it the most bloody and heaven-daring arrangement ever made by men for the continuance and protection of a system of the most atrocious villainy ever exhibited upon the earth. Yes, we recognize the compact, but with feelings of shame and indignation; and it will be held in everlasting infamy by the friends of justice and humanity throughout the world. It was a compact formed at the sacrifice of the bodies and souls of millions of our race, for the sake of achieving a political object—an unblushing and monstrous coalition to do evil that good might come. Such a compact was in the nature of things, and according to the law of God, null and void from the beginning. No body of men ever had the right to guarantee the holding of human beings in bondage.

"Who or what were the framers of our Government that they should dare confirm and authorize such high-handed villainy— such a flagrant robbery of the inalienable rights of man—such a glaring violation of all the precepts and injunctions of the Gospel— such a savage war upon a sixth part of our whole population? They were men, like ourselves—as fallible, as sinful, as weak, as ourselves. By the infamous bargain which they made between themselves, they virtually dethroned the Most High God, and trampled beneath their feet their own solemn and heaven-attested Declaration, that all men are created equal, and endowed by their Creator with certain inalienable rights—among which are life, liberty, and the pursuit of happiness. They had no lawful power to bind themselves or their posterity for one hour—for one moment—by such an unholy alliance. It was not valid then—it is not valid now. Still they persisted in maintaining it—and still do their successors, the people of Massachusetts, of New England, and of the twelve free States, persist in maintaining it. A sacred compact! a sacred compact! What, then, is wicked and ignominious?

"It is said that if you agitate this question you will divide the Union. Believe it not; but should disunion follow, the fault will not be yours. You must perform your duty, faithfully, fearlessly and promptly, and leave the consequences to God: that duty clearly is, to cease from giving countenance and protection to Southern kidnappers. Let them separate, if they can muster courage enough—and the liberation of their slaves is certain. Be assured that slavery will very speedily destroy this Union *if it be let alone;* but even if the Union can be preserved by treading upon the necks, spilling the blood, and destroying the souls of millions of your race, we say it is not worth a price like this, and that it is in the highest degree criminal for you to continue the present compact. Let the pillars thereof fall—let the superstructure crumble into dust—if it must be upheld by robbery and oppression."

This statement of Garrison's is, to my mind, the best thing ever said about slavery in the United States. There is no exaggeration in the statement: it is absolutely true. It is a complete answer to the Constitutional point; and makes all our ante-bellum public men (including Lincoln) appear a little benighted. They are like men who have been born in a darkness and have lived always in a twilight. They all have a slight, congenital weakness of the eye, which prevents them from taking the daylight view of this whole matter.

We ourselves to-day are so habituated to the historic obfuscation of our ancestors that we make allowance for it—more allowance, indeed, than we ought to make. We have, by inheritance, rather weak eyes on this subject ourselves. The true cause for wonder as to the age of Abolition is not that Garrison was right, but that there should have been only one person in America with a clear head. Let us now turn forward over ten years of history—including all the pictures of struggle and incidents referred to in the earlier pages, and let us read Garrison's most famous exposition of his theme uttered in 1842:

"We affirm that the Union is not of heaven. It is founded in unrighteousness and cemented with blood. It is the work of men's hands, and they worship the idol which they have made. It is a horrible mockery of freedom. In all its parts and proportions it is misshapen, incongruous, unnatural. The message of the prophet to the people in Jerusalem describes the exact character of our 're- publican' Compact: 'Hear the Word of the Lord, ye scornful men that rule this people. Because ye have said, We have made a cov- enant with Death, and with Hell are we at agreement; when the overflowing scourge shall pass through, it shall not come unto us: for we have made lies our refuge, and under falsehood have we hid ourselves: Therefore thus saith the Lord God, Judgment will I lay to the line, and righteousness to the plummet: and the hail shall sweep away the refuge of lies, and the water shall overflow the hiding-place. And your covenant with Death *shall be annulled,* and your agreement with Hell *shall not stand;* when the overflowing scourge shall pass through then ye shall be trodden down by it.'

"Another message of the same inspired prophet is equally appli- cable: 'Thus saith the Holy One of Israel, Because ye despised this word, and trust in oppression and perverseness, and stay thereon: Therefore, this iniquity shall be to you *as a breach ready to fall,* swelling out in a high wall, whose breaking cometh suddenly, AT AN INSTANT. And he shall break it as the breaking of a potter's vessel that is broken to pieces; he shall not spare: so that there shall not be found in the bursting of it, a sherd to take fire from the hearth, or to take water withal out of the pit.'

"Slavery is a combination of Death and Hell, and with it the North have made a covenant and are at agreement. As an element of the Government it is omnipotent, omniscient, omnipresent. As a component part of the Union it is necessarily a national interest. Divorced from Northern protection it dies; with that protection, it enlarges its boundaries, multiplies its victims, and extends its rav- ages."

These passages are too direct to be called extravagant. They are appalling. They are magnificent. And they came much nearer to expressing the general opinion of the country in 1842 than the milder words quoted above came to expressing the contemporary opinion of 1832. Education was marching, the case was beginning to be understood. Within three years after Garrison's denunciation of the Constitution as an agreement with Hell, the Annexation of Texas brought thousands of the most conservative minds in the country, including Channing, to the point of abandoning the Constitution; and when in 1854 Garrison publicly burned the Constitution on the Fourth of July, the incident was of slight importance. Civil War was already inevitable: the dragon's teeth had been sown: the blades of bright bayonets could be seen pushing up through the soil in Kansas.

We see, then, the profound unity of Garrison's whole course, and may examine with indulgence some minor failures in logic which are very characteristic of him—very characteristic, indeed, of all practical-minded men who, after making one fault of logic, proceed to joggle themselves back again to their true work by committing a second. It is apparent that a man who assumes Garrison's grounds as to the importance of the spirit, and the unimportance of everything else, can never turn aside and adopt any institution, without doing violence to his own principles. To disparage all government because it is "the letter that killeth," and thereafter to swear fealty to some party, or adopt a symbol, or advise a friend to vote with the Whigs is inconsistent. One who believes in standing for *absolute* principle can never indorse some political scheme on the ground that "this time it doesn't count." One who believes it wrong to meet force with force cannot retain the privilege of approving some particular war or some particular act of self-defense, which seems to him to be useful. Garrison had not the mental training to perceive this, and to do so would have involved his retirement from the camp to the closet: it would have involved his being someone else. Suffice it to say that from time to time his nature drew a veil over his theories, and so obscured them that he was able to support the Constitution of the United States, to rejoice in bloodshed, to take active part in political contests,—both in the great occasional National elections (as when he came out for Lincoln or

Frémont), and in the continuous petty politics of the Anti-slavery cause.

After having supported one of these human institutions with zeal, and having justified his conduct with facile and self-deceiving casuistry, he would again ascend the mountain, the veil would be withdrawn from his intellect, and he would see his true vision once more and proclaim it with renewed fervor: the vision, namely, that no institution should be held sacred.

Let us now look upon Garrison's dealings with Anti-slavery societies, newspapers, and meetings by the light of the foregoing views. When a new religious movement begins to stir in a community, its members are drawn together through the spiritual likeness of one to the other. They are few: they are held together by persecution: they have all things in common. They need no creed; they all feel as one. This stage cannot endure; for someone arises who wishes to hold office. The Apostles began quarreling as to who should be greatest even during Christ's lifetime. As soon as any organization is formed, there arise differences of opinion, and the era of politics is reached. With our modern ideas of club organization for everything, a political element enters into any cause whenever two or three are gathered together in it. It ought to be a lesson to us to observe how completely all men, even great men, are the children of their age. Garrison took up the propagation of the Anti-slavery cause by means of Democratic societies—a means which ties up any cause into little tight knots as it goes along, much as certain forms of crochet work progress by adding little groups of hard knots to other groups of hard knots. The machinery of his movement made vigilance essential. He might be outvoted, his newspaper might be taken from him, his control might be destroyed at any juncture. He is obliged, at intervals, to throw himself into the intrigue of Anti-slavery government, with the words of Moses on his lips and some vote-getting, hall-packing device in his mind. This was not true of the earliest years of the movement; but came about through the mighty logic of natural law as the movement spread.

Persecution purifies any new religion. As the wave of persecution which had held the Abolitionists together from 1830 to 1837 began to subside, quarrels broke out. It was not until 1850 when the triumph of the Slave Power in the passage of the Compromise Bill, gave rise to a new and short persecution, that the Anti-slavery people enjoyed again a short period of unity and peace. The inevitable quarrels over creed and dogma set in in 1839. Anti-slavery developed a complex and bitter political activity. This is the epoch of mutual proscriptions. The purity of the faith is ever at stake, New Organization is branded by Old Organization "as the worst form of pro-slavery." The *Tocsin of Liberty* maintained: "The simple truth is, the American A. S. Society has linked itself to pro-slavery, to get friends—and, like the Colonization Society, it has become an obstacle to progress which must be removed." Mr. Garrison reported from the business committee, "that we cannot regard any man as a consistent Abolitionist who, while holding to the popular construction of the Constitution, makes himself a party to that instrument, by taking any office under it requiring an oath, or voting for its support."

We can see to-day that it was through these very struggles that the new thought was penetrating the community. It is at first through the multiplication of new agencies, and later through an attack upon existing agencies, and an absorption into the older organs of society, that new thought always sinks and spreads, touching and changing society both visibly and invisibly. This process is inevitable, but Garrison quarreled with it. He was ever wanting to keep the faith pure. He saw that no one else cared so much about the subject as he himself did; and he thought that he must keep the precious ichor from pollution. As late as 1857, he moaned that if it had not been for the split in the Anti-slavery ranks in 1840, slavery might have been abolished before then. It was not given to him to see that he could have kept himself and all his following clear of all entanglements, and could have exerted the maximum of influence with the minimum of effort, if he had simply formed no organization, but had merely taken in subscriptions for the cause, in his own name, and to do with as he pleased. His organization and his *Liberator* were in any case, and always, mere personal organs of his own: they followed his mental vagaries, they stuck to him, they were himself; and this same result could have been accomplished with infinite heart's ease instead of infinite heart's anguish, had Garrison but seen how to do it. In adopting a formal organization he was adopting part of the very element that his thought rejected: he was fighting the cause of no-government by means of a "machine"; he was supporting the spirit by votes.

Hence Garrison's share in all the wearisome, little, and at times, degraded bickering between Anti-slavery societies; hence much personal vilification and heated talk over trifles. We see here also that these defects in Garrison proceed from a want of philosophic continuity of thought. Philosophic insight he had, but philosophic continuity he had not. There came a time in the forties when he seems to have half-perceived the nature of his own mission—to have half-seen, at least for a moment, that there were to be no simon-pure Abolitionists except himself, and that his function was to influence the world from where he stood. This insight was probably the result of watching the same phenomena occur again and again, of seeing his Cause move constantly forward through an infinite series of failures: "As fast as we, the Old Organization, make Abolitionists, the new converts run right into the Liberty Party, and become almost wholly hostile to us. This results from the strong leaning of our National character to politics. . . . It is disheartening to see that every blow we strike thus tells in a degree against ourselves, and yet duty bids us keep on striking." It is Wendell Phillips who in this passage is accurately describing the operation of a great law of influence, and who yet seems to see in it merely evidence of human perversity. Later on, and especially during the war, Garrison became reconciled to that law, which his own life had ever blindly obeyed and exemplified.

I must now speak of the matter of strong language. The prophet, great or small, is not so much an individual, as a part of the consciousness of all men. He acts in a particular way upon the force of life, just as a prism acts in a particular way upon light. He is formed by pressure of some sort, and appears at critical times, just as a prism is created by pressure in the womb of the mountain. His understanding of his own function is uncertain, and there have been many plain-minded prophets who could suffer martyrdom, but not explain. I cannot find that even Socrates exactly understood the theory of agitation. The world sometimes thinks of these men as stupid people who know not what they would be at. We should think of them as spirits who enact a lesson rather than as moralists who read a lecture. Let every man carry home what he can from the auto-da-fé. The prophets are hot volcanic lava, rolling out of some hidden furnace—which is really a distributive furnace, and overflows to a lesser degree in other men.

The aerolites which fall in Terra del Fuego show much the same chemical nature as those of Iceland. So of these accusing, flaming aerolites of politics. The Jewish prophet is the most soft-hearted of them all, and it is to this variety that Garrison belongs. These men see the suffering of the world, and they see or feel the relation between the suffering of one man and the selfishness of the next. The greatest of them all speaks thus:

"For they bind heavy burdens and grievous to be borne, and lay them on men's shoulders; but they themselves will not move them with one of their fingers. But all their works they do for to be seen of men: they make broad their phylacteries, and enlarge the borders of their garments, and love the uppermost rooms at feasts, and the chief seats in the synagogues, and greetings in the markets, and to be called of men, Rabbi, Rabbi.

"But woe unto you, scribes and Pharisees, hypocrites! for ye shut up the kingdom of heaven against men: for ye neither go in yourselves, neither suffer ye them that are entering to go in. Woe unto ye, scribes and Pharisees, hypocrites! for ye devour widows' houses, and for a pretence make long prayers: therefore ye shall receive the greater damnation. Woe unto you, scribes and Pharisees, hypocrites! for ye compass sea and land to make one proselyte; and when he is made, ye make him twofold more the child of hell than yourselves. Woe unto you, ye blind guides, which say, Whosoever shall swear by the temple, it is nothing; but whosoever shall swear by the gold of the temple he is a debtor!

"Ye fools and blind: for whether is greater, the gold, or the temple that sanctifieth the gold? Woe unto ye, scribes and Pharisees, hypocrites! for ye pay tithe of mint, and anise, and cummin, and have omitted the weightier matters of the law, judgment, mercy, and faith: these ought ye to have done and not leave the other undone. Woe unto ye, scribes and Pharisees, hypocrites! because ye build the tombs of the prophets, and garnish the sepulchres of the righteous, and say, If we had been in the days of our fathers, we would not have been partakers with them in the blood of the prophets. Wherefore ye be witnesses unto yourselves, that ye are the children of them which killed the prophets. Fill ye up then the measure of your fathers.

"Ye serpents, ye generation of vipers, how can ye escape the damnation of hell? Wherefore, behold, I send unto you prophets, and wise men, and scribes: and some of them ye shall kill and crucify, and some of them ye shall scourge in your synagogues, and persecute them from city to city: that upon you may come all the righteous blood shed upon the earth, from the blood of righteous Abel unto the blood of Zacharias, son of Barachias, whom ye slew between the temple and the altar. Verily I say unto you, all these things shall come upon this generation. O Jerusalem, Jerusalem, thou that killest the prophets, and stonest them which are sent unto thee, how often would I have gathered thy children together, even as a hen gathereth her chickens under her wings, and ye would not! Behold your house is left unto you desolate. For I say unto you, Ye shall not see me henceforth, till ye shall say, Blessed is he that cometh in the name of the Lord."

The tone of these denunciations is not an accidental characteristic of Christ's. It is an organic product, a concomitant of the hottest, most personal love of men that has ever been known upon the earth. Here then is an outpouring of lava. Vainly might we call this passion, idle, unphilosophical, lacking in courtesy; or say that it fails to distinguish between the sinner and the sin. Granted: granted. Yet this is the way a man speaks who feels as Christ felt. If Christ's way of feeling be right, there is something right about his mode of expression. Somewhere, somehow, this heat is valuable. In some sense these whirling words are true, just, adequate and scientific. They do something which nothing else will do. You say there is evil in them. You are mistaken: there is no evil in them: there is nothing uncharitable in them. They are the terrible music of social agony. You would speak thus yourself, could you see as clearly, feel as keenly, as did Christ. Your calmness is only possible because your heart is cold, or your eyes dim.

Let us now remember what mild gentlemen those Pharisees were, to whom Christ used such strong language. How inoffensive their vices—a little usury, some business villainy, perhaps, a good deal of conventional hypocrisy, front pews in church, public charity-giving. That old Jewish society was probably the most moral society that ever existed. If we consider its thousand years of prophets, its literature of ethics and of devotion, its popular passion for theology, its passion for those discussions which went on constantly in temple and marketplace, and which show a deeper clutch upon truth than Athens at her best could show—if we consider what sort of men those scribes and Pharisees probably were, we shall have to confess that Christ's rebuke fell on men whose faults were mild compared to the atrocities visible in the modern world. Examine the morning newspaper and you will find fiendish cruelties unknown in Judæa.

At the back of the prophet's emotion is his vision of a relation between innocent suffering and half-innocent selfishness. If you should see a man being burned alive by respectable rate-payers, you would cry out, you—yet not you but something in you—would burst into agonized protest, accusing those rate-payers; and your language would be harsh. Such is the explanation of the strong language of Anti-slavery. The Abolitionists were the only people in the country who effectually saw what was going on. They saw the slave-block, they saw the child reft from the mother, they saw the floggings and the despair. A hundred volumes might be compiled out of old newspapers by culling advertisements like the following from the *Charleston Courier* in 1825:

"Twenty dollars reward. Ran away from the subscriber, on the 14th instant, a negro girl named Molly. She is 16 or 17 years of age, slim made, lately branded on her left cheek, thus, 'R,' and a piece is taken off her left ear on the same side; the same letter is branded on the inside of both her legs.

"ABNER ROSS

"Fairfield District, S. C."

Let any serious-minded man read a few pages of the Key to "Uncle Tom's Cabin," or of Theodore D. Weld's book on American Slavery, before he decides to discountenance strong language. The people of the South did not know about the horrors of slavery, and taught their children not to see them; they glossed them over, as the inevitable unpleasantnesses of life are always glossed over. John S. Wise was a typical child of the South, save that he had a Northern mother. He was the son of Henry A. Wise, the famous Governor of Virginia, and he has given us a book of memoirs, "The End of An Era," which will be read as long as the Civil War is remembered. John S. Wise had never heard of a slave-auction, till a Northern uncle, whom he met or visited in Philadelphia, took him to see "Uncle Tom's Cabin" on the stage. This was in the fif-

ties, and when John S. Wise was a young lad. On returning to
Richmond he visited a slave-auction, and was as much horrified as
a Northern boy would have been. The horrors of slavery were unknown to the South, and ten times more unknown to the North,
when the Abolitionists discovered them.

I have noticed in recent years one or two denunciations of business wickedness, in which a fierce invective seemed to tear the skin
from the victim's body. One writer pictured the descent of disease
upon the bad man—how his hair fell from his scalp. Now in all
these cases—in the case of Christ, of the Abolitionists, and of the de-
nouncers of business wickedness—the delicate mind is shocked. It
is shocked because it reads in cold blood what is merely the instinctive expression of hot feeling. It sees malice where there is no
malice. The truth is that instinctive expression does something
which philosophic analysis can not do: it reaches the soul, it raises
the temperature and lets in light. The danger of denunciation lies
in the temptation to use denunciation as a method of reform. The
spontaneous cry of pity ought never to be transformed into a lash;
nor should the flames of righteous indignation be exploited politi-
cally, and used to cook up reform. There is nothing of this kind in
the New Testament, but there was a good deal of it in Anti-slavery history. Garrison made a method of personal vilification; he
would cover the wicked with "thick infamy." He was a gadfly and
a fury in his own conception. His utterances are not always, like
Christ's, lyrical utterances; they are calculated attacks. This is hardly
a matter, however, upon which one can make a general statement
that will cover all cases. The particular thing uttered by Garrison
must, in each case, be considered by itself. There are moments when
Garrison is inspired. His faith is perfect. In reviewing the first year
of the *Liberator's* activity, he wrote: "Last year I felt as if I were
fighting single-handed against the great enemy; now I see around
me a host of valiant warriors, armed with weapons of an immortal
temper, whom nothing can daunt, and who are pledged to the end
of the contest. The number is increasing with singular rapidity.
The standard which has been lifted up in Boston is attracting the
gaze of the nation, and inspiring the drooping hearts of thousands
with hope and courage.

"As for myself, whatever may be my fate—whether I fall in the
spring-time of manhood by the hand of the assassin, or be immured

in a Georgia cell, or be permitted to live to a ripe old age—I know that the success of your cause depends nothing upon my existence. I am but as a drop in the ocean, which, if it be separated, cannot be missed. My own faith is strong—my vision, clear—my consolation, great. 'Who art thou O great mountain? Before Zerubbabel thou shalt become a plain: and he shall bring the headstone thereof with shoutings, crying, Grace, grace unto it!' " Surely this is beautiful: it is inspired; it is unconscious.

The following description of the Colonization Society seems to me to be truly Hebraic in its celestial rage—"Upon this pamphlet I shall be willing to stake my reputation for honesty, prudence, benevolence, truth, and sagaciousness. If I do not prove the Colonization spirit to be a creature without heart, without brains, eyeless, unnatural, hypocritical, relentless, unjust, then nothing is capable of demonstration." The reader may turn over Garrison's utterances and pick out the lyrical from the political by the light of his own feeling. In doing so he will find himself forgiving more, the more he becomes acquainted with Garrison's world. The following words about Henry Clay seem cruel: "Henry Clay—with one foot in the grave, and just ready to have body and soul cast into Hell—as if eager to make his damnation doubly sure, rises in the United States Senate and proposes an inquiry into the expediency of passing yet another law, by which every one who shall dare peep or mutter against the execution of the Fugitive Slave Law shall have his life crushed out."

When we learn, however, that the Fugitive Slave Law of 1850 provided that the negro in Massachusetts might be identified through the mere affidavit of the slaveholder agent; that the slave could not testify himself; that there was no trial by jury; that the commissioner's fee was doubled if the slaveholder prevailed; that the bystander could be summoned to aid in preventing an escape, and that, in case any person assisted the escape, such person should be fined a thousand dollars, or imprisoned not exceeding six months; when we learn that modern historians have accounted for its diabolical provisions by suggesting that this Fugitive Slave Bill was intended to involve such humiliation to the North that the North would not swallow it, but would reject it and thereby give the South grounds for secession; when we reflect that the North did swallow this law, and that thousands of free colored people throughout the Northern cities, innocent and industrious citizens, were at that time fleeing to Canada;—when we remember these facts, we begin to feel that Garrison's language was by no means too strong.

When all has been said in his favor, there remains a certain debauchery of language in Garrison, which came from his occupation: he was a journalist. If a man writes all the time, his mannerisms become intensified. Garrison became a common scold—and yet not a common scold, because his inner temper was perfect, and his subject the great subject of the age. He is ever driving his Cause, and feels he must evoke immediate response at every instant. His lack of good taste is not unconnected with his weakness in abstract thinking. To him Slavery in the concrete was the evil. He had not the philosophic power to perceive that sin was the real evil. The evils were injustice, cruelty, murder, lust, egoism. These things he believed to be the outcome of Slavery.

It is not, however, the harshness of language that we are quarreling with. What displeases us in Garrison is the element of policy, the *wholesale* element in his method. But let us beware lest in straining at a gnat we swallow a camel; and let us remember that what is offensive to us, physicked the nation. The young Garrison, the man of twenty-four, when he discovered Immediate Emancipation, was the vortex of an unseen whirlpool. Through his brain spun the turbillion. Something was to break forth; for the power was bursting its envelope. The flood issued in the form in which we know it—with purposed vilification, with excoriating harshness, with calculated ferocity. Only in this manner could it issue: the dam could hold the flood no longer, nor lift it into poetic expression.

If you take the great political agitators of the world like Luther, Calvin, Savonarola, Garibaldi, or certain of the English church reformers, you will find that these men always live under a terrible strain, and they generally give way somewhere. No one can imagine how fierce is the blast upon a man's nervous system, when he stands in the midst of universal antagonism, solitary and at bay. The continuousness of the trial is apt to wear upon the character of reformers. Through vanity, or love of power, or through sheer nervous exhaustion, they become guilty of cruelty or tainted with ambition. There is generally something to forgive in the history of such men. Now Garrison is almost perfect: he is perfect in his lack of personal ambition, in his indifference to power, in his courage, his faith, his persistence, his benevolence. When he breaks down it is in driblets, and every day—in the bad taste and self-indulgence of a disgusting rhetoric, in his inability to "shut up" about anything, in his use of the personal pronoun. Through these channels his nervous exhaustion is worked off, and the inner heart of the creature is left free from the great temptations.

All this armor of language was the paraphernalia of the arena, which was, as it were, handed to Garrison from without—from on high, from within. He puts it on, and enters the lists: he puts it off, and takes supper with his family. As for the kind of man which he really was, the testimony is universal and uniform. I copy one or two phrases almost at random, from among the innumerable descriptions of him. Richard D. Webb, an Irish Abolitionist, and a very old friend of all the Anti-slavery people, wrote: "I . . . spent three weeks with the Garrisons in Paris and Switzerland. It was a time of intense enjoyment, for I exceedingly liked my companions. . . . As to Mr. Garrison himself, he is the most delightful man I have ever known—magnanimous, generous, considerate, and, as far as I can see, every way morally excellent. I can perceive that he has large faith, is very credulous, is not deeply read, and has little of the curiosity or thirst for knowledge which educated people are prone to. But, take him for all in all, I know no such other man. His children are most affectionate and free with him—yet they have their own opinions and express them freely, even when they differ most widely from his. . . . People who travel together have an excellent opportunity of knowing and testing one another. . . . I have never on the whole known a man who bears to be more thoroughly known, or is so sure to be loved and reverenced."

Harriet Martineau has left us a record of her first impressions in all their freshness:—"At ten o'clock he came, accompanied by his introducer. His aspect put to flight in an instant what prejudices his slanderers had raised in me. I was wholly taken by surprise. It was a countenance glowing with health, and wholly expressive of purity, animation, and gentleness. I did not wonder at the citizen who, seeing a print of Garrison at a shop window without a name to it, went in and bought it, and framed it as the most saintlike of countenances. The end of the story is, that when the citizen found whose portrait he had been hanging up in his parlor, he took the print out of the frame and huddled it away."

The lion and the lamb dwelt together in Garrison; but the lion was a peculiar lion, he was never really in control of Garrison, as the lion in Luther was sometimes in control of Luther. The following anecdote from Mr. May's reminiscences gives us a glimpse of the social side of Garrison and shows the perplexities into which his methods of agitation naturally led the public. The scene is upon a steamboat.

"There was much earnest talking by other parties beside our own. Presently a gentleman turned from one of them to me and said, 'What, sir, are the Abolitionists going to do in Philadelphia?' I informed him that we intended to form a National Anti-Slavery Society. This brought from him an outpouring of the commonplace objections to our enterprise, which I replied to as well as I was able. Mr. Garrison drew near, and I soon shifted my part of the discussion into his hands, and listened with delight to the admirable manner in which he expounded and maintained the doctrines and purposes of those who believed with him that the slaves—the blackest of them—were men, entitled as much as the whitest and most exalted men in the land to their liberty, to a residence here, if they chose, and to acquire as much wisdom, as much property, and as high a position as they may.

"After a long conversation, which attracted as many as could get within hearing, the gentleman said, courteously: 'I have been much interested, sir, in what you have said, and in the exceedingly frank and temperate manner in which you have treated the subject. If all Abolitionists were like you, there would be much less opposition to your enterprise. But, sir, depend upon it, that hair-brained, reckless, violent fanatic, Garrison, will damage, if he does not shipwreck, any cause.' Stepping forward, I replied, 'Allow me, sir, to introduce you to Mr. Garrison, of whom you entertain so bad an opinion. The gentleman you have been talking with is he.'"

The gayety of temperament and a certain bubbling power of enjoyment which Garrison possessed he shared with all, or almost all, the Abolitionists; their work made them happy. "I have seen him intimately," said Wendell Phillips, "for thirty years, while raining on his head was the hate of the community, when by every possible form of expression malignity let him know that it wished him all sorts of harm. I never saw him unhappy. I never saw the moment that serene abounding faith in the rectitude of his motive, the soundness of his method, and the certainty of success did not lift him above all possibility of being reached by any clamor about him."

## VIII. THE RYNDERS MOB

THE ANTI-SLAVERY MEETING at the Broadway Tabernacle on May 7, 1850, which goes by the name of the Rynders Mob, has an interest quite beyond the boundaries of its epoch. It gives an example of how any disturbance that arises in a public meeting ought to be handled by the managers of the meeting. It has a lesson for all agitators and popular speakers. It gives, indeed, a picture of humanity during a turbulent crisis, a picture that is Athenian, Roman, Mediæval, modern—a scene of democratic life, flung to us from the ages. I shall copy the account of this meeting almost verbatim from the large Life of Garrison. No comment can add to the power of it.

We have to remember that Webster had made his famous Compromise speech just two months before this meeting; and that the phalanxes of all conservative people, from George Ticknor, in Boston, to the rowdies on the Bowery in New York, were being marshalled to repress Abolition as they had not been marshalled since 1835. It must be noted also that this attempt succeeded on the whole. In spite of the triumph which the Abolitionists scored at this particular meeting, it became impossible for them to hold meetings in great cities for some time afterwards. The complicity of the Churches with Slavery is now almost forgotten. Among the Abolitionists during the critical epoch there was to be found no Episcopal clergyman (save the Rev. E. M. P. Wells, of Boston, who early withdrew from the Cause) and no Catholic priest. The Abolition leaders were, nevertheless, drawn largely from the clerical ranks; but they were Unitarians, Methodists, Congregationalists, Baptists, etc., and were generally driven from their own pulpits in consequence of their opinions about Slavery. The Ecclesiastical Apologists for Slavery founded their case upon the New Testament. A literature of exegesis was in existence of which the "View of Slavery" by John Henry Hopkins, D.D., LL.D., Episcopal Bishop of the Diocese of Vermont, is a late example. At this time Zachary Taylor, a slave-

holder and a devout Episcopalian, was president of the United
States.

The situation was a difficult one for the Evangelical, anti-sectarian
mind to deal with. What was the use of quoting the New Testament
to slaveholders, who were already fortified out of that very volume?
The effect of the situation on Garrison's temperament may be
seen in the meeting at the Tabernacle. There is a demonic element
in what he says: his utterance is forced out of him: it is not calculated. You could not reproduce the spirit of this utterance except
at the cost of two centuries of human passion. There is a demonic
element also in Garrison's courage. He displays, on this occasion,
at least two kinds of genius, the genius of satire,—Voltaire might
have uttered the scathing slashes about "Christ in the presidential
chair,"—and the all but antipodal genius of infinite sweetness of
temperament.

The *New York Herald* in advance of the meeting denounced
Garrison for many days in succession, and advised the breaking up
of the meeting by violence. According to the *Herald,* "Garrison
boldly urges the utter overthrow of the churches, the Sabbath, and
the Bible. Nothing has been sacred with him but the ideal intellect
of the Negro race. To elevate this chimera, he has urged the necessity of an immediate overthrow of the Government, a total disrespect for the Constitution, actual disruption and annihilation of
the Union, and a cessation of all order, legal or divine, which does
not square with his narrow views of what constitutes human liberty.
Never, in the time of the French Revolution and blasphemous
atheism, was there more malevolence and unblushing wickedness
avowed than by this same Garrison. Indeed, he surpasses Robes-
pierre and his associates, for he has no design of building up. His
only object is to destroy. . . . In Boston, a few months ago, a convention was held, the object of which was the overthrow of Sunday
worship. Thus it appears that nothing divine or secular is respected
by these fanatics. . . . When free discussion does not promote the
public good, it has no more right to exist than a bad government
that is dangerous and oppressive to the common weal. It should be
overthrown. On the question of usefulness to the public of the
packed, organized meetings of these Abolitionists, socialists, Sabbath-
breakers, and anarchists, there can be but one result arrived at by
prudence and patriotism. They are dangerous assemblies—calcu-

lated for mischief, and treasonable in their character and purposes. Though the law cannot reach them, public opinion can; and as, in England, a peaceful dissent from such doctrines as these fellows would promulgate—a strong expression of hisses and by counter statements and expositions, so here in New York we may anticipate that there are those who will enter the arena of discussion, and send out the true opinion of the public. . . ."

The meeting of May 7, at the Tabernacle, was a vast assembly which contained many respectable people, intermingled with whom was an organized element of impending mob. The leader of the mob was a well-known ruffian called Isaiah Rynders, "native American, of mixed German and Irish lineage, now some forty-six years of age. He began life as a boatman on the Hudson River, and, passing easily into the sporting class, went to seek his fortunes as a professional gambler in the paradise of the Southwest. In this region he became familiar with all forms of violence, including the institution of slavery. After many personal hazards and vicissitudes, he returned to New York city, where he proved to be admirably qualified for local political leadership in connection with Tammany Hall. A sporting-house which he opened became a Democratic rendezvous and the headquarters of the Empire Club, an organization of roughs and desperadoes who acknowledged his 'captaincy.' His campaigning in behalf of Polk and Dallas in 1844 secured him the friendly patronage of the successful candidate for Vice-President, and he took office as Weigher in the Custom-house of the metropolis. He found time, while thus employed, to engineer the Astor Place riot on behalf of the actor Forrest against his English rival Macready, on May 10, 1849, and the year 1850 opened with his trial for this atrocity and his successful defense by John Van Buren. On February 16 he and his Club broke up an anti-Wilmot-Proviso meeting in New York—a seeming inconsistency, but it was charged against Rynders that he had offered to 'give the State of New York to Clay' in the election of 1844 for $30,000, and had met with reluctant refusal. In March he was arrested for a brutal assault on a gentleman in a hotel, but the victim and the witnesses found it prudent not to appear against a ruffian who did not hesitate to threaten the district-attorney in open court. Meanwhile, the new Whig Administration quite justifiably discharged Rynders from the Custom-house, leaving him free to pose as a savior of the Union against traitors—a savior of society against blasphemers and infidels wherever encountered. . . ."

When the meeting was brought to order Mr. Garrison, as an opening exercise, read certain passages of the Bible, chosen with reference to their bearing upon the slave trade: "The Lord standeth up to plead, and standeth to judge the people. . . . What mean ye that ye beat my people to pieces, and grind the faces of the poor? saith the Lord God of Hosts. . . . Associate yourselves, O ye people, and ye shall be broken in pieces; gird yourselves, and ye shall be broken in pieces. . . . They all lie in wait for blood; they hunt every man his brother with a net. . . . Hide the outcasts, bewray not him that wandereth; let mine outcasts dwell with thee; be thou a covert to them from the face of the spoiler."

"To Dr. Furness, who sat beside Mr. Garrison, these selections (in full, not in our abstract) seemed 'most admirably adapted to the existing state of our country. His reading, however, was not remarkably effective. It was like the ordinary reading of the pulpit, —and hence not calculated to stir the wrath of the ungodly.

"The reading of the Treasurer's report followed, and then Mr. Garrison, resigning the chair to Francis Jackson, proceeded to make the first speech of the day.

"He began," says Dr. Furness, "with stating that they, the members of the Anti-Slavery Society, regarded the Anti-slavery cause as emphatically *the* Christian movement of the day. Nothing could be more explicit than his recognition of the truth and divine authority of the Christianity of the New Testament. He went on to examine the popular tests of religion, and to show their defectiveness. In so doing, his manner was grave and dignified. There was no bitterness, no levity. His manner of speaking was simple, clerical, and Christian. His subject was, substantially, that we have, over and over again, in all the pulpits of the land—the inconsistency of our profession and practice—although not with the same application. . . . Mr. Garrison said great importance was attached to a belief in Jesus. We were told that we must believe in Jesus. And yet this faith in Jesus had no vitality, no practical bearing on conduct and character. He had previously, however, passed in rapid review the chief religious denominations, showing that they uttered no protest against the sins of the nation. He spoke first in this connection of the Roman Catholic Church, stating that its priests and members held slaves without incurring the rebuke of the Church."

Up to this time the only symptoms of opposition had been some ill-timed and senseless applause—or what seemed such. And as it came from one little portion of the audience, Dr. Furness asked Wendell Phillips at his side what it meant. " 'It means,' he said, 'that there is to be a row.' The reference to the Catholic Church gave the first opening to the leader of the gang."

The following is from the *New York Herald's* account of the meeting: "Captain Rynders (who occupied a position in the background, at one side of the organ-loft, and commanding a bird's-eye view of the whole scene beneath) here said: Will you allow me to ask you a question? (Excitement and confusion.)

"Mr. Garrison—Yes, sir.

"Captain Rynders—The question I would ask is, whether there are no other churches as well as the Catholic Church, whose clergy and lay members hold slaves?

"Mr. Garrison—Will the friend wait for a moment, and I will answer him in reference to other churches." (Cheers.)

(Dr. Furness says that Mr. Garrison expressed no surprise at the interruption. There was not the slightest change in his manner or his voice. He simply said: "My friend, if you will wait a moment, your question shall be answered," or something to that effect. There instantly arose a loud clapping around the stranger in the gallery, and from the outskirts of the audience, at different points.)

Captain Rynders then resumed his seat. Mr. Garrison thus proceeded: "Shall we look to the Episcopal Church for hope? It was the boast of John C. Calhoun, shortly before his death, that that church was impregnable to Anti-slavery. That vaunt was founded on truth, for the Episcopal clergy and laity are buyers and sellers of human flesh. We cannot, therefore, look to them. Shall we look to the Presbyterian Church? The whole weight of it is on the side of oppression. Ministers and people buy and sell slaves, apparently without any compunctious visitings of conscience. We cannot, therefore, look to them, nor to the Baptists, nor the Methodists; for they, too, are against the slave, and all the sects are combined to prevent that jubilee which it is the will of God should come. . . .

"Be not startled when I say that a belief in Jesus is no evidence of goodness (hisses); no, friends.

"Voice—Yes it is.

"Mr. Garrison—Our friend says 'yes'; my position is 'no.' It is worthless as a test, for the reason I have already assigned in reference to the other tests. His praises are sung in Louisiana, Alabama, and the other Southern States just as well as in Massachusetts.

"Captain Rynders—Are you aware that the slaves in the South have their prayermeetings in honor of Christ?

"Mr. Garrison—Not a slaveholding or a slave-breeding Jesus. (Sensation.) The slaves believe in a Jesus that strikes off chains. In this country, Jesus has become obsolete. A profession in him is no longer a test. Who objects to his course in Judæa? The old Pharisees are extinct, and may safely be denounced. Jesus is the most respectable person in the United States. (Great sensation, and murmurs of disapprobation.) Jesus sits in the President's chair of the United States. (A thrill of horror here seemed to run through the assembly.) Zachary Taylor sits there, which is the same thing, for he believes in Jesus. He believes in war, and the Jesus 'that gave the Mexicans hell.' (Sensation, uproar, and confusion.)

"The name of Zachary Taylor had scarcely passed Mr. Garrison's lips when Captain Rynders, with something like a howl, forsaking his strategic position on the border-line of the gallery and the platform, dashed headlong down towards the speaker's desk, followed, with shouting and imprecations and a terrifying noise, by the mass of his backers. The audience, despite a natural agitation, gave way to no panic. The Abolitionist leaders upon the platform remained imperturbable. 'I was not aware,' writes Dr. Furness, 'of being under any apprehension of personal violence. We were all like General Jackson's cotton-bales at New Orleans. Our demeanor made it impossible for the rioters to use any physical force against us.' Rynders found himself in the midst of Francis and Edmund Jackson, of Wendell Phillips, of Edmund Quincy, of Charles F. Hovey, of William H. Furness, of Samuel May, Jr., of Sydney Howard Gay, of Isaac T. Hopper, of Henry C. Wright, of Abby Kelley Foster, of Frederick Douglass, of Mr. Garrison—against whom his menaces were specially directed. Never was a human being more out of his element."

The following, according to the *Herald,* was what greeted Mr. Garrison's ear:

"Captain Rynders (clenching his fist)—I will not allow you

to assail the President of the United States. You shan't do it (shaking his fist at Mr. Garrison).

"Many voices—Turn him out, turn him out!

"Captain Rynders—If a million of you were there, I would not allow the President of the United States to be insulted. As long as you confined yourself to your subject, I did not interfere; but I will not permit you or any other man to misrepresent the President."

Mr. Garrison, as the Rev. Samuel May testifies, "calmly replied that he had simply quoted some recent words of General Taylor, and appealed to the audience if he had said aught in disrespect of him." "You ought not to interrupt us," he continued to Rynders—in the quietest manner conceivable, as Dr. Furness relates. "We go upon the principle of hearing everybody. If you wish to speak, I will keep order, and you shall be heard." The din, however, increased. "The Hutchinsons," continues Dr. Furness, "who were wont to sing at the Anti-slavery meetings, were in the gallery, and they attempted to raise a song, to soothe the savages with music. But it was of no avail. Rynders drowned their fine voices with noise and shouting." Still, a knockdown argument with a live combatant would have suited him better than mere Bedlamitish disturbance. He was almost gratified by young Thomas L. Kane, son of Judge Kane of Philadelphia, who, seeing the rush of the mob upon the platform, had himself leaped there, to protect his townsman, Dr. Furness. "They shall not touch a hair of your head," he said in a tone of great excitement; and, as the strain became more intense, he rushed up to Rynders and shook his fist in his face. "He said to me [Dr. Furness] with the deepest emphasis: 'If he touches Mr. Garrison I'll *kill* him.'" But Mr. Garrison's composure was more than a coat of mail.

The knot was cut by Francis Jackson's formal offer of the floor to Rynders as soon as Mr. Garrison had finished his remarks; with an invitation meanwhile to take a seat on the platform. This, says Mr. May, he scoutingly refused; but, seeing the manifest fairness of the president's offer, drew back a little, and stood, with folded arms, waiting for Mr. Garrison to conclude, which soon he did—offering a resolution in these terms:

"Resolved, That the Anti-slavery movement, instead of being 'infidel,' in an evil sense (as is falsely alleged), is truly Christian, in the primitive meaning of that term, and the special embodiment in this country of whatever is loyal to God and benevolent to man; and that, in view of the palpable enormity of slavery—of the religious and political professions of the people—of the age in which we live, blazing with the concentrated light of many centuries—indifference or hostility to this movement indicates a state of mind more culpable than was manifested by the Jewish nation in rejecting Jesus as the Messiah, eighteen hundred years ago."

With these words the speaker retired, to resume the presidency of the meeting.

"The close of Mr. Garrison's address," says Dr. Furness, "brought down Rynders again, who vociferated and harangued, at one time on the platform, and then pushing down into the aisles, like a madman followed by his keepers. Through the whole, nothing could be more patient and serene than the bearing of Mr. Garrison. I have always revered Mr. Garrison for his devoted, uncompromising fidelity to his great cause. To-day I was touched to the heart by his calm and gentle manners. There was no agitation, no scorn, no heat, but the quietness of a man engaged in simple duties."

After some parleying, it appeared that Rynders had a spokesman who preferred to speak after Dr. Furness.

"Accordingly," says the latter, "I spoke my little, anxiously prepared word. I never recall that hour without blessing myself that I was called to speak precisely at that moment. At any other stage of the proceedings, it would have been wretchedly out of place. As it was, my speech fitted in almost as well as if it had been impromptu, although a sharp eye might easily have discovered that I was speaking *memoriter*. Rynders interrupted me again and again, exclaiming that I lied, that I was personal; but he ended with applauding me!"

No greater contrast to what was to follow could possibly be imagined than the genial manner, firm tones, and self-possession, the refined discourse, of this Unitarian clergyman, who was felt to have turned the current of the meeting. There uprose, as per agreement, one "Professor" Grant, a seedy-looking personage, having one hand tied round with a dirty cotton cloth. Mr. Garrison recognized him as a former pressman in the *Liberator* office. His thesis was that the blacks were not men, but belonged to the monkey tribe. His speech proved dull and tiresome, and was made sport of by his own set, whom Mr. Garrison had to call to order. There were now loud cries for Frederick Douglass, who came forward to where Rynders stood in the conspicuous position he had taken when he thought the meeting was his, and who remained in it, too mortified even to creep away, when he found it was somebody else's. "Now you can speak," said he to Douglass; "but mind what I say: if you speak disrespectfully (of the South, or Washington, or Patrick Henry) I'll knock you off the stage." Nothing daunted, the ex-fugitive from greater terrors began:

"The gentleman who has just spoken has undertaken to prove that the blacks are not human beings. He has examined our whole conformation, from top to toe. I cannot follow him in his argument. I will assist him in it, however. I offer myself for your examination. Am I a man?"

The audience responded with a thunderous affirmative, which Captain Rynders sought to break by exclaiming: *"You* are not a black man; you are only half a nigger." "Then," replied Mr. Douglass, turning upon him with the blandest of smiles and an almost affectionate obeisance, "I am half-brother to Captain Rynders!" He would not deny that he was the son of a slaveholder, born of Southern "amalgamation"; a fugitive, too, like Kossuth— "another half-brother of mine" (to Rynders). He spoke of the difficulties thrown in the way of industrious colored people at the North, as he had himself experienced—this by way of answer to Horace Greeley, who had recently complained of their inefficiency and dependence. Criticism of the editor of the *Tribune* being grateful to Rynders, a political adversary, "he added a word to Douglass's against Greeley. 'I am happy,' said Douglass, *'to have the assent of my half-brother here,'* pointing to Rynders, and convulsing the audience with laughter. After this, Rynders, finding how he was played with, took care to hold his peace; but someone of Rynders' company in the gallery undertook to interrupt the speaker. 'It's of no use,' said Mr. Douglass, *'I've Captain Rynders here to back me.'* We were born here," he said finally, "we are not dying out, and we mean to stay here. We made the clothes you have on, the sugar you put into your tea. We would do more if allowed." "Yes," said a voice in the crowd, "you would cut our throats for us." "No," was the quick response, "but we would cut your hair for you."

Douglass concluded his triumphant remarks by calling upon the

Rev. Samuel R. Ward, editor of the *Impartial Citizen,* to succeed him. "All eyes," says Dr. Furness, "were instantly turned to the back of the platform, or stage rather, so dramatic was the scene; and there, amidst a group, stood a large man, so black that, as Wendell Phillps said, when he shut his eyes you could not see him. As he approached, Rynders exclaimed: 'Well, this is the original nigger.' 'I've heard of the magnanimity of Captain Rynders,' said Ward, 'but the half has not been told me!' And then he went on with a noble voice and his speech was such a strain of eloquence as I never heard excelled before or since." The mob had to applaud him, too, and it is the highest praise to record that his unpremeditated utterance maintained the level of Douglass's, and ended the meeting with a sense of climax—demonstrating alike the humanity and the capacity of the full-blooded Negro.

"When he ceased speaking, the time had expired for which the Tabernacle was engaged, and we had to adjourn. Never," continues Dr. Furness, "was there a grander triumph of intelligence, of mind, over brute force. Two colored men, whose claim to be considered human was denied, had, by mere force of intellect, overwhelmed their maligners with confusion. As the audience was thinning out, I went down on the floor to see some friends there. Rynders came by. I could not help saying to him: 'How shall I thank you for what you have done for us to-day?' 'Well,' said he, 'I do not like to hear my country abused, but that last thing that you said, that's the truth.' That last thing was, I believe, a simple assertion of the right of the people to think and speak freely."

### IX. GARRISON AND EMERSON

THESE TWO MEN were almost exactly the same age; for Emerson was born in 1803 and Garrison in 1805. The precocity of Garrison, however, who became one of the figure-heads of his day at the age of twenty-four, and the tardy, inward development of Emerson, who did not become widely known till almost twenty years later, seem to class them in separate generations. Each of the men was a specialist of the extremest kind; Garrison, devoted to the visible and particular evils of his times, Emerson, seeking always the abstraction, and able to see the facts before his face only by the aid of general laws; Garrison all heart, Emerson all head; Garrison determined to remake the world, Emerson convinced that he must keep his eyes on the stars and wait for his message. Each of these men was, nevertheless, twin to the other. Their spirit was the same, and the influence of each was a strand in the same reaction, a cry from the same abyss. Emerson, no less than Garrison, was the voice of Abolition, and the dying Theodore Parker names him as a prophet. I should sum up Garrison's whole life-work in one word, Courage. And I cannot find another word, except Courage, to sum up Emerson.

The function of Garrison was to crack up, to dissolve. He cannot bear to see two men agree about anything, he cannot tolerate assent; toleration is the enemy, toleration is the sin of the age. In like manner is Emerson a sphinx who puts questions to his age. His thought cannot be understood without a thorough pulling-down of extant prejudices. Both men are dissolvents. With Emerson, this was *idea;* with Garrison, it was *function*. Garrison does, he knows not what—he talks foaming, he cannot fit two conceptions together; but he is generally, and on the whole, the agent of dissolution and re-crystallization. Emerson has only one note. He sits helplessly on his perch and utters his note;—waits a while, and again utters his note; and he is everywhere and always the agent of dissolution and re-crystallization. To compare the relations of these men to each other brings out very vividly the strong and the weak sides of each of them; for each seems to split the age, and show the sutures in the skull of the world; each is the key to the puzzle, and each is the missing half of the other's nature. That they did not understand one another, that there was no plane on which they could meet (except for a flash), is a sort of proof, by paradox, that they stood for the same thing expressed in different symbols.

Never in all literature has there been such a passionate proclamation of the individual as Emerson makes; and one of the few men that ever lived, who best fulfills Emerson's ideal picture of the influential individual, is Garrison. It is indeed strange to reflect that Emerson's life was given up to picturing the strong man who sheds all positive influence upon his age, and receives nothing from it, and yet to remember that Garrison's activity in real life was unsympathetic and even repulsive to Emerson.

The fame of the two men is unequal; because Emerson had about him a dry glint of the eternal, and his mind was a unity; whereas Garrison was a professional agitator and his mind was sometimes at odds with itself. The power that counts towards fame seems to be the power of vision. A man with vision leaves behind him a clear picture, consistent with itself, easily understood, popular, enduring; and though there be but few strokes in the sketch, his thought carries. The practical man, though he have the heart of the Samaritan, and do the work of a Titan, deals in more ephemeral symbols and is sooner forgotten. There was no single contemporary whose nature covered the divergent fields of both of these men. The Anti-slavery cause was always badly crippled for lack of a philosopher; and Emerson's influence has always stood in need of more animal life as a vehicle to float it towards mankind. Let us review the points at which the careers of the two men touched each other; remembering all the time that any age is a unity, that all men who live in it are members of each other, and that the Unconscious is the important part of life.

Emerson, after the loss of his first wife, followed by a breakdown in health and a year of gloomy travel in Europe, returned to Boston in 1833, a frail man of thirty, with a theological training, the tastes of a recluse, and an immense, unworldly ambition. To live in a village, to write in his journal, to walk in the woods and ruminate, —such was to be his existence. The organic reticence of Emerson has all but concealed the strong current of purpose that ran beneath the apparent futility of his external life. He was indeed a man of iron; and both he and Garrison might be compared to Ignatius Loyola in respect to their will. Emerson writes in his journal in 1834:

"The philosophy of *Waiting* needs sometimes to be unfolded. Thus he who is qualified to act upon the public, if he does not act on many, may yet act intensely on a few; if he does not act much upon any, but, from insulated condition and unfit companions, seems quite withdrawn into himself, still, if he know and feel his obligations, he may be (unknown and unconsciously) hiving knowledge and concentrating powers to act well hereafter, and a very remote hereafter." "A remote hereafter,"—this was ever in Emerson's mind. He feels himself to be an outpost or advance guard of future wisdom. "It is a manifest interest which comes home to my bosom and every man's bosom," he continues a page or two later, "that there should be on every tower Watchers set to observe and report of every new ray of light, in what quarter soever of Heaven it should appear, and their report should be eagerly and reverently received. There is no offense done, certainly, to the community in distinctly stating the claims of this office. It is not a coveted office: it is open to all men."

Never for one moment was Emerson's mission far from his thought. His fear of approaching it, his excessive reverence for it, is due to his artistic instinct; just as Garrison's blatancy about his mission—the same mission—is a part of Garrison's lack of artistic instinct. With that gleam of practical sagacity which distinguished him, Emerson had resigned from the Church at the first whisper of coercion. He was a free man. He was freer than Channing. He was freer even than Garrison; for Garrison kept founding Societies which gave him endless trouble. Emerson's early and unobtrusive retirement from office shows us an amusing exchange of rôles between the two; for in this instance Emerson, the recluse, knew the world better than Garrison, the man of action. But Emerson knew the world only in spots. His diary shows us a mind that is almost callow.

"Never numbers," he writes, "but the simple and wise shall judge, not the Whartons and Drakes, but some divine savage like Webster, Wordsworth, and Reed, whom neither the town nor the college ever made, shall say that we shall all believe. How we thirst for a natural thinker." Emerson's "natural thinking" leads him to collocate the names of great men very unexpectedly and somewhat mysteriously. Entries like the foregoing seem more like the work of a man of twenty than of thirty. We must note in the following not only the lack of emotional life which is implied: we must note also its perfect intellectual poise.

"You affirm," says Emerson in his journal, "that the moral development contains all the intellectual, and that Jesus was the perfect man. I bow in reverence unfeigned before that benign man. I know more, hope more, am more, because he has lived. But, if you tell me that in your opinion, he hath fulfilled all the conditions of man's existence, carried out to the utmost, at least by implication, all man's powers, I suspend my assent. I do not see in him cheerfulness: I do not see in him the love of natural science: I see in him no kindness for art: I see in him nothing of Socrates, of Laplace, of Shakespeare. The perfect man should remind us of all great men. Do you ask me if I would rather resemble Jesus than any other man? If I should say Yes, I should suspect myself of superstition."

This passage is like the stalk of the pieplant without the sap. But nature had gifts in her lap for the youth that penned it; and imagination can detect some sort of power even here. Here is at least a creature who will test other persons by himself, and not himself by others. The lacking element seems to be experience— experience of persons, experience of literature, experience of emotion. He has the coldness of crystal, but also its transparent purity. You would not suspect the man who writes thus of holding a pastorate over souls—of secretly regarding himself as a bishop and an apostle to lost sheep. Yet such was the fact. A care for men, a love of mankind, is the motive power in him.

Emerson is a man whom we are obliged to understand all the time by the light of what only breaks out of him once in seven years and endures but for two seconds. By the spark of this betrayal we know him: witness the opening of his Cooper Union address which I shall quote shortly.

The Abolitionists, of course, made a descent upon Emerson in their diocesan rounds—for they visited and proselytized everyone. May and Thompson, two of Garrison's lieutenants, called upon Emerson. Their mission was incomprehensible to Emerson, who writes in his journal: "Our good friend, Samuel J. May, may instruct us in many things." He admired May but not Thompson, of whom he says: "He belongs I fear to that great class of the Vanity-stricken. An inordinate thirst for notice cannot be gratified until it has found in its gropings what is called a cause that men will bow to; tying himself fast to that, the small man is then at liberty to consider all objections made to him as proofs of folly and the devil in the objector, and, under that screen, if he gets a rotten egg or two, yet his name sounds through the world and he is praised and praised."

Any one who has followed May and Thompson through good and evil report, who has felt the heat and depth of their devotion to truth, must almost wince at seeing what effect a visit from them produced upon the chill-blooded young parson who sat in his meager study, reading his threadbare library in the village of Concord.

We are brought to see by such anecdotes as this that Anti-slavery was a sort of special illumination. The greatest saints lived without an understanding of Abolition till, suddenly one day, Abolition broke out in their hearts and made them miserable. Abolition was a disease—the disease caused by the flooding of withered natures with new health. The infection jumped from one man to another. Genius and talent had nothing to do with it; learning and piety seem to have been immune to it. Emerson was no nearer to an understanding of it than if he had been a clerk in a drugshop. He had, moreover, a dry disposition,—a cold wind seemed to blow out of him,—and the sweat and unction of emotion were always antipathetic to him. Nevertheless Emerson *thought* about the Abolitionists. It cannot be said that he thought about slavery. He neither saw nor knew much about slavery. But he looked out of his window and saw Garrison and the Abolitionists shouting in the streets. They invaded his musings: they troubled his solitude. He tries to shelve them in his mind by a final analysis; but he never quite suits himself, and so tries again. His lecture on "The Times" in 1841, is in reality a lecture upon Garrison and Garrison's multitudinous causes. The rather old-maidish young Emerson was disgusted by the miscellaneous and ramping enthusiasm of Garrison. He says, for instance, in the lecture on "The Times":

"These reforms are our contemporaries; they are ourselves; our own light and sight, and conscience; they only name the relation which subsists between us and the vicious institutions which they go to rectify." This is complimentary to the reformers: they have at any rate, *discovered* the evils. But Emerson goes on almost immediately: "The young men who have been vexing society these last years with regenerative methods, seem to have made this mistake; they all exaggerated some special means, and all failed to see that the Reform of Reforms must be accomplished without means. . . . Those who are urging with most ardor what are called the greatest benefits to mankind, are narrow, self-pleasing, conceited men, and affect us as the insane do. They bite us and we run mad also. I think the work of the reformers as innocent as other work that is done around them; but when I have seen it near I do not like it better."

It appears, then, through these last-quoted phrases, that Emerson thinks the reformers are quite off the track, after all. But in the final sentence of the essay there is another phrase to the effect "that the highest compliment man receives from Heaven is the sending to him its disguised and discredited angels." So Garrison, it appears, was a disguised angel, after all. The essay on "The Times" is a glacial attempt to explain the function of the Reformer. It contains valuable ideas, and beautiful ideas; but it leaves unbridged the chasm between the apparent odiousness of the reformer and his real utility. It explains nothing: it demonstrates only that Emerson did not understand these particular "times" but was greatly puzzled by them. Dr. Holmes has said "that it would have taken a long time to get rid of slavery if some of Emerson's teachings in this lecture had been accepted as the whole gospel of liberty." "But," he adds, "how much its last sentence covers with its soothing tribute!"

Sometimes in reading this essay on "The Times," it has seemed to me as if the whole of it were tinctured with condescension;— just as the paragraph about Christ quoted above is unpleasant through its crudity of feeling. There is, however, no condescension in either passage. Emerson was the last man in the world to feel condescension. If he had had an inkling of what Garrison's activity signified he would have shouted approval. Emerson's humility was abundantly approved in the outcome. Let this be noted: Emerson was a perfectly courageous person; regard for appearance has nothing to do with the ineffectuality of his perceptions. Upon Lovejoy's murder, in 1837, Emerson "sternly rejoiced," says Dr. Edward W. Emerson, "that one was found to die for humanity and the rights of free speech and opinion"; and soon thereafter Emerson delivered a lecture in Boston in which "he suddenly looked the Boston audience in the eyes" as he said these words about Lovejoy, "and a shudder seemed to run through the audience, yet unprepared for this bold word, for a martyr of an unpopular Cause." Dr. Emerson cites this episode twice over, once in the Journals, and once in the Works, and he adds, "of course Lovejoy had other defenders in Boston." Yes, Lovejoy certainly had other defenders in Boston; and it is fortunate for us that he had.

Emerson's words of approbation for Lovejoy seem to have been carefully weighed, and he does not mention slavery. He belonged, in fact, to that large class of people who were shocked because *free speech* was murdered in Lovejoy's murder. Now, inasmuch as Emerson was lecturing before very conservative people, even this reference to "free speech and opinion" called up before the imagination of the audience the spectre of the Abolition Cause;—and a shudder warmed the room. Even so remote an approval of Abolition as this, was thought to be very bold in Mr. Emerson.

I believe that had it not been for Garrison and his crew, Mr. Emerson would have seen nothing in the street as he looked out of his window in the years 1833–1840. He would, therefore, have turned his eyes upon the heavens, and continued to develop a neo-platonic philosophy. The thing which he did develop during these years, and while he was thinking a good deal about Garrison, and wondering what was the matter with Garrison,—the outcome of Emerson's reflections upon Garrison,—was that picture of the Just Man which runs through Emerson's thought; that theory of the perfect man, the Overman, the Apollonian saint, who accomplishes all reforms without using any visible means.

In 1844, Emerson gives us a glimpse of this Overman in an essay entitled "The New England Reformers." The essay records a lack of progress in Emerson's thought, and shows that he had as yet no idea of the difference between Anti-slavery and the other many and clamoring reforms of the day. Like the essay on "The Times" it contains beautiful ideas, but betrays ignorance of this particular matter—Anti-slavery. "The man who shall be born," he says, "whose advent men and events prepare and foreshow, is one who shall enjoy his connection with a higher life, with the man within man; shall destroy distrust by his trust, shall use his native but forgotten methods, shall not take counsel of flesh and blood, but shall rely on the Law alive and beautiful which works over our heads and under our feet." "If," he says on another page, "we start objections to your project, oh, friend of the slave, or friend of the poor or of the race, understand well it is because we wish to drive you to drive us into your measures. We wish to hear ourselves confuted. We are haunted with a belief that you have a secret which it would highliest advantage us to learn, and we would force you to impart it to us, though it should bring us to prison or to worse extremity."

This last passage is an echo of the admirable fooling of Plato's dialogues. But it is not in phrases like these that men show their understanding of a subject like slavery. The time shall come when the fire shall descend on Emerson and he shall tear his mantle and put dust upon his head. If you would see how a man speaks when the virus of Anti-slavery has really entered his veins, you must turn to the address that Emerson delivered at Cooper Union in New York on March 7th, 1854. It is the Fugitive Slave Law that has aroused the seer and wrenched him from his tripod. He hates to leave his study, yet must leave it. His voice is strident; he forgets the amenities, and begins speaking almost without making a bow to his audience, and while he is still removing his overcoat.

"I do not often speak to public questions;—they are odious and hurtful, and it seems like meddling or leaving your work. I have my own spirits in prison;—spirits in deeper prisons, whom no man visits if I do not. And then I see what havoc it makes with any good mind, a dissipated philanthropy. The one thing not to be forgiven to intellectual persons is, not to know their own tasks, or to take their ideas from others. From this want of manly rest in their own and rash acceptance of other people's watchwords, come the imbecility and fatigue of their conversation." He continues to speak in haste, making use of the personal pronoun—belligerent, reckless. "I have lived all my life without suffering any known inconvenience from American Slavery: I never saw it; I never heard the whip; I never felt the check on my free speech and action, until, the other day, when Mr. Webster, by his personal influence, brought the Fugitive Slave Law on the country. I say Mr. Webster, for though the Bill was not his, it is yet notorious that he was the life and soul of it, that he gave it all he had: it cost him his life, and under the shadow of his great name inferior men sheltered themselves, threw their ballots for it and made the law. I say inferior men. There were all sorts of what are called brilliant men, accomplished men, men of high station, a President of the United States, Senators, men of eloquent speech, but men without self-respect, without character, and it was strange to see that office, age, fame, talent, even a repute for honesty, all count for nothing."

Emerson next discovers that Webster (formerly one of his gods) had never said anything of any consequence anyway. "If his moral sensibility had been proportioned to the force of his understanding, what limits could have been set to his genius and beneficent power? But he wanted that deep source of inspiration. Hence a sterility of thought, the want of generalization in his speeches, and the curious fact that, with a general ability which impresses all the world, there is not a single general remark, not an observation on life and manners, not an aphorism that can pass into literature from his writings."

Emerson now has the disease of Anti-slavery. The proof is that he feels obliged to take some sort of personal action. He feels responsible to the community for the educated classes. "The way in which the country was dragged to consent to this (the Fugitive Slave Law), and the disastrous defection (on the miserable cry of Union) of the men of letters, of the colleges, of educated men, nay, of some preachers of religion—was the darkest passage in the history." And again: "Yet the lovers of liberty may with reason tax the coldness and indifferentism of scholars and literary men. They are lovers of liberty in Greece and Rome and in the English Commonwealth, but they are lukewarm lovers of the liberty of America in 1854. The Universities are not, as in Hobbes's time, 'the core of rebellion,' no, but the seat of inertness." We find no avoidance of the word "slavery" in this address. Every other word seems to be "Slavery, slavery!" "A man who steals another man's labor steals away his own faculties; his integrity, his humanity is flowing away from him. The habit of oppression cuts out the moral eyes, and, though the intellect goes on simulating the moral as before, its sanity is gradually destroyed. It takes away the presentiments." And finally in the last paragraph, comes a fierce, frank, almost incoherent, acknowledgment of the country's debt to the Abolitionists. "I respect the Anti-Slavery Society. It is the Cassandra that has foretold all that has befallen, fact for fact, years ago; foretold all, and no man laid it to heart. It seemed, as the Turks say, 'Fate makes that a man should not believe his own eyes.' But the Fugitive Slave Law did much to unglue the eyes of men, and now the Nebraska Bill leaves us staring. The Anti-Slavery Society will add many members this year. The Whig Party will join it: the Democrats will join it. The population of the Free States will join it. I doubt not, at last, the Slave States will join it. But be that sooner or later and whoever comes or stays away, I hope we have reached the end of our unbelief, have come to a belief that there is a divine Providence in the world, which will not save us but through our own coöperation."

Happy Emerson, who has lived to be so moved! Now what is it that has brought Emerson to this pass? It is Daniel Webster's defection. Webster's defection was like the falling of a mighty tower that jarred whole classes and categories of men into an understanding of the Slave Power. It did what neither Lovejoy's murder, nor the Annexation of Texas was able to do:—it waked up "the better element." To this group, the better element, Emerson belonged by education and tradition. He crossed the Jordan along with the rest of his caste. This was just twenty-five years after Garrison's discovery of Immediate Emancipation: for these things were hidden from the wise and prudent and were revealed unto babes. The Abolitionists had been studying Daniel Webster for fifteen years. They had seen the menace in sticks and straws; Emerson sees it in the earthquake. They had then left their desks and hearths as he does now, and had talked on street corners to any one who would listen about "slavery,—slavery, slavery!"

Now it seems to me clear that Emerson had, from the beginning, been dealing with souls in slavery. This was the vision he saw, a vision which was consequent upon the Slave Epoch, a vision of moral slavery. And the man of Emerson's imagination, who is to set free these slaves is Emerson himself. This Overman is certainly a beautiful person. He does suggest truths,—this Apollo-like person of Emerson's,—he is valuable and he is beautiful. All of Emerson's abstractions and summaries of moral idea bear somewhat the same sort of relation to the real world that this Overman bears to Garrison. They are spirit-pictures, drawn from the life, a life never fully understood in its throb and passion; yet the pictures are given with such accuracy, such nobility, such power, that they speak forever. They are the artistic outcome of our Anti-slavery period. Garrison set a great brazen trumpet to his lips and blew; and the walls of Jericho fell. Garrison dies, and his trumpet sounds no more. Nevertheless, the small, inner, silver trumpet of Emerson caught and sounded the same note, and it continues to sound the note, shaking down the walls of inner Jerichoes in men of later and ever later generations.

## X. FOREIGN INFLUENCE; SUMMARY

IN EVERY GREAT FLUCTUATION that takes place in human society,—whether it be a moral, a political, or even an industrial phenomenon,—force converges upon some one man, and makes him the metaphysical center and thought-focus of the movement. The man is always a little metamorphosed by his office, a little deified by it. He is endued with supernatural sagacity, or piety, or resiliency. He is fed with artificial life, through the fact that thousands of men are sustaining him by their attention and in their hope. Thus in 1858, Lincoln suddenly became the great general-agent of political Anti-slavery in America; because his brain was exactly fitted for this work, which deified him quite rapidly. So of a hundred other cases of deification or demonization:—leaders seem to be grabbed, used and flung aside by immaterial and pitiless currents of force, which had as lief destroy as benefit their darlings. Witness the career of Stephen A. Douglas.

Garrison was the leader of Abolition from its inception to its triumph. His genius, and his activity kept it a unity, despite the incessant tearing and crumbling that were the normal accompaniment of its spreading influence. "I have never met the man or woman," said Wendell Phillips in 1865, "who had struck any effectual blow at the slave system in this country, whose action was not born out of the heart and conscience of William Lloyd Garrison." There is a certain verbal exaggeration in Phillips' statement; but the idea conveyed is true. Garrison's preëminence is incontestable. In agitation, as elsewhere, the great man eats up the little man; he sets the clock in the little man's bosom by his own chronometer— or rather, all this is done for both of them by the stress of the times. There never was a leader of men more completely consumed by his mission than Garrison. His life was sucked up into Anti-slavery. He had no attention for other things. How he obtained food and lodging for his family during all these years is a mystery. From time to time, it seems, his friends would relieve his wants, or pay a doctor's bill. He was supported by his Cause: the benevolence which he generated fed him. At the close of the war Garrison occupied a position of great eminence; and he could have cut a figure in public had he wished it. For, although the Abolitionists and Lincoln's Administration found some difficulty in coming to understand each other at the outset, they were in moral union before long; and they fought the war through together. "It was my privilege once, and once only, to talk with Abraham Lincoln, at Petersburg, Va., April 6, 1865," says Daniel H. Chamberlain. "His face, his figure, his attitudes, his words, form the most remarkable picture in my memory, and will, while memory lasts. I spoke to him of the country's gratitude for his great deliverance of the slaves. His sad face beamed for a moment with happiness as he answered in exact substance, and very nearly in words: 'I have been only an instrument. The logic and moral power of Garrison, and the Anti-slavery people of the country, and the army have done all.'"

Garrison had no worldly ambition; he even declined to favor Governor Andrew for a cabinet office in the days of the triumph of Abolition at the close of the war. He neglected and refused to write his own memoirs though offered large sums of money to do so. He sank into private life as easily as if he had truly been the benevolent, self-educated clockmaker of a Pickwickian kind, whose type he physically resembled. The storm which had engendered this dragon passed over, and left behind it a placid old man.

We must now revert to certain antebellum doings of the Abolitionists which had a profound influence upon the diplomatic history of the country during the war. While the demoniac Garrison was, in 1833, stirring his American caldron with his right hand, he reached over with his left and set a-going another vessel in England, which was destined to be of enormous importance to this country. Garrison made five journeys to England, namely in 1833, 1840, 1846 and 1867, and 1877. In the first, he clasped hands with all the philanthropists in England who were, at that time, assembled to witness the final triumph of the law abolishing Slavery in the West Indies. His immediate object in this journey was to unmask the American Colonization Society before the British public, and to bring the non-conformist conscience of England into true relations with American Abolition. He visited the venerable Clarkson, he met Wilberforce, Zachary Macaulay, Samuel Gurney, Thomas Fowell Buxton, and many other men and women of this kind. At the suggestion of Daniel O'Connell he held a meeting in Exeter Hall, where O'Connell spoke. Garrison was at one with these warm-hearted people in England as water is at one with water. They loved him; they doted on him, and he on them.

As we have seen, George Thompson came to America in 1835, as an apostle to the Abolition Cause. Harriet Martineau came as a traveler in the same year. By her writings, and especially by her "Martyr Age in America," she explained to the English mind the

Anti-slavery situation in this country. After the year 1835 there existed a bond between the philanthropists of England and of America. Constant intercourse, the sending of money and articles from England to the Cause in America, and an affectionate personal correspondence between the most unselfish classes in each country, led to the consolidation of a sort of Anglo-Saxon alliance of the only desirable kind—an alliance between loving and public-spirited persons in each country. As the outcome of this international union, which was inaugurated in 1833, a spiritual alliance of private persons succeeded thirty years later in controlling the diplomatic relations between the two countries and in averting war. It was, perhaps, the first time in history that such a thing could have occurred; and the incident shows us that the influence of private morality upon world politics is by no means imperceptible.

In 1840 a good many of the Abolitionists went to England to attend a World's Convention, and to renew their acquaintance with O'Connell, Buxton, Elizabeth Fry, the Howetts, Elizabeth Pease and others. The later visit of Garrison to England in 1846, was due to a picturesque episode in Anti-slavery history. A free church in Scotland had accepted money subscribed by slaveholders in Charleston; and Edinburgh became for a few weeks the focus of Anti-slavery agitation. "Send back the money" was placarded upon the streets, while English and American Abolitionists flocked to the fray. Garrison took this occasion to go to London and attend a World's Temperance Convention, then in session at the London Literary Institute. Immediately thereafter he organized an Anti-Slavery League, and held "a real old-fashioned Anti-slavery meeting," the first that had ever been held in London. The astonishing freedom with which he dealt out blows and caresses to the British public, the perfectly popular, jocular, boisterous tone of his speech on this occasion reminds one of Luther, and shows a new side to Garrison's powers. His success with the public was great. Now it happened that there was still another World's Conference going on in London at that time, namely a meeting of the *Evangelical Alliance,* which was a union of protestant clergy from various parts of the world. Garrison and Thompson took, of course, no share in the deliberations of these clergymen, but watched their proceedings with interest. The slave question was already burning hotly in the Alliance. The contested point was whether slaveholders were to be admitted to fellowship. After much wrangling and reference to committees, etc., the Alliance decided for the admission of slaveholders. Imagine the state of mind of Thompson and Garrison! They instantly called a meeting at Exeter Hall under the auspices of their own newborn League: and they proceeded to denounce the Evangelical Alliance—yes, they denounced it out of existence—to the great encouragement of the whole Abolition movement in America and elsewhere. This procedure occupied but a few days, and shows how much an active man can do, even upon a foreign soil, when he is dealing with matters peculiarly within his own province of understanding.

Garrison's personal relations with the British philanthropists can best be understood by reflecting upon his social isolation in America and upon the natural warmth of temperament in himself and in these English friends. "I did not hear without great emotion that you are returned to England, and I look forward with great happiness to meeting you in these better times," writes the Duchess of Sutherland in 1867. Harriet Martineau wrote just before her death in 1876: "I can say no more. My departure is evidently near, and I hold the pen with difficulty. Accept the sympathy and reverent blessing of your old friend, Harriet Martineau."

"I have watched his career with no common interest, even when I was too young to take much part in public affairs; and I have kept within my heart his name and the names of those who have been associated with him in every step he has taken." It is John Bright who spoke thus, at the great Garrison banquet given in London in 1867. The voice of Bright here spoke for that whole world of liberal sentiment in England which first rose to power through the passage of the Reform Bill of 1832. It spoke for Glasgow and Edinburgh, for Lancashire and Yorkshire—for the new Burgherdom which came into the world heralding religious freedom, popular education, and the protection of the humbler classes.

Garrison was better known to the working classes in Great Britain than in his own country. "During my visit to England," said Henry Ward Beecher, speaking in 1863, "it was my privilege to address, in various places, very large audiences, and I never made mention of the names of any of those men whom you most revere and love, without calling down the wildest demonstrations of popular enthusiasm. I never mentioned the names of Mr. Phillips or Mr. Garrison, that it did not call forth a storm of approbation."

It was through all this intercourse between the Abolitionists and the liberals of England that there grew up that understanding which the middle classes of England possessed as to the nature of the American struggle in 1860 to 1865; and which alone averted the recognition of the Southern Confederacy by the British Government. In reading the life of Charles Francis Adams, it has always been a surprise to me to find how well informed the cotton spinners, operatives, and small tradesmen of England were upon the very point which the governing classes were so unwilling to understand. The story of the support given to the Northern cause by the cotton spinners of Lancashire, who were being starved to death by the blockade of our Southern ports, is among the most moving stories in history. They could not be induced to protest or to ask their own Government for relief against that blockade. They would not take sides against the United States Government whose action was crushing them, because that Government stood for the freedom of the slave. The tale resembles the story of some siege at which not merely the safety of a city, but the fate of all humanity is at stake. These humble creatures saved us. It was due to their fortitude that Great Britain did not openly recognize the Confederacy. Had the masses of England sustained the official classes in regard to the American question, some sort of intervention by England in American affairs would in all probability have followed.

The Englishmen whose influence educated and sustained the working classes upon this whole matter were John Stuart Mill, John Bright, Richard Cobden, Lord Houghton, William E. Forster, George Thompson, Goldwin Smith, Justin McCarthy, Thomas Hughes, Herbert Spencer, Professor J. E. Cairnes—as well as the Gurneys, Buxtons, Webbs, and Clarksons of the previous generation: that is to say they were the heart and conscience of England of which Garrison had found himself to be a part in the early days, and by which the whole Anti-slavery movement had been comprehendingly followed during thirty years. The lower classes in England saw that the battle raging in America was their own battle, and that upon the maintenance of the cause of free labor the progress of popular institutions all over the world largely depended.

When Garrison visited England in 1867 he was greeted as the Giant of an Idea ought to be greeted. Public receptions and lunches were given in his honor in London, Manchester, Newcastle, Edinburgh, and Glasgow; and many names of note were to be found subscribed under words of welcome. Charles Darwin wrote, twelve years later, to young Garrison: "Thank you for the memorials of Garrison, a name to be forever revered." I would not cite the fêtes and ovations given to Garrison in London in 1867 as proving more than they do prove. We ought to examine the list of guests at the banquets and read the current newspaper editorials by the light of the events of that day, before deciding that Garrison's virtue was alone responsible for all this enthusiasm. I believe that Great Britain seized upon the London Banquet to Garrison as an opportunity for making a sort of *amende* for her unfriendly conduct during our crisis; and that persons attended this breakfast in 1867 who would not have been found at such a celebration if it had occurred in June, 1863. But whatever may have been the intentions of the Englishmen who, in 1867, gave Garrison a banquet, they did right to honor him; and their action gives the cue to posterity. It was Garrison who saved this nation. In his youth he gave us the issue through which alone salvation could come; and by his life he created the spirit through which that issue triumphed.

When the strands of this great web are brought together, they are seen to be as light as gossamer: the whole expanding Cosmos of Slavery may be drawn backward through a gold ring. Slavery in the North American Colonies was an outcome of that geographical remoteness which has so much hampered our progress. Slavery was a form of outrage which could linger on in outlying corners of the globe, long after it had become impossible in the centers of Western civilization. It had no legal inception in our Colonies: it was older than law. But it grew with our growth. The arrangement between the Colonies which goes by the name of the "New England Confederation of 1643" contained a clause for the rendition of fugitive slaves. Before the year 1862 there was never a moment in our history when slavery could have been abolished by the popular will. The United States Constitution of 1789 could never have been adopted by the Southern States had it not contained clauses protecting slavery. Slavery was in the blood of our people. During the thirty years, from 1830 to 1860, while the system was being driven out of the blood of our people through the power of the New Testament, there grew up a natural illusion, that the whole matter was one of municipal law. In reality the matter was one of influence, in which law only played a part.

The American temperament had thus been under the harrow of iniquity for two hundred years. During all this time slavery had been commercially an error, intellectually a blight, in every social aspect a poison. The toxin of it engendered in the Southerner that subtle quality, known and feared by the Greeks—an un-awed self-will. This quality is a mere inability to give way, and shows that the inner will of the man is closed to the great creative force of the universe. If he cannot let this force in, he will be destroyed by it. Nature conspires against him; humanity joins hands against him. His fall is certain.

The toxin of slavery engendered also in the Northerner the correlative sin to self-will, namely, a mean submission. The Southerner could not give way: he did not know how to yield. The Northerner could not stand fast: he always yielded. If you subtract the slave, who stands between these two samples of damaged temperament, you will still have a symbol of the institution of slavery in these two divergent attitudes of degradation. Do not seek for the fault in conventions or in Constitutions. There is no fault: there is only a moral situation, having a geographical origin.

During all this time the stars were fighting against slavery. They fought behind clouds and darkly for two hundred years; and at last their influence began to develop visible symptoms of cure. A very small part of life or history is ever visible, and it is only by inference that we know what powers have been at work; but in 1829 it is plain that some terrible drug is in operation in America. Whether this hot liquid was first born in the vitals of the slave we do not know. It seems to me that the origin of it must have been in the slave himself; and that it was mystically transmitted to the Abolitionist, in whom it appeared as pity. We know that the drops of this pity had a peculiar, stimulating power on the earth—a dynamic, critical power, a sort of prison-piercing faculty, which sent voltages of electrical shock through humanity. It is plain that all this conductivity to the ideas of Abolition was a part of Abolition.

The sensitiveness of the South to criticism was also a part of Abolition.

There began, therefore, in about 1830, a course of shuttling passion, which seems ever to repeat itself and to run upon a circuit. A wave of criticism from the North arouses violent opposition at the South: this awakens the North to new criticism. As the result of each reaction the South loses a little and the North gains a little. Now the relative numbers and resources of the North were, during all this time, increasing so rapidly that nothing but hypnotism could keep her in subjection to the Slave Power. And the days of hypnotism were plainly at an end; the days of shock and question were come. Whatever the South did, turned out to be shocking, and to be mistaken. Whatever the South did, returned to plague the inventor. The Missouri Compromise of 1820 was a Southern victory and jarred upon the Northern conscience a little. Nine years thereafter arises Abolition. The offer of a reward for Garrison by the State of Georgia in 1831 weakened the South; the elaborate attempts to suppress the Abolitionists in 1835 weakened the South; the Annexation of Texas weakened her. The Fugitive Slave Law in 1850, the Repeal of the Missouri Compromise in 1854, the Kansas-Nebraska Bill, the invasion of Kansas by the Border Ruffians, the Dred Scott Decision—each one of these things, though apparently a victory, proved in the end to be a boomerang, which operated to weaken the South and to awaken the North. On the other hand the North seemed to be protected from the consequences of moral error. The greatest illustration of this is the case of John Brown, whose crimes were at first not credited, and later were sanctified by contemporary Northern opinion.

Curiously enough, the *political* control of the South went on growing stronger and stronger while the basis for this control— its hold on the Northern imagination—was growing weaker and weaker. In other words, the Southern leaders always won: their cause always lost. Some Nemesis was working out. The *mécanique* of each successive step in the process was always the same. The weapon of the South was her threat of disunion. This threat seems to have had the effect of a spell upon our Northern ancestors. Disunion was in their opinion too horrible to be named, and much too terrible to be executed. The mere thought of it shattered Northern nerves. A world without the United States Constitution seemed to Northern men like a world before God's arrival—chaos come again. It was this threat of disunion that carried the Missouri Compromise in 1820, gave the moral victory to the Nullifiers in 1832, carried the Compromise measures of 1850, repealed the Missouri Compromise in 1854, elected Buchanan in 1856, and ruled the fortunes of the Republic in collateral matters between these crises.

The North was so accustomed to knuckling under at the sound of that threat that when Secession actually took place in 1860,—when the worst had happened and the Union was irretrievably shattered,—the North begged for more compromises: it proposed to woo the South back through new concessions. It offered another Fugitive Slave Law which should be embodied in the Constitution. The triumphant Republican Party seems to have been *stunned,* and could not believe that the long-dreamed-of catastrophe had actually occurred. It will be observed that both North and South upon this occasion merely played their stock parts. The South, through the habit of self-will, seceded. The North, through the tradition of self-abasement, begged her to come back.

Then occurred a thing which no one expected. The submerged courage, the abased self-assertion of the Northern people broke suddenly into expression. Fort Sumter was fired on, and every one of twenty millions of people received a shock that gave him a new kind of an organ for a heart. The dramatic nature of this climax was greatly enhanced by the slow manner of its coming on, by the dreadful waiting of the previous months, by the cowardice and inefficiency of the politicians, and by the dumbness of all the oracles. Garrison, at this juncture, is as empty as the prophets of Baal: he knows nothing. Earth's remedies have failed. No one is abreast of the situation. Lincoln only waits. At this moment, when the catastrophe is in the sky and the thud of Fate's footsteps can be heard, there occurred that thing which Herndon had spoken of in a prophetic letter one year earlier. Herndon wrote his last letter to Theodore Parker on December 15, 1859. "The Republicans in Congress," he says, "are grinding off the flesh from their kneecaps, attempting to convince the South that we are cowards. We *are* cowards, that is, our representatives are. . . . The South is now catechising the North. To this question, 'What is the true end of man?' it stands and shiveringly answers, 'The chief end of man is to support the nigger institutions, and to apologize to despots.' The Senators are all on their knees. So are the Representatives. Let them shrive themselves there, and mankind will avenge the humiliation in the future. This is God's constant mode of operation. The race will pull the trigger which the individual refused to touch. God will cry to the race 'Fire' and it will fire."

Never did the calculating human intellect more completely break down in the whole legal history of America. Never did so much ability prove so impotent to understand or to assist a social development. Salvation came in spite of all men—through the invisible. Courage came back with the war,—a certain great, gross courage,—mixed with carnage and barbarity as the courage of war ever must be,—yet still courage. This was the precious part of the war; for this courage was but a sample thread of a new kind of life which trusts generous feelings, relies upon the unseen, is in union with the unconscious operations of the spirit.

## EPILOGUE

*The harvest is past, the summer is ended and we are not saved.—*
Jeremiah 8: 20.

# EPILOGUE

THE ANTI-SLAVERY EPOCH presents a perfect example of the rise, progress, and victory of a moral cause. This cause was so obvious, so inevitable, its roots were so deep in human nature and in history, that its victory was assured from the beginning. In studying it, all our wonder and all our attention may be reserved for the manner of its rise, the form of its advance, and the mode of its victory.

Historians are apt to apportion praise and blame to the Abolitionists, to the Southern leaders, to the Republican Party, to the generals during the war, to the troops upon one side or the other in the terrible conflict. But such appraisements are either the aftermath of partisan feeling, or they are the judgments of men who have not realized the profundity and the complexity of the whole movement—the inevitability not only of the outcome, but of the process. That Garrison should have disapproved of the entry of Abolition into party politics, and that he should have raved like a hen upon the river bank when he saw the ducklings he had hatched rush into political waters; that the great intellect of Calhoun should have been driven forward by a suicidal logic into theories that were at war with the world's whole inheritance of truth; that Webster should have been now right, now wrong, or the Supreme Court now enlightened by a flickering compassion or again overshadowed by the Spirit of Crime;—such facts as these are parts of the great story, and can hardly be handled or sampled by themselves, hardly separated, even for a moment, from their context.

The private judgments which we are tempted to utter concerning critical phases or moments in any great cycle and sweep of destiny, are never conclusive, never important. We cannot know the truth about any of these things. No one can be sure that Garrison did not exert greater influence upon practical politics through his dogma of non-resistance than he could have done through an active participation in government. No one can state the precise value of the Liberty Party and the Free Soil Movement; no one can weigh the influence of "Uncle Tom's Cabin." All that we can be sure of is the great movement itself, which emerges, winds, coils, progresses, now gleaming and flashing beneath the surface, now emerging above the surface of social and political life in America, like a great golden serpent,—a mysterious all-pervading influence, supernal, mythological,—typifying the regeneration of a people.

The Legend is so vast, and moves at such a pace from beginning to end, that no two minds can agree about its details. Yet that Legend is at all points illuminated with the inner light of poetry and religion. It has an artistic unity, it moves like a very complicated sonata; so that we who regard it, somehow see our own souls in it, and draw out of it only what we put into it. The Anti-slavery Legend will reflect the spiritual history of any mind that looks into it; it is a mirror of the soul. It is a sort of thesaurus of moral illustration. The reason is that we were deeply diseased; we were in immense danger; we were covered with scales, and our mind was threatened. Our whole civilization was iridescent with the same poison. But we were healed, we were saved. And in the course of our cure every process and function of health was revealed.

To talk about the present is always difficult. The past is easy; but when in the course of any discussion we approach the present, we approach the unknowable. The present can by no means be brought into historic focus. If then we look about us in America to-day, having in our minds some reminiscence of history, let us beware of certitude: let us touch upon what we see with merely a hint and a query. I will, then, do no more than name three shapes which I see or seem to see and which may be thought of as apparitions or as passing fancies;—the first is a kind of specter, the second is a visitation from on high, the third is a prophecy. They are namely: the Decay of Learning, the Rise of Love, and the ultimate Revival of Spiritual Interests.

The dying-off of our older cultivation, which gives so much concern to all intelligent persons in America, does not indicate death. It is due to two causes, one of them being the historic and withering influence of isolation and of commerce; the other being the present preoccupation of our noblest minds with philanthropic work. New life is at hand, though it exists in forms which the intellect has never grasped, and never can grasp. Before, however, speaking of the future, we must look back once more upon the discouraging side of life in America—on the decay of learning.

From an external point of view, the Anti-slavery epoch can be very simply seen as the epoch during which America was returning to the family of European nations from the exile which her connection with slavery had imposed upon her. The struggle over slavery while it lasted left her citizens neither time nor attention for general education. In 1830, we found ourselves isolated and it took us thirty years of work to break down the barriers between ourselves and the modern world. The intellect and passion of the country was given up during this time to a terrible conflict between prophetic morality on the one hand and the unprofitable sophistries of law, politics and government on the other. Our attitude towards Europe was unintelligent; our experience in ideas (other than prophetic ethics and Constitutional Law) was nil. The consequence was that the American fell tremendously behind the European in general cultivation.

Now the period after our return to social life—the period, namely, between 1865 and the present time—coincides with the rise of modern commerce, so that we no sooner got free from one enemy to the soul than we were fastened upon by another—and that other the half-brother and blood relation of the first. I will not try to analyze America nor define her relation to Europe. I will only point out our most dreadful defects, and this only as a prelude to mentioning our hopes of salvation.

I confess that a certain hard-eyed, cold-hearted look in the American sometimes causes me to remember that Slavery was always Commerce, and that Commerce is to some extent always Slavery. Such great wealth as has been created in America since 1865 would have hardened the eyes of any generation that looked on it. We have indeed been born to calamity in America, and our miseries have come thickly upon us. If you will walk back across the whole history of the world, you will find that respect for learning has never before fallen so low as it has fallen in the United States to-day. If you start anywhere in Europe and trace your way back to ancient Egypt, you will find no age without its savants, its thinkers, men who know something of the past, living sometimes in caves and sometimes in drawing-rooms, yet always, in a certain sense, the publicists of their times. These are the men through whom, to some extent, religion, education, and the traditions of spiritual life are transmitted from age to age. There have always been enough of such men in every age to secure popular respect for the idea for which they stand, the idea of continuity. There has been no real break in European culture. During the dark ages the most visible and most powerful influence upon popular imagination consisted in the monuments of a gigantic past. Indeed, for many centuries thereafter, the overwhelming influence of antiquity cowed the world. That element has endured in European education in the form of a reverence for the past. It stands behind every man as a sort of soundingboard in his mind, an invisible chamber of consciousness that gives resonance to his voice.

If to-day you fall into casual conversation with almost any European, you will feel the influence of these vistas of education. The man's mind is inured to thought. What you say to him is native to his soul. He has heard something like it before. He knows of the existence of the Empire of the Intellect. He is interested in the spiritual history of the world. All this illumination is no personal merit in the individual you speak to. He has lived near to the scholar, the musician, the painter, the antiquarian, the philologist, the mathematician.

It happened that a series of misfortunes so widowed America that we have all but lost the past. Much baggage was jettisoned in the original transit across the sea, much lost during our colonial and frontier period, and finally—we were stripped bare by the pirate Slavery, and marooned for seventy years in a sort of Babylonian captivity. I think there is enough in all this to account for the bleakness of American life as contrasted with European life. I think that the emotions must in youth be fed upon a sort of pabulum that comes down out of the past—songs, aspirations, stories, prayers, reverence for humanity, knowledge of God;—or else some dreadful barrenness will set in and paralyze the intellect of a race. The question sometimes forces itself upon me, Is not the German citizen of the second generation, who walks the streets of New York to-day, more truly a barbarian than his Gothic ancestor who invaded Europe in the fourth century A.D., and whose magnificent vernacular is preserved in Ulfilas' translation of the Scriptures? In piety, in knowledge of poetry, in reverence, the Goth was more advanced than his American descendant. I say, the Swabian peasant of to-day seems to me to be superior to the American farmer in many of those things that make life deep and cause society to endure.

To cut loose, to cast away, to destroy, seems to be our impulse. We do not want the past. This awful loss of all the terms of thought, this beggary of intellect, is shown in the unwillingness of the average man in America to go to the bottom of any subject, his mental inertia, his hatred of impersonal thought, his belief in labor-saving, his indifference to truth. The state of mind in which commercial classes spend their lives is not that of pure, self-sacrificing spiritual perception. The commercial mind seems, in its essence, to be the natural enemy of love, religion, and truth; and when, as at the present moment in America, we have commerce dominant in an era whose characteristic note is contempt for the past, we can hardly expect a picturesque, pleasing, or harmonious social life.

Much is lost sight of, much is forgotten among us; much is unknown that in any European country would be familiar. For instance, this very man, William Lloyd Garrison, is almost forgotten among us. He lived a life of heroism and of practical achievement; the beauty of his whole course was extraordinary, and his type of character is very rare. Had he lived in Europe he would have been classified at once among the great figures of his own generation. Indeed he was so classified from across the sea. His character would have been prized thereafter as a national possession. But in America all that the educated man of to-day knows of Garrison is that he was one who held impractical views and used over-strong language during the Anti-slavery struggle.

All this feebleness, whose evidences I have been reviewing, comes, I believe, from a central deficiency of life in the American people. It is not a thing which can be cured in the college, or in the school, or in the drawing-room; though the cure will show in all such places as fast as the great patient improves.

During the very epoch (the decade succeeding the close of the war) when our intellectual blight was at its worst, there began to appear among us compassionate persons founding newsboys' halls in the Five Points, prison angels, and police court visitors, saints knocking at the doors of the poor—men filled with love and pity. This new gospel of love now absorbs whole classes of people in American life, and swallows the young as the Crusades once swallowed them. I hear schoolmasters and learned men complain that their most brilliant classical scholars insist upon doing settlement work the moment they graduate. Why do the young people of both sexes take this course? What planetary influence depletes the exhausted ranks of scholarship, and makes traitors of these trained minds to the cause of learning? In their new career their old education goes apparently for nothing. They themselves cannot tell you. And yet they are justified. These young people are being governed by that higher law which governed St. Francis—the law which he also knew how to obey but could not explain. Our young people express by their conduct a more potent indictment of the cultivation and science of the older, dying epoch than could be written with the pen of Ezekiel. The age has nothing in it that satisfies them: they therefore turn away from it: they satisfy themselves elsewhere. In so doing they create a new age. The deeper needs of humanity can only be met slowly. It required several hundred years for the meaning and importance of St. Francis to become apparent. To his contemporaries he seemed to be a disciple sent to the poor; yet his influence ultimately qualified the art and letters, and tinged the philosophy of life of several centuries.

All these new saints of ours—new Christians, and loving persons who crowd the slums, and rediscover Christ in themselves and in others—lack power to explain; they merely exist. Through them, or rather through the heart which they infuse, literature and intellect will return, art and mental vigor will be restored to us. It would seem that the bowels and viscera of society must be heated first, and thereafter in time—it may be a century or two—a warmer life will reach the mind. These new grubs that creep out of the ground, these golden bees that dart by us in the sunshine, going so directly to their work like camp nurses, are more perfect creatures than we are, in that they deal with humanity as a unit. You and I are nothing to them. They have a relation to the whole. They are living in a beam which we do not see, they are the servants of a great cure which we cannot give, and do not understand.

So also in regard to the Anti-Slavery Movement; the importance of that Movement comes from the fact that it meant piety, truth, and love. The rest is illusion. In a certain sense the slaves were freed too soon. That short-sighted element in the philosophy of Abolition, which saw Slavery as the Antichrist (whereas the spiritual domination of evil was the real Antichrist), ended by putting Slavery to its purgation so quickly and so convulsively that many features and visiting cards of slavery were left behind in the nervous system of the people. This was no one's fault: it was the method of nature. An after-cure was necessary; and we have been undergoing an after-cure, and need more of it.

I regret the loss of the old cultivation; and yet I know that none of our older cultivation was ever quite right. The American has never lived from quite the right place in his bosom. Nevertheless if we are but patient the loss will be restored to us tenfold. We are living in the age of a great regeneration. There is hardly a man in whose face I do not see some form of it. New hope is with us. Very different is our mission from that of the Abolitionist, though both are forms of the same power. Anti-slavery was the narrow, burning gate of heaven, seen by a few men, who fought their way towards it, paying with their lives for every step in their progress. Crags overhung them: society hated them: every man was their enemy. In our new crusade no one is our enemy. The spirit is felt in all men. In some, it moves in the heart crying, Abba, Father. Others it leaves speechless, but makes their lives beautiful through unselfish labor. Still others it illuminates with visions, so that we see men and women who live like angels, running up and down in the celestial light, passing forward and back between God and man, bringing health to many. In other hearts it has broken the old shackles of prejudice, and shown to them the common bond that lives in all religion. The churches have been growing liberal—for the first time in the history of Christianity. Other classes of men glow with an enthusiasm for science which is becoming a form of worship for truth, differing chiefly in name from religion. It is as if a truce had been sounded in that antique war that has raged forever over creed form and scientific theory, and as if every one were standing in silence, thinking of the realities which lie and which have always lain behind the noisy dogmas and the certified formulas of human thought. The wrecks of many creeds are being clashed together like the cakes of ice in the Hudson during a great February thaw; while the strong river bears them all forward in triumph.

Great and small, learned and unlearned meet upon that plane of common humility which is their only meeting ground. It is a period when the power and first-hand mystery of life is recognized on every side, and when the conventions and lies that dam and deny that power are for the time being widely broken down. I do not say that the dams will remain down forever. People are building at them all the time. Trade interests, personal selfishnesses are indefatigably at work like ants—contesting every inch of the damage, inventing new dykes, denying that any permanent change has taken place.

Let us be glad that we are born in this age and within the swirl and current of the new freedom. Let us do each our share to leave the dams down, and not build them up in our own bosoms; for it is in peoples' bosoms that all these dams exist. We must permit the floods of life to run freely. It is not from any one of our reforms, arts, sciences, and churches but out of all of them that salvation flows. What shall we do to assist in this great process? What relation do we bear to the movement? That is the question which requires a lifetime for its answer. Our knowledge of the subject changes constantly under experience. At first we desire to help vigorously; and we do all in our power to assist mankind. As time goes on, we perceive more and more clearly that the advancement of the world does not depend upon us, but that we, rather, are bound up in it, and can command no foothold of our own. At last we see that our very ambitions, desires and hopes in the matter are a part of the Supernal Machinery moving through all things, and that our souls can be satisfied and our power exerted only in so far as we are taken up into that original motion, and merged in that primal power. Our minds thus dissolve under the grinding analysis of life, and leave behind nothing except God. Towards him we stand and look; and we, who started out with so many gifts for men, have nothing left in our satchel for mankind except a blessing.

# PART TWO

# Walt Whitman

It would be an ill turn for an essay-writer to destroy Walt Whitman,—for he was discovered by the essayists, and but for them his notoriety would have been postponed for fifty years. He is the mare's nest of "American Literature," and scarce a contributor to *The Saturday Review* but has at one time or another raised a flag over him.

The history of these chronic discoveries of Whitman as a poet, as a force, as a something or a somebody, would write up into the best possible monograph on the incompetency of the Anglo-Saxon in matters of criticism.

English literature is the literature of genius, and the Englishman is the great creator. His work outshines the genius of Greece. His wealth outvalues the combined wealth of all modern Europe. The English mind is the only unconscious mind the world has ever seen. And for this reason the English mind is incapable of criticism.

There has never been an English critic of the first rank, hardly a critic of any rank; and the critical work of England consists either of an academical bandying of a few old canons and shibboleths out of Horace or Aristotle, or else of the merest impressionism, and wordy struggle to convey the sentiment awakened by the thing studied.

Now, true criticism means an attempt to find out what something is, not for the purpose of judging it, or of imitating it, nor for the purpose of illustrating something else, nor for any other ulterior purpose whatever.

The so-called canons of criticism are of about as much service to a student of literature as the Nicene Creed and the Lord's Prayer are to the student of church history. They are a part of his subject, of course, but if he insists upon using them as a tape measure and a divining-rod he will produce a judgment of no possible value to any one, and interesting only as a record of a most complex state of mind.

The educated gentlemen of England have surveyed literature with these time-honored old instruments, and hordes of them long ago rushed to America with their theodolites and their quadrants in their hands. They sized us up and they sized us down, and they never could find greatness in literature among us till Walt Whitman appeared and satisfied the astrologers.

Here was a comet, a man of the people, a new man, who spoke no known language, who was very uncouth and insulting, who proclaimed himself a "barbaric yawp," and who corresponded to the English imagination with the unpleasant and rampant wildness of everything in America,—with Mormonism and car factories, steamboat explosions, strikes, repudiation, and whiskey; whose form violated every one of their minor canons as America violated every one of their social ideas.

Then, too, Whitman arose out of the war, as Shakespeare arose out of the destruction of the Armada, as the Greek poets arose out of the repulse of the Persians. It was impossible, it was unprecedented, that a national revulsion should not produce national poetry —and lo! here was Whitman.

It may safely be said that the discovery of Whitman as a poet caused many a hard-thinking Oxford man to sleep quietly at night. America was solved.

The Englishman travels, but he travels after his mind has been burnished by the university, and at an age when the best he can do in the line of thought is to make an intelligent manipulation of the few notions he leaves home with. He departs an educated gentleman, taking with him his portmanteau and his ideas. He returns a travelled gentleman, bringing with him his ideas and his portmanteau. He would as soon think of getting his coats from Kansas as his thoughts from travel. And therefore every impression of America which the travelling Englishman experienced confirmed his theory of Whitman. Even Rudyard Kipling, who does not in any sense fall under the above description, has enough Anglo-Saxon blood in him to see in this country only the fulfilment of the fantastic notions of his childhood.

But imagine an Oxford man who had eyes in his head, and who should come to this country, never having heard of Whitman. He would see an industrious and narrow-minded population, commonplace and monotonous, so uniform that one man can hardly be distinguished from another, law-abiding, timid, and traditional; a community where the individual is suppressed by law, custom, and instinct, and in which, by consequence, there are few or no great men, even counting those men thrust by necessary operation of the laws of trade into commercial prominence, and who claim scientific rather than personal notice.

The culture of this people, its architecture, letters, drama, etc., he would find were, of necessity, drawn from European models; and in its poetry, so far as poetry existed, he would recognize a somewhat feeble imitation of English poetry. The newspaper verses very fairly represent the average talent for poetry and average appreciation of it, and the newspaper verse of the United States is precisely what one would expect from a decorous and unimaginative population,—intelligent, conservative, and uninspired.

Above the newspaper versifiers float the minor poets, and above these soar the greater poets; and the characteristics of the whole hierarchy are the same as those of the humblest acolyte,—intelligence, conservatism, conventional morality.

Above the atmosphere they live in, above the heads of all the American poets, and between them and the sky, float the Constitution of the United States and the traditions and forms of English literature.

This whole culture is secondary and tertiary, and it truly represents the respectable mediocrity from which it emanates. Whittier and Longfellow have been much read in their day,—read by mill-hands and clerks and school-teachers, by lawyers and doctors and divines, by the reading classes of the republic, whose ideals they truly spoke for, whose yearnings and spiritual life they truly expressed.

Now, the Oxford traveller would not have found Whitman at all. He would never have met a man who had heard of him, nor seen a man like him.

The traveller, as he opened his *Saturday Review* upon his return to London, and read the current essay on Whitman, would have been faced by a problem fit to puzzle Montesquieu, a problem to floor Goethe.

And yet Whitman is representative. He is a real product, he has a real and most interesting place in the history of literature, and he speaks for a class and type of human nature whose interest is more than local, whose prevalence is admitted,—a type which is one of the products of the civilization of the century, perhaps of all centuries, and which has a positively planetary significance.

There are, in every country, individuals who, after a sincere attempt to take a place in organized society, revolt from the drudgery of it, content themselves with the simplest satisfactions of the grossest need of nature, so far as subsistence is concerned, and rediscover the infinite pleasures of life in the open air.

If the roadside, the sky, the distant town, the soft buffeting of the winds of heaven, are a joy to the æsthetic part of man, the freedom from all responsibility and accountability is Nirvana to his moral nature. A man who has once tasted these two joys together, the joy of being in the open air and the joy of being disreputable and unashamed, has touched an experience which the most close-knit and determined nature might well dread. Life has no terrors for such a man. Society has no hold on him. The trifling inconveniences of the mode of life are as nothing compared with its satisfactions. The worm that never dies is dead in him. The great mystery of consciousness and of effort is quietly dissolved into the vacant happiness of sensation,—not base sensation, but the sensation of the dawn and the sunset, of the mart and the theatre, and the stars, the panorama of the universe.

To the moral man, to the philosopher or the business man, to any one who is a cog in the wheel of some republic, all these things exist for the sake of something else. He must explain or make use of them, or define his relation to them. He spends the whole agony of his existence in an endeavor to docket them and deal with them. Hampered as he is by all that has been said and done before, he yet feels himself driven on to summarize, and wreak himself upon the impossible task of grasping this cosmos with his mind, of holding it in his hand, of subordinating it to his purpose.

The tramp is freed from all this. By an act as simple as death, he has put off effort and lives in peace.

It is no wonder that every country in Europe shows myriads of these men, as it shows myriads of suicides annually. It is no wonder, though the sociologists have been late in noting it, that specimens of the type are strikingly identical in feature in every country of the globe.

The habits, the physique, the tone of mind, even the sign-language and some of the catch-words, of tramps are the same everywhere. The men are not natally outcasts. They have always tried civilized life. Their early training, at least their early attitude of mind towards life, has generally been respectable. That they should be criminally inclined goes without saying, because their minds have been freed from the sanctions which enforce law. But their general innocence is, under the circumstances, very remarkable, and distinguishes them from the criminal classes.

When we see one of these men sitting on a gate, or sauntering down a city street, how often have we wondered how life appeared to him; what solace and what problems it presented. How often have we longed to know the history of such a soul, told, not by the police-blotter, but by the poet or novelist in the heart of the man!

Walt Whitman has given utterance to the soul of the tramp. A man of genius has passed sincerely and normally through this entire experience, himself unconscious of what he was, and has left a record of it to enlighten and bewilder the literary world.

In Whitman's works the elemental parts of a man's mind and the fragments of imperfect education may be seen merging together, floating and sinking in a sea of insensate egotism and rhapsody, repellent, divine, disgusting, extraordinary.

Our inability to place the man intellectually, and find a type and reason for his intellectual state, comes from this: that the revolt he represents is not an intellectual revolt. Ideas are not at the bottom of it. It is a revolt from drudgery. It is the revolt of laziness.

There is no intellectual coherence in his talk, but merely pathological coherence. Can the insulting jumble of ignorance and effrontery, of scientific phrase and French paraphrase, of slang and inspired adjective, which he puts forward with the pretence that it represents thought, be regarded, from any possible point of view, as a philosophy, or a system, or a belief? Is it individualism of any statable kind? Do the thoughts and phrases which float about in it have a meaning which bears any relation to the meaning they bear in the language of thinkers? Certainly not. Does all the patriotic talk, the talk about the United States and its future, have any significance as patriotism? Does it poetically represent the state of feeling of any class of American citizens towards their country? Or would you find the nearest equivalent to this emotion in the breast of the educated tramp of France, or Germany, or England? The speech of Whitman is English, and his metaphors and catchwords are apparently American, but the emotional content is cosmic. He put off patriotism when he took to the road.

The attraction exercised by his writings is due to their flashes of reality. Of course the man was a poseur, a most horrid mountebank and ego-maniac. His tawdry scraps of misused idea, of literary smartness, of dog-eared and greasy reminiscence, repel us. The world of men remained for him as his audience, and he did to civilized society the continuous compliment of an insane self-consciousness in its presence.

Perhaps this egotism and posturing is the revenge of a stilled conscience, and we ought to read in it the inversion of the social instincts. Perhaps all tramps are poseurs. But there is this to be said for Whitman, that whether or not his posing was an accident of a personal nature, or an organic result of his life, he was himself an authentic creature. He did not sit in a study and throw off his saga of balderdash, but he lived a life, and it is by his authenticity, and not by his poses, that he has survived.

The descriptions of nature, the visual observation of life, are first-hand and wonderful. It was no false light that led the Oxonians to call some of his phrases Homeric. The pundits were right in their curiosity over him; they went astray only in their attempt at classification.

It is a pity that truth and beauty turn to cant on the second delivery, for it makes poetry, as a profession, impossible. The lyric poets have always spent most of their time in trying to write lyric poetry, and the very attempt disqualifies them.

A poet who discovers his mission is already half done for; and even Wordsworth, great genius though he was, succeeded in half drowning his talents in his parochial theories, in his own self-consciousness and self-conceit.

Walt Whitman thought he had a mission. He was a professional poet. He had purposes and theories about poetry which he started out to enforce and illustrate. He is as didactic as Wordsworth, and is thinking of himself the whole time. He belonged, morever, to that class of professionals who are always particularly self-centred, autocratic, vain, and florid,—the class of quacks. There are, throughout society, men, and they are generally men of unusual natural powers, who, after gaining a little unassimilated education, launch out for themselves and set up as authorities on their own account. They are, perhaps, the successors of the old astrologers, in that what they seek to establish is some personal professorship or predominance. The old occultism and mystery was resorted to as the most obvious device for increasing the personal importance of the magician; and the chief difference today between a regular physician and a quack is, that the quack pretends to know it all.

Brigham Young and Joseph Smith were men of phenomenal capacity, who actually invented a religion and created a community by the apparent establishment of supernatural and occult powers. The phrenologists, the venders of patent medicine, the Christian Scientists, the single-taxers, and all who proclaim panaceas and nostrums make the same majestic and pontifical appeal to human nature. It is this mystical power, this religious element, which floats them, sells the drugs, cures the sick, and packs the meetings.

By temperament and education Walt Whitman was fitted to be a prophet of this kind. He became a quack poet, and hampered his talents by the imposition of a monstrous parade of rattletrap theories and professions. If he had not been endowed with a perfectly marvellous capacity, a wealth of nature beyond the reach and plumb of his rodomontade, he would have been ruined from the start. As it is, he has filled his work with grimace and vulgarity. He writes a few lines of epic directness and cyclopean vigor and naturalness, and then obtrudes himself and his mission.

He has the bad taste bred in the bone of all missionaries and palmists, the sign-manual of a true quack. This bad taste is nothing more than the offensive intrusion of himself and his mission into the matter in hand. As for his real merits and his true mission, too much can hardly be said in his favor. The field of his experience was narrow, and not in the least intellectual. It was narrow because of his isolation from human life. A poet like Browning, or Heine, or Alfred de Musset deals constantly with the problems and struggles that arise in civilized life out of the close relationships, the ties, the duties and desires of the human heart. He explains life on its social side. He gives us some more or less coherent view of an infinitely complicated matter. He is a guide-book or a note-book, a highly trained and intelligent companion.

Walt Whitman has no interest in any of these things. He was fortunately so very ignorant and untrained that his mind was utterly incoherent and unintellectual. His mind seems to be sub-merged and to have become almost a part of his body. The utter lack of concentration which resulted from living his whole life in the open air has left him spontaneous and unaccountable. And the great value of his work is, that it represents the spontaneous and unaccountable functioning of the mind and body in health.

It is doubtful whether a man ever enjoyed life more intensely than Walt Whitman, or expressed the physical joy of mere living more completely. He is robust, all tingling with health and the sen-sations of health. All that is best in his poetry is the expression of bodily well-being.

A man who leaves his office and gets into a canoe on a Canadian river, sure of ten days' release from the cares of business and house-keeping, has a thrill of joy such as Walt Whitman has here and there thrown into his poetry. One might say that to have done this is the greatest accomplishment in literature. Walt Whitman, in some of his lines, breaks the frame of poetry and gives us life in the throb.

It is the throb of the whole physical system of a man who breathes the open air and feels the sky over him. "When lilacs last in the dooryard bloomed" is a great lyric. Here is a whole poem without a trace of self-consciousness. It is little more than a description of nature. The allusions to Lincoln and to the funeral are but a word or two—merest suggestions of the tragedy. But grief, overwhelming grief, is in every line of it, the grief which has been transmuted into this sensitiveness to the landscape, to the song of the thrush, to the lilac's bloom, and the sunset.

Here is truth to life of the kind to be found in King Lear or Guy Mannering, in Æschylus or Burns.

Walt Whitman himself could not have told you why the poem was good. Had he had any intimation of the true reason, he would have spoiled the poem. The recurrence and antiphony of the thrush, the lilac, the thought of death, the beauty of nature, are in a balance and dream of natural symmetry such as no cunning could come at, no conscious art could do other than spoil.

It is ungrateful to note Whitman's limitations, his lack of human passion, the falseness of many of his notions about the American people. The man knew the world merely as an observer, he was never a living part of it, and no mere observer can understand the life about him. Even his work during the war was mainly the work of an observer, and his poems and notes upon the period are picturesque. As to his talk about comrades and Manhattanese car-drivers, and brass-founders displaying their brawny arms round each other's brawny necks, all this gush and sentiment in Whitman's poetry is false to life. It has a lyrical value, as representing Whitman's personal feelings, but no one else in the country was ever found who felt or acted like this.

In fact, in all that concerns the human relations Walt Whitman is as unreal as, let us say, William Morris, and the American mechanic would probably prefer Sigurd the Volsung, and understand it better than Whitman's poetry.

This falseness to the sentiment of the American is interwoven with such wonderful descriptions of American sights and scenery, of ferryboats, thoroughfares, cataracts, and machine-shops that it is not strange the foreigners should have accepted the gospel.

On the whole, Whitman, though he solves none of the problems of life and throws no light on American civilization, is a delightful appearance, and a strange creature to come out of our beehive. This man committed every unpardonable sin against our conventions, and his whole life was an outrage. He was neither chaste, nor industrious, nor religious. He patiently lived upon cold pie and tramped the earth in triumph.

He did really live the life he liked to live, in defiance of all men, and this is a great desert, a most stirring merit. And he gave, in his writings, a true picture of himself and of that life,—a picture which the world had never seen before, and which it is probable the world will not soon cease to wonder at.

# Emerson

## I

"LEAVE THIS HYPOCRITICAL PRATING about the masses. Masses are rude, lame, unmade, pernicious in their demands and influence, and need not to be flattered, but to be schooled. I wish not to concede anything to them, but to tame, drill, divide, and break them up, and draw individuals out of them. The worst of charity is that the lives you are asked to preserve are not worth preserving. Masses! The calamity is the masses. I do not wish any mass at all, but honest men only, lovely, sweet, accomplished women only, and no shovel-handed, narrow-brained, gin-drinking million stockingers or lazzaroni at all. If government knew how, I should like to see it check, not multiply the population. When it reaches its true law of action, every man that is born will be hailed as essential. Away with this hurrah of masses, and let us have the considerate vote of single men spoken on their honor and their conscience."

This extract from The Conduct of Life gives fairly enough the leading thought of Emerson's life. The unending warfare between the individual and society shows us in each generation a poet or two, a dramatist or a musician who exalts and deifies the individual, and leads us back again to the only object which is really worthy of enthusiasm or which can permanently excite it,—the character of a man. It is surprising to find this identity of content in all great deliverances. The only thing we really admire is personal liberty. Those who fought for it and those who enjoyed it are our heroes.

But the hero may enslave his race by bringing in a system of tyranny; the battle-cry of freedom may become a dogma which crushes the soul; one good custom may corrupt the world. And so the inspiration of one age becomes the damnation of the next. This crystallizing of life into death has occurred so often that it may almost be regarded as one of the laws of progress.

Emerson represents a protest against the tyranny of democracy. He is the most recent example of elemental hero-worship. His opinions are absolutely unqualified except by his temperament. He expresses a form of belief in the importance of the individual which is independent of any personal relations he has with the world. It is as if a man had been withdrawn from the earth and dedicated to condensing and embodying this eternal idea—the value of the individual soul—so vividly, so vitally, that his words could not die, yet in such illusive and abstract forms that by no chance and by no power could his creed be used for purposes of tyranny. Dogma cannot be extracted from it. Schools cannot be built on it. It either lives as the spirit lives, or else it evaporates and leaves nothing. Emerson was so afraid of the letter that killeth that he would hardly trust his words to print. He was assured there was no such thing as literal truth, but only literal falsehood. He therefore resorted to metaphors which could by no chance be taken literally. And he has probably succeeded in leaving a body of work which cannot be made to operate to any other end than that for which he designed it. If this be true, he has accomplished the inconceivable feat of eluding misconception. If it be true, he stands alone in the history of teachers; he has circumvented fate, he has left an unmixed blessing behind him.

The signs of those times which brought forth Emerson are not wholly undecipherable. They are the same times which gave rise to every character of significance during the period before the war. Emerson is indeed the easiest to understand of all the men of his time, because his life is freest from the tangles and qualifications of circumstance. He is a sheer and pure type and creature of destiny, and the unconsciousness that marks his development allies him to the deepest phenomena. It is convenient, in describing him, to use language which implies consciousness on his part, but he himself had no purpose, no theory of himself; he was a product.

The years between 1820 and 1830 were the most pitiable through which this country has ever passed. The conscience of the North was pledged to the Missouri Compromise, and that Compromise neither slumbered nor slept. In New England, where the old theocratical oligarchy of the colonies had survived the Revolution and kept under its own waterlocks the new flood of trade, the conservatism of politics reinforced the conservatism of religion; and as if these two inquisitions were not enough to stifle the soul of man, the conservatism of business self-interest was superimposed. The history of the conflicts which followed has been written by the radicals, who negligently charge up to self-interest all the resistance which establishments offer to change. But it was not solely self-interest, it was conscience that backed the Missouri Compromise, nowhere else, naturally, so strongly as in New England. It was conscience that made cowards of us all. The white-lipped generation of Edward Everett were victims, one might even say martyrs, to conscience. They suffered the most terrible martyrdom that can fall to man, a martyrdom which injured their immortal volition and dried up the springs of life. If it were not that our poets have too seldom deigned to dip into real life, I do not know what more awful subject for a poem could have been found than that of the New England judge enforcing the fugitive slave law. For lack of such a poem the heroism of these men has been forgotten, the losing heroism of conservatism. It was this spiritual power of a committed conscience which met the new forces as they arose, and it deserves a better name than these new forces afterward gave it. In 1830 the social fruits of these heavy conditions could be seen in the life of the people. Free speech was lost.

"I know no country," says Tocqueville, who was here in 1831, "in which there is so little independence of mind and freedom of discussion as in America." Tocqueville recurs to the point again and again. He cannot disguise his surprise at it, and it tinged his whole philosophy and his book. The timidity of the Americans of this era was a thing which intelligent foreigners could not understand. Miss Martineau wrote in her Autobiography: "It was not till months afterwards that I was told that there were two reasons why I was not invited there [Chelsea] as elsewhere. One reason was that I had avowed, in reply to urgent questions, that I was disappointed in an oration of Mr. Everett's; and another was that I had publicly condemned the institution of slavery. I hope the Boston people have outgrown the childishness of sulking at opinions not in either case volunteered, but obtained by pressure. But really, the subservience to opinion at that time seemed a sort of mania."

The mania was by no means confined to Boston, but qualified this period of our history throughout the Northern States. There was no literature. "If great writers have not at present existed in America, the reason is very simply given in the fact that there can be no literary genius without freedom of opinion, and freedom of opinion does not exist in America," wrote Tocqueville. There were no amusements, neither music nor sport nor pastime, indoors or out of doors. The whole life of the community was a life of the intelligence, and upon the intelligence lay the weight of intellectual tyranny. The pressure kept on increasing, and the suppressed forces kept on increasing, till at last, as if to show what gigantic power was needed to keep conservatism dominant, the Merchant Province put forward Daniel Webster.

The worst period of panic seems to have preceded the anti-slavery agitations of 1831, because these agitations soon demonstrated that the sky did not fall nor the earth yawn and swallow Massachusetts because of Mr. Garrison's opinions, as most people had sincerely believed would be the case. Some semblance of free speech was therefore gradually regained.

Let us remember the world upon which the young Emerson's eyes opened. The South was a plantation. The North crooked the hinges of the knee where thrift might follow fawning. It was the era of Martin Chuzzlewit, a malicious caricature,—founded on fact. This time of humiliation, when there was no free speech, no literature, little manliness, no reality, no simplicity, no accomplishment, was the era of American brag. We flattered the foreigner and we boasted of ourselves. We were over-sensitive, insolent, and cringing. As late as 1845, G. P. Putnam, a most sensible and modest man, published a book to show what the country had done in the field of culture. The book is a monument of the age. With all its good sense and good humor, it justifies foreign contempt because it is explanatory. Underneath everything lay a feeling of unrest, an instinct,—"this country cannot permanently endure half slave and half free,"—which was the truth, but which could not be uttered.

So long as there is any subject which men may not freely discuss, they are timid upon all subjects. They wear an iron crown and talk in whispers. Such social conditions crush and maim the individual, and throughout New England, as throughout the whole North, the individual was crushed and maimed.

The generous youths who came to manhood between 1820 and 1830, while this deadly era was maturing, seem to have undergone a revulsion against the world almost before touching it; at least two of them suffered, revolted, and condemned, while still boys sitting on benches in school, and came forth advancing upon this old society like gladiators. The activity of William Lloyd Garrison, the man of action, preceded by several years that of Emerson, who is his prophet. Both of them were parts of one revolution. One of Emerson's articles of faith was that a man's thoughts spring from his actions rather than his actions from his thoughts, and possibly the same thing holds good for society at large. Perhaps all truths, whether moral or economic, must be worked out in real life before they are discovered by the student, and it was therefore necessary that Garrison should be evolved earlier than Emerson.

The silent years of early manhood, during which Emerson passed through the Divinity School and to his ministry, known by few, understood by none, least of all by himself, were years in which the revolting spirit of an archangel thought out his creed. He came forth perfect, with that serenity of which we have scarce another example in history,—that union of the man himself, his beliefs, and his vehicle of expression that makes men great because it makes them comprehensible. The philosophy into which he had already transmuted all his earlier theology at the time we first meet him consisted of a very simple drawing together of a few ideas, all of which had long been familiar to the world. It is the wonderful use he made of these ideas, the closeness with which they fitted his soul, the tact with which he took what he needed, like a bird building its nest, that make the originality, the man.

The conclusion of Berkeley, that the external world is known to us only through our impressions, and that therefore, for aught we know, the whole universe exists only in our own consciousness, cannot be disproved. It is so simple a conception that a child may understand it; and it has probably been passed before the attention of every thinking man since Plato's time. The notion is in itself a mere philosophical catch or crux to which there is no answer. It may be true. The mystics made this doctrine useful. They were not content to doubt the independent existence of the external world. They imagined that this external world, the earth, the planets, the phenomena of nature, bore some relation to the emotions and destiny of the soul. The soul and the cosmos were somehow related, and related so intimately that the cosmos might be regarded as a sort of projection or diagram of the soul.

Plato was the first man who perceived that this idea could be made to provide the philosopher with a vehicle of expression more powerful than any other. If a man will once plant himself firmly on the proposition that *he is* the universe, that every emotion or expression of his mind is correlated in some way to phenomena in the external world, and that he shall say how correlated, he is in a position where the power of speech is at a maximum. His figures of speech, his tropes, his witticisms, take rank with the law of gravity and the precession of the equinoxes. Philosophical exaltation of the individual cannot go beyond this point. It is the climax.

This is the school of thought to which Emerson belonged. The sun and moon, the planets, are mere symbols. They signify whatever the poet chooses. The planets for the most part stay in conjunction just long enough to flash his thought through their symbolism, and no permanent relation is established between the soul and the zodiac. There is, however, one link of correlation between the external and internal worlds which Emerson considered established, and in which he believed almost literally, namely, the moral law. This idea he drew from Kant through Coleridge and Wordsworth, and it is so familiar to us all that it hardly needs stating. The fancy that the good, the true, the beautiful,—all things of which we instinctively approve,—are somehow connected together and are really one thing; that our appreciation of them is in its essence the recognition of a law; that this law, in fact all law and the very idea of law, is a mere subjective experience; and that hence any external sequence which we coördinate and name, like the law of gravity, is really intimately connected with our moral nature,—this fancy has probably some basis of truth. Emerson adopted it as a corner-stone of his thought.

Such are the ideas at the basis of Emerson's philosophy, and it is fair to speak of them in this place because they antedate everything else which we know of him. They had been for years in his mind before he spoke at all. It was in the armor of this invulnerable idealism and with weapons like shafts of light that he came forth to fight.

In 1836, at the age of thirty-three, Emerson published the little pamphlet called Nature, which was an attempt to state his creed. Although still young, he was not without experience of life. He had been assistant minister to the Rev. Dr. Ware from 1829 to 1832, when he resigned his ministry on account of his views regarding the Lord's Supper. He had married and lost his first wife in the same interval. He had been abroad and had visited Carlyle in 1833. He had returned and settled in Concord, and had taken up the profession of lecturing, upon which he in part supported himself ever after. It is unnecessary to review these early lectures. "Large portions of them," says Mr. Cabot, his biographer, "appeared afterward in the Essays, especially those of the first series." Suffice it that through them Emerson had become so well known that although Nature was published anonymously, he was recognized as the author. Many people had heard of him at the time he resigned his charge, and the story went abroad that the young minister of the Second Church had gone mad. The lectures had not discredited the story, and Nature seemed to corroborate it. Such was the impression which the book made upon Boston in 1836. As we read it to-day, we are struck by its extraordinary beauty of language. It is a supersensuous, lyrical, and sincere rhapsody, written evidently by a man of genius. It reveals a nature compelling respect,—a Shelley, and yet a sort of Yankee Shelley, who is mad only when the wind is nor'-nor'west; a mature nature which must have been nourished for years upon its own thoughts, to speak this new language so eloquently, to stand so calmly on its feet. The deliverance of his thought is so perfect that this work adapts itself to our mood and has the quality of poetry. This fluency Emerson soon lost; it is the quality missing in his poetry. It is the efflorescence of youth.

"In good health, the air is a cordial of incredible virtue. Crossing a bare common, in snow puddles, at twilight, under a clouded sky, without having in my thoughts any occurrence of special good fortune, I have enjoyed a perfect exhilaration. I am glad to the brink of fear. In the woods, too, a man casts off his years, as the snake his slough, and at what period soever of life is always a child. In the woods is perpetual youth. Within these plantations of God, a decorum and sanctity reign, a perennial festival is dressed, and the guest sees not how he should tire of them in a thousand years. . . . It is the uniform effect of culture on the human mind, not to shake our faith in the stability of particular phenomena, as heat, water, azote; but to lead us to regard nature as phenomenon, not a substance; to attribute necessary existence to spirit; to esteem nature as an accident and an effect."

Perhaps these quotations from the pamphlet called Nature are enough to show the clouds of speculation in which Emerson had been walking. With what lightning they were charged was soon seen.

In 1837 he was asked to deliver the Phi Beta Kappa oration at Cambridge. This was the opportunity for which he had been waiting. The mystic and eccentric young poet-preacher now speaks his mind, and he turns out to be a man exclusively interested in real life. This recluse, too tender for contact with the rough facts of the world, whose conscience has retired him to rural Concord, pours out a vial of wrath. This cub puts forth the paw of a full-grown lion.

Emerson has left behind him nothing stronger than this address, The American Scholar. It was the first application of his views to the events of his day, written and delivered in the heat of early manhood while his extraordinary powers were at their height. It moves with a logical progression of which he soon lost the habit. The subject of it, the scholar's relation to the world, was the passion of his life. The body of his belief is to be found in this address, and in any adequate account of him the whole address ought to be given.

"Thus far," he said, "our holiday has been simply a friendly sign of the survival of the love of letters amongst a people too busy to give to letters any more. As such it is precious as the sign of an indestructible instinct. Perhaps the time is already come when it ought to be, and will be, something else; when the sluggard intellect of this continent will look from under its iron lids and fill the postponed expectation of the world with something better than the exertions of mechanical skill. . . . The theory of books is noble. The scholar of the first age received into him the world around; brooded thereon; gave it the new arrangement of his own mind, and uttered it again. It came into him life; it went out from him truth. . . . Yet hence arises a grave mischief. The sacredness which attaches to the act of creation, the act of thought, is transferred to the record. The poet chanting was felt to be a divine man: henceforth the chant is divine, also. The writer was a just and wise spirit: henceforward it is settled the book is perfect; as love of the hero corrupts into worship of his statue. Instantly the book becomes noxious: the guide is a tyrant. . . . Books are the best of things, well used; abused, among the worst. What is the right use? What is the one end which all means go to effect? They are for nothing but to inspire. . . . The one thing in the world, of value, is the active soul. This every man is entitled to; this every man contains within him, although in almost all men obstructed, and as yet unborn. The soul active sees absolute truth and utters truth, or creates. In this action it is genius; not the privilege of here and there a favorite, but the sound estate of every man. . . . Genius is always sufficiently the enemy of genius by over-influence. The literature of every nation bears me witness. The English dramatic poets have Shakespearized now for two hundred years. . . . These being his functions, it becomes him to feel all confidence in himself, and to defer never to the popular cry. He, and he only, knows the world. The world of any moment is the merest appearance. Some great decorum, some fetish of a government, some ephemeral trade, or war, or man, is cried up by half mankind and cried down by the other half, as if all depended on this particular up or down. The odds are that the whole question is not worth the poorest thought which the scholar has lost in listening to the controversy. Let him not quit his belief that a popgun is a popgun, though the ancient and honorable of the earth affirm it to be the crack of doom."

Dr. Holmes called this speech of Emerson's our "intellectual Declaration of Independence," and indeed it was. "The Phi Beta Kappa speech," says Mr. Lowell, "was an event without any former parallel in our literary annals,—a scene always to be treasured in the memory for its picturesqueness and its inspiration. What crowded and breathless aisles, what windows clustering with eager heads, what enthusiasm of approval, what grim silence of foregone dissent!"

The authorities of the Divinity School can hardly have been very careful readers of Nature and The American Scholar, or they would

not have invited Emerson, in 1838, to deliver the address to the
graduating class. This was Emerson's second opportunity to apply
his beliefs directly to society. A few lines out of the famous address
are enough to show that he saw in the church of his day signs of
the same decadence that he saw in the letters: "The prayers and
even the dogmas of our church are like the zodiac of Denderah and
the astronomical monuments of the Hindoos, wholly insulated from
anything now extant in the life and business of the people. They
mark the height to which the waters once rose. . . . It is the office
of a true teacher to show us that God is, not was; that he speaketh,
not spake. The true Christianity—a faith like Christ's in the infinitude of man—is lost. None believeth in the soul of man, but
only in some man or person old and departed. Ah me! no man
goeth alone. All men go in flocks to this saint or that poet, avoiding
the God who seeth in secret. They cannot see in secret; they love
to be blind in public. They think society wiser than their soul, and
know not that one soul, and their soul, is wiser than the whole
world."

It is almost misleading to speak of the lofty utterances of these
early addresses as attacks upon society, but their reception explains
them. The element of absolute courage is the same in all natures.
Emerson himself was not unconscious of what function he was
performing.

The "storm in our wash-bowl" which followed this Divinity
School address, the letters of remonstrance from friends, the advertisements by the Divinity School of "no complicity," must have been
cheering to Emerson. His unseen yet dominating ambition is shown
throughout the address, and in this note in his diary of the following year:—

"*August* 31. Yesterday at the Phi Beta Kappa anniversary. Steady,
steady. I am convinced that if a man will be a true scholar he shall
have perfect freedom. The young people and the mature hint at
odium and the aversion of forces to be presently encountered in
society. I say No; I fear it not."

The lectures and addresses which form the latter half of the first
volume in the collected edition show the early Emerson in the ripeness of his powers. These writings have a lyrical sweep and a
beauty which the later works often lack. Passages in them remind
us of Hamlet:—

"How silent, how spacious, what room for all, yet without space to insert an atom;—in graceful succession, in equal fulness, in balanced beauty, the dance of the hours goes forward still. Like an odor of incense, like a strain of music, like a sleep, it is inexact and boundless. It will not be dissected, nor unravelled, nor shown. . . . The great Pan of old, who was clothed in a leopard skin to signify the beautiful variety of things and the firmament, his coat of stars,— was but the representative of thee, O rich and various man! thou palace of sight and sound, carrying in thy senses the morning and the night and the unfathomable galaxy; in thy brain, the geometry of the City of God; in thy heart, the bower of love and the realms of right and wrong. . . . Every star in heaven is discontent and insatiable. Gravitation and chemistry cannot content them. Ever they woo and court the eye of the beholder. Every man who comes into the world they seek to fascinate and possess, to pass into his mind, for they desire to republish themselves in a more delicate world than that they occupy. . . . So it is with all immaterial objects. These beautiful basilisks set their brute glorious eyes on the eye of every child, and, if they can, cause their nature to pass through his wondering eyes into him, and so all things are mixed."

Emerson is never far from his main thought:—

"The universe does not attract us till it is housed an in individual."

"A man, a personal ascendency, is the only great phenomenon."

"I cannot find language of sufficient energy to convey my sense of the sacredness of private integrity."

On the other hand, he is never far from his great fear: "But Truth is such a fly-away, such a sly-boots, so untransportable and unbarrelable a commodity, that it is as bad to catch as light."

"Let him beware of proposing to himself any end. . . . I say to you plainly, there is no end so sacred or so large that if pursued for itself will not become carrion and an offence to the nostril."

There can be nothing finer than Emerson's knowledge of the world, his sympathy with young men and with the practical difficulties of applying his teachings. We can see in his early lectures before students and mechanics how much he had learned about the structure of society from his own short contact with the organized church.

"Each finds a tender and very intelligent conscience a disqualifica-

tion for success. Each requires of the practitioner a certain shutting
of the eyes, a certain dapperness and compliance, an acceptance of
customs, a sequestration from the sentiments of generosity and
love, a compromise of private opinion and lofty integrity. . . . The
fact that a new thought and hope have dawned in your breast,
should apprise you that in the same hour a new light broke in
upon a thousand private hearts. . . . And further I will not dis-
semble my hope that each person whom I address has felt his own
call to cast aside all evil customs, timidity, and limitations, and to
be in his place a free and helpful man, a reformer, a benefactor,
not content to slip along through the world like a footman or a
spy; escaping by his nimbleness and apologies as many knocks as
he can, but a brave and upright man who must find or cut a straight
road to everything excellent in the earth, and not only go honorably
himself, but make it easier for all who follow him to go in honor
and with benefit. . . ."

Beneath all lay a greater matter,—Emerson's grasp of the forms
and conditions of progress, his reach of intellect, which could
afford fair play to every one.

His lecture on The Conservative is not a puzzling *jeu d'esprit*,
like Bishop Blougram's Apology, but an honest attempt to set up
the opposing chessmen of conservatism and reform so as to represent real life. Hardly can such a brilliant statement of the case be
found elsewhere in literature. It is not necessary to quote here the
reformer's side of the question, for Emerson's whole life was devoted to it. The conservatives' attitude he gives with such accuracy
and such justice that the very bankers of State Street seem to be
speaking:—

"The order of things is as good as the character of the population
permits. Consider it as the work of a great and beneficent and
progressive necessity, which, from the first pulsation in the first
animal life up to the present high culture of the best nations, has
advanced thus far. . . .

"The conservative party in the universe concedes that the radical
would talk sufficiently to the purpose if we were still in the garden
of Eden; he legislates for man as he ought to be; his theory is
right, but he makes no allowance for friction, and this omission
makes his whole doctrine false. The idealist retorts that the conservative falls into a far more noxious error in the other extreme.

The conservative assumes sickness as a necessity, and his social frame is a hospital, his total legislation is for the present distress, a universe in slippers and flannels, with bib and pap-spoon, swallowing pills and herb tea. Sickness gets organized as well as health, the vice as well as the virtue."

It is unnecessary to go, one by one, through the familiar essays and lectures which Emerson published between 1838 and 1875. They are in everybody's hands and in everybody's thoughts. In 1840 he wrote in his diary: "In all my lectures I have taught one doctrine, namely, the infinitude of the private man. This the people accept readily enough, and even with commendation, as long as I call the lecture Art or Politics, or Literature or the Household; but the moment I call it Religion they are shocked, though it be only the application of the same truth which they receive elsewhere to a new class of facts." To the platform he returned, and left it only once or twice during the remainder of his life.

His writings vary in coherence. In his early occasional pieces, like the Phi Beta Kappa address, coherence is at a maximum. They were written for a purpose, and were perhaps struck off all at once. But he earned his living by lecturing, and a lecturer is always recasting his work and using it in different forms. A lecturer has no prejudice against repetition. It is noticeable that in some of Emerson's important lectures the logical scheme is more perfect than in his essays. The truth seems to be that in the process of working up and perfecting his writings, in revising and filing his sentences, the logical scheme became more and more obliterated. Another circumstance helped make his style fragmentary. He was by nature a man of inspirations and exalted moods. He was subject to ecstasies, during which his mind worked with phenomenal brilliancy. Throughout his works and in his diary we find constant reference to these moods, and to his own inability to control or recover them. "But what we want is consecutiveness. 'Tis with us a flash of light, then a long darkness, then a flash again. Ah! could we turn these fugitive sparkles into an astronomy of Copernican worlds!"

In order to take advantage of these periods of divination, he used to write down the thoughts that came to him at such times. From boyhood onward he kept journals and commonplace books, and in the course of his reading and meditation he collected innumerable notes and quotations which he indexed for ready use. In these mines he "quarried," as Mr. Cabot says, for his lectures and essays. When he needed a lecture he went to the repository, threw together what seemed to have a bearing on some subject, and gave it a title. If any other man should adopt this method of composition, the result would be incomprehensible chaos; because most men have many interests, many moods, many and conflicting ideas. But with Emerson it was otherwise. There was only one thought which could set him aflame, and that was the thought of the unfathomed might of man. This thought was his religion, his politics, his ethics, his philosophy. One moment of inspiration was in him own brother to the next moment of inspiration, although they might be separated by six weeks. When he came to put together his star-born ideas, they fitted well, no matter in what order he placed them, because they were all part of the same idea.

His works are all one single attack on the vice of the age, moral cowardice. He assails it not by railings and scorn, but by positive and stimulating suggestion. The imagination of the reader is touched by every device which can awake the admiration for heroism, the consciousness of moral courage. Wit, quotation, anecdote, eloquence, exhortation, rhetoric, sarcasm, and very rarely denunciation, are launched at the reader, till he feels little lambent flames beginning to kindle in him. He is perhaps unable to see the exact logical connection between two paragraphs of an essay, yet he feels they are germane. He takes up Emerson tired and apathetic, but presently he feels himself growing heady and truculent, strengthened in his most inward vitality, surprised to find himself again master in his own house.

The difference between Emerson and the other moralists is that all these stimulating pictures and suggestions are not given by him in illustration of a general proposition. They have never been through the mill of generalization in his own mind. He himself could not have told you their logical bearing on one another. They have all the vividness of disconnected fragments of life, and yet they all throw light on one another, like the facets of a jewels. But whatever cause it was that led him to adopt his method of writing, it is certain that he succeeded in delivering himself of his thought with an initial velocity and carrying power such as few men ever attained. He has the force at his command of the thrower of the discus.

His style is American, and beats with the pulse of the climate. He is the only writer we have had who writes as he speaks, who makes no literary parade, has no pretensions of any sort. He is the only writer we have had who has wholly subdued his vehicle to his temperament. It is impossible to name his style without naming his character: they are one thing.

Both in language and in elocution Emerson was a practised and consummate artist, who knew how both to command his effects and to conceal his means. The casual, practical, disarming directness with which he writes puts any honest man at his mercy. What difference does it make whether a man who can talk like this is following an argument or not? You cannot always see Emerson clearly; he is hidden by a high wall; but you always know exactly on what spot he is standing. You judge it by the flight of the objects he throws over the wall,—a bootjack, an apple, a crown, a razor, a volume of verse. With one or other of these missiles, all delivered with a very tolerable aim, he is pretty sure to hit you. These catchwords stick in the mind. People are not in general influenced by long books or discourses, but by odd fragments of observation which they overhear, sentences or head-lines which they read while turning over a book at random or while waiting for dinner to be announced. These are the oracles and orphic words that get lodged in the mind and bend a man's most stubborn will. Emerson called them the Police of the Universe. His works are a treasury of such things. They sparkle in the mine, or you may carry them off in your pocket. They get driven into your mind like nails, and on them catch and hang your own experiences, till what was once his thought has become your character.

"God offers to every mind its choice between truth and repose. Take which you please; you can never have both." "Discontent is want of self-reliance; it is infirmity of will." "It is impossible for a man to be cheated by any one but himself."

The orchestration with which Emerson introduces and sustains these notes from the spheres is as remarkable as the winged things themselves. Open his works at a hazard. You hear a man talking.

"A garden is like those pernicious machineries we read of every month in the newspapers, which catch a man's coat-skirt or his hand, and draw in his arm, his leg, and his whole body to irresistible destruction. In an evil hour he pulled down his wall and added a field to his homestead. No land is bad, but land is worse. If a man own land, the land owns him. Now let him leave home if he dare. Every tree and graft, every hill of melons, row of corn, or quickset hedge, all he has done and all he means to do, stand in his way like duns, when he would go out of his gate."

Your attention is arrested by the reality of this gentleman in his garden, by the first-hand quality of his mind. It matters not on what subject he talks. While you are musing, still pleased and patronizing, he has picked up the bow of Ulysses, bent it with the ease of Ulysses, and sent a shaft clear through the twelve axes, nor missed one of them. But this, it seems, was mere byplay and marksmanship; for before you have done wondering, Ulysses rises to his feet in anger, and pours flight after flight, arrow after arrow, from the great bow. The shafts sing and strike, the suitors fall in heaps. The brow of Ulysses shines with unearthly splendor. The air is filled with lightning. After a little, without shock or transition, without apparent change of tone, Mr. Emerson is offering you a biscuit before you leave, and bidding you mind the last step at the garden end. If the man who can do these things be not an artist, then must we have a new vocabulary and rename the professions.

There is in all this effectiveness of Emerson, no prose, no literary art; nothing that corresponds even remotely to the pretended modesty and ignorance with which Socrates lays pitfalls for our admiration in Plato's dialogues.

It was the platform which determined Emerson's style. He was not a writer, but a speaker. On the platform his manner of speech was a living part of his words. The pauses and hesitation, the abstraction, the searching, the balancing, the turning forward and back of the leaves of his lecture, and then the discovery, the illumination, the gleam of lightning which you saw before your eyes descend into a man of genius,—all this was Emerson. He invented this style of speaking, and made it express the supersensuous, the incommunicable. Lowell wrote, while still under the spell of the magician: "Emerson's oration was more disjointed than usual, even with him. It began nowhere, and ended everywhere, and yet, as always with that divine man, it left you feeling that something beautiful had passed that way, something more beautiful than anything else, like the rising and setting of stars. Every possible criticism might have been made on it but one,—that it was not noble. There was a tone in it that awakened all elevating associations. He boggled, he lost his place, he had to put on his glasses; but it was as if a creature from some fairer world had lost his way in our fogs, and it was *our* fault, not his. It was chaotic, but it was all such stuff as stars are made of, and you couldn't help feeling that, if you waited awhile, all that was nebulous would be whirled into planets, and would assume the mathematical gravity of system. All through it I felt something in me that cried, 'Ha! ha!' to the sound of the trumpets."

It is nothing for any man sitting in his chair to be overcome with the sense of the immediacy of life, to feel the spur of courage, the victory of good over evil, the value, now and forever, of all great-hearted endeavor. Such moments come to us all. But for a man to sit in his chair and write what shall call up these forces in the bosom of others—that is desert, that is greatness. To do this was the gift of Emerson. The whole earth is enriched by every moment of converse with him. The shows and shams of life become transparent, the lost kingdoms are brought back, the shutters of the spirit are opened, and provinces and realms of our own existence lie gleaming before us.

It has been necessary to reduce the living soul of Emerson to mere dead attributes like "moral courage" in order that we might talk about him at all. His effectiveness comes from his character; not from his philosophy, nor from his rhetoric nor his wit, nor from any of the accidents of his education. He might never have heard of Berkeley or Plato. A slightly different education might have led him to throw his teaching into the form of historical essays or of stump speeches. He might, perhaps, have been bred a stonemason, and have done his work in the world by travelling with a panorama. But he would always have been Emerson. His weight and his power would always have been the same. It is solely as character that he is important. He discovered nothing; he bears no relation whatever to the history of philosophy. We must regard him and deal with him simply as a man.

Strangely enough, the world has always insisted upon accepting him as a thinker: and hence a great coil of misunderstanding. As a thinker, Emerson is difficult to classify. Before you begin to assign him a place, you must clear the ground by a disquisition as to what is meant by "a thinker," and how Emerson differs from other thinkers. As a man, Emerson is as plain as Ben Franklin.

People have accused him of inconsistency; they say that he teaches one thing one day, and another the next day. But from the point of view of Emerson there is no such thing as inconsistency. Every man is each day a new man. Let him be to-day what he is to-day. It is immaterial and waste of time to consider what he once was or what he may be.

His picturesque speech delights in fact and anecdote, and a public which is used to treatises and deduction cares always to be told the moral. It wants everything reduced to a generalization. All generalizations are partial truths, but we are used to them, and we ourselves mentally make the proper allowance. Emerson's method is, not to give a generalization and trust to our making the allowance, but to give two conflicting statements and leave the balance of truth to be struck in our own minds on the facts. There is no inconsistency in this. It is a vivid and very legitimate method of procedure. But he is much more than a theorist: he is a practitioner. He does not merely state a theory of agitation: he proceeds to agitate. "Do not," he says, "set the least value on what I do, or the least discredit on what I do not, as if I pretended to settle anything as false or true. I unsettle all things. No facts are to me sacred, none are profane. I simply experiment, an endless seeker with no past at my back." He was not engaged in teaching many things, but one thing,—Courage. Sometimes he inspires it by pointing to great characters,—Fox, Milton, Alcibiades; sometimes he inspires it by bidding us beware of imitating such men, and, in the ardor of his rhetoric, even seems to regard them as hindrances and dangers to our developments. There is no inconsistency here. Emerson might logically have gone one step further and raised inconsistency into a jewel. For what is so useful, so educational, so inspiring, to a timid and conservative man, as to do something inconsistent and regrettable? It lends character to him at once. He breathes freer and is stronger for the experience.

Emerson is no cosmopolitan. He is a patriot. He is not like Goethe, whose sympathies did not run on national lines. Emerson has America in his mind's eye all the time. There is to be a new religion, and it is to come from America; a new and better type of man, and he is to be an American. He not only cared little or nothing for Europe, but he cared not much for the world at large. His thought was for the future of this country. You cannot get into any chamber in his mind which is below this chamber of patriotism. He loves the valor of Alexander and the grace of the Oxford athlete; but he loves them not for themselves. He has a use for them. They are grist to his mill and powder to his gun. His admiration of them he subordinates to his main purpose,—they are his blackboard and diagrams. His patriotism is the backbone of his significance. He came to his countrymen at a time when they lacked, not thoughts, but manliness. The needs of his own particular public are always before him.

"It is odd that our people should have, not water on the brain, but a little gas there. A shrewd foreigner said of the Americans that 'whatever they say has a little the air of a speech.'"

"I shall not need to go into an enumeration of our national defects and vices which require this Order of Censors in the State. . . . The timidity of our public opinion is our disease, or, shall I say, the publicness of opinion, the absence of private opinion."

"Our measure of success is the moderation and low level of an individual's judgment. Dr. Channing's piety and wisdom had such weight in Boston that the popular idea of religion was whatever this eminent divine held."

"Let us affront and reprimand the smooth mediocrity, the squalid contentment of the times."

The politicians he scores constantly.

"Who that sees the meanness of our politics but congratulates Washington that he is long already wrapped in his shroud and forever safe." The following is his description of the social world of his day: "If any man consider the present aspects of what is called by distinction *society*, he will see the need of these ethics. The sinew and heart of man seem to be drawn out, and we are become timorous, desponding whimperers."

It is the same wherever we open his books. He must spur on, feed up, bring forward the dormant character of his countrymen. When he goes to England, he sees in English life nothing except those elements which are deficient in America life. If you wish a catalogue of what America has not, read English Traits. Emerson's patriotism had the effect of expanding his philosophy. To-day we know the value of physique, for science has taught it, but it was hardly discovered in his day, and his philosophy affords no basis for it. Emerson in this matter transcends his philosophy. When in England, he was fairly made drunk with the physical life he found there. He is like Caspar Hauser gazing for the first time on green fields. English Traits is the ruddiest book he ever wrote. It is a hymn to force, honesty, and physical well-being, and ends with the dominant note of his belief: "By this general activity and by this sacredness of individuals, they [the English] have in seven hundred years evolved the principles of freedom. It is the land of patriots, martyrs, sages, and bards, and if the ocean out of which it emerged should wash it away, it will be remembered as an island famous for immortal laws, for the announcements of original right which make the stone tables of liberty." He had found in England free speech, personal courage, and reverence for the individual.

No convulsion could shake Emerson or make his view unsteady even for an instant. What no one else saw, he saw, and he saw nothing else. Not a boy in the land welcomed the outbreak of the war so fiercely as did this shy village philosopher, then at the age of fifty-eight. He saw that war was the cure of cowardice, moral as well as physical. It was not the cause of the slave that moved him; it was not the cause of the Union for which he cared a farthing. It was something deeper than either of these things for which he had been battling all his life. It was the cause of character against convention. Whatever else the war might bring, it was sure to bring in character, to leave behind it a file of heroes; if not heroes, then villains, but in any case strong men. On the 9th of April, 1861, three days before Fort Sumter was bombarded, he had spoken with equanimity of "the downfall of our character-destroying civilization. . . . We find that civilization crowed too soon, that our triumphs were treacheries; we had opened the wrong door and let the enemy into the castle."

"Ah," he said, when the firing began, "sometimes gunpowder smells good." Soon after the attack on Sumter he said in a public address, "We have been very homeless for some years past, say since 1850; but now we have a country again. . . . The war was an eye-opener, and showed men of all parties and opinions the value of those primary forces that lie beneath all political action." And it was almost a personal pledge when he said at the Harvard Commemoration in 1865, "We shall not again disparage America, now that we have seen what men it will bear."

The place which Emerson forever occupies as a great critic is defined by the same sharp outlines that mark his work, in whatever light and from whatever side we approach it. A critic in the modern sense he was not, for his point of view is fixed, and he reviews the world like a search-light placed on the top of a tall tower. He lived too early and at too great a distance from the forum of European thought to absorb the ideas of evolution and give place to them in his philosophy. Evolution does not graft well upon the Platonic Idealism, nor are physiology and the kindred sciences sympathetic. Nothing aroused Emerson's indignation more than the attempts of the medical faculty and of phrenologists to classify, and therefore limit individuals. "The grossest ignorance does not disgust me like this ignorant knowingness."

We miss in Emerson the underlying conception of growth, of development, so characteristic of the thought of our own day, and which, for instance, is found everywhere latent in Browning's poetry. Browning regards character as the result of experience and as an ever changing growth. To Emerson, character is rather an entity complete and eternal from the beginning. He is probably the last great writer to look at life from a stationary standpoint. There is a certain lack of the historic sense in all he has written. The ethical assumption that all men are exactly alike permeates his work. In his mind, Socrates, Marco Polo, and General Jackson stand surrounded by the same atmosphere, or rather stand as mere naked characters surrounded by no atmosphere at all. He is probably the last great writer who will fling about classic anecdotes as if they were club gossip. In the discussion of morals, this assumption does little harm. The stories and proverbs which illustrate the thought of the moralist generally concern only those simple relations of life which are common to all ages. There is charm in this familiar dealing with antiquity. The classics are thus domesticated and made real to us. What matter if Æsop appear a little too much like an American citizen, so long as his points tell?

It is in Emerson's treatment of the fine arts that we begin to notice his want of historic sense. Art endeavors to express subtle and ever changing feelings by means of conventions which are as protean as the forms of a cloud; and the man who in speaking on the plastic arts makes the assumption that all men are alike will reveal before he has uttered three sentences that he does not know what art is, that he has never experienced any form of sensation from it. Emerson lived in a time and clime where there was no plastic art, and he was obliged to arrive at his ideas about art by means of a highly complex process of reasoning. He dwelt constantly in a spiritual place which was the very focus of high moral fervor. This was his enthusiasm, this was his revelation, and from it he reasoned out the probable meaning of the fine arts. "This," thought Emerson, his eye rolling in a fine frenzy of moral feeling, "this must be what Apelles experienced, this fervor is the passion of Bramante. I understand the Parthenon." And so he projected his feelings about morality into the field of the plastic arts. He deals very freely and rather indiscriminately with the names of artists,— Phidias, Raphael, Salvator Rosa,—and he speaks always in such a way that it is impossible to connect what he says with any impression we have ever received from the works of those masters.

In fact, Emerson has never in his life felt the normal appeal of any painting, or any sculpture, or any architecture, or any music. These things, of which he does not know the meaning in real life, he yet uses, and uses constantly, as symbols to convey ethical truth. The result is that his books are full of blind places, like the notes which will not strike on a sick piano.

It is interesting to find that the one art of which Emerson did have a direct understanding, the art of poetry, gave him some insight into the relation of the artist to his vehicle. In his essay on Shakespeare there is a full recognition of the debt of Shakespeare to his times. This essay is filled with the historic sense. We ought not to accuse Emerson because he lacked appreciation of the fine arts, but rather admire the truly Goethean spirit in which he insisted upon the reality of arts of which he had no understanding. This is the same spirit which led him to insist on the value of the Eastern poets. Perhaps there exist a few scholars who can tell us how far Emerson understood or misunderstood Saadi and Firdusi and the Koran. But we need not be disturbed for his learning. It is enough that he makes us recognize that these men were men too, and that their writings mean something not unknowable to us. The East added nothing to Emerson, but gave him a few trappings of speech. The whole of his mysticism is to be found in Nature, written before he knew the sages of the Orient, and it is not improbable that there is some real connection between his own mysticism and the mysticism of the Eastern poets.

Emerson's criticism on men and books is like the test of a great chemist who seeks one or two elements. He burns a bit of the stuff in his incandescent light, shows the lines of it in his spectrum, and there an end.

It was a thought of genius that led him to write Representative Men. The scheme of this book gave play to every illumination of his mind, and it pinned him down to the objective, to the field of vision under his miscroscope. The table of contents of Representative Men is the dial of his education. It is as follows: Uses of Great Men; Plato, or The Philosopher; Plato, New Readings; Swedenborg, or The Mystic; Montaigne, or The Sceptic; Shakespeare, or The Poet; Napoleon, or The Man of the World; Goethe, or The Writer. The predominance of the writers over all other types of men is not cited to show Emerson's interest in The Writer, for we know his interest centred in the practical man,—even his ideal scholar is a practical man,—but to show the sources of his illustration. Emerson's library was the old-fashioned gentleman's library. His mines of thought were the world's classics. This is one reason why he so quickly gained an international currency. His very subjects in Representative Men are of universal interest, and he is limited only by certain inevitable local conditions. Representative Men is thought by many persons to be his best book. It is certainly filled with the strokes of a master. There exists no more profound criticism than Emerson's analysis of Goethe and of Napoleon, by both of whom he was at once fascinated and repelled.

## II

THE ATTITUDE of Emerson's mind toward reformers results so logically from his philosophy that it is easily understood. He saw in them people who sought something as a panacea or as an end in itself. To speak strictly and not irreverently, he had his own panacea,—the development of each individual; and he was impatient of any other. He did not believe in association. The very idea of it involved a surrender by the individual of some portion of his identity, and of course all the reformers worked through their associations. With their general aims he sympathized. "These reforms," he wrote, "are our contemporaries; they are ourselves, our own light and sight and conscience; they only name the relation which subsists between us and the vicious institutions which they go to rectify." But with the methods of the reformers he had no sympathy: "He who aims at progress should aim at an infinite, not at a special benefit. The reforms whose fame now fills the land with temperance, anti-slavery, non-resistance, no-government, equal labor, fair and generous as each appears, are poor bitter things when prosecuted for themselves as an end." Again: "The young men who have been vexing society for these last years with regenerative methods seem to have made this mistake: they all exaggerated some special means, and all failed to see that the reform of reforms must be accomplished without means."

Emerson did not at first discriminate between the movement of the Abolitionists and the hundred and one other reform movements of the period; and in this lack of discrimination lies a point of extraordinary interest. The Abolitionsists, as it afterwards turned out, had in fact got hold of the issue which was to control the fortunes of the republic for thirty years. The difference between them and the other reformers was this: that the Abolitionists were men set in motion by the primary and unreasoning passion of pity. Theory played small part in the movement. It grew by the excitement which exhibitions of cruelty will arouse in the minds of sensitive people.

It is not to be denied that the social conditions in Boston in 1831 foreboded an outbreak in some form. If the abolition excitement had not drafted off the rising forces, there might have been a Merry Mount, an epidemic of crime or insanity, or a mob of some sort. The abolition movement afforded the purest form of an indulgence in human feeling that was ever offered to men. It was intoxicating. It made the agitators perfectly happy. They sang at their work and bubbled over with exhilaration. They were the only people in the United States, at this time, who were enjoying an exalted, glorifying, practical activity.

But Emerson at first lacked the touchstone, whether of intellect or of heart, to see the difference between this particular movement and the other movements then in progress. Indeed, in so far as he sees any difference between the Abolitionists and the rest, it is that

the Abolitionists were more objectionable and distasteful to him.
"Those," he said, "who are urging with most ardor what are called
the greatest benefits to mankind are narrow, conceited, self-pleasing men, and affect us as the insane do." And again: "By the side
of these men [the idealists] the hot agitators have a certain cheap
and ridiculous air; they even look smaller than others. Of the two, I
own I like the speculators the best. They have some piety which
looks with faith to a fair future unprofaned by rash and unequal attempts to realize it." He was drawn into the abolition cause by having
the truth brought home to him that these people were fighting for
the Moral Law. He was slow in seeing this, because in their methods they represented everything he most condemned. As soon, however, as he was convinced, he was ready to lecture for them and to
give them the weight of his approval. In 1844 he was already practically an Abolitionist, and his feelings upon the matter deepened
steadily in intensity ever after.

The most interesting page of Emerson's published journal is the
following, written at some time previous to 1844; the exact date is
not given. A like page, whether written or unwritten, may be read
into the private annals of every man who lived before the war.
Emerson has, with unconscious mastery, photographed the half-
spectre that stalked in the minds of all. He wrote: "I had occasion
to say the other day to Elizabeth Hoar that I like best the strong
and worthy persons, like her father, who support the social order
without hesitation or misgiving. I like these; they never incommode
us by exciting grief, pity, or perturbation of any sort. But the professed philanthropists, it is strange and horrible to say, are an altogether odious set of people, whom one would shun as the worst of
bores and canters. But my conscience, my unhappy conscience re-
spects that hapless class who see the faults and stains of our social
order, and who pray and strive incessantly to right the wrong; this
annoying class of men and women, though they commonly find the
work altogether beyond their faculty, and their results are, for the
present, distressing. They are partial, and apt to magnify their own.
Yes, and the prostrate penitent, also,—he is not comprehensive, he
is not philosophical in those tears and groans. Yet I feel that under
him and his partiality and exclusiveness is the earth and the sea
and all that in them is, and the axis around which the universe re-
volves passes through his body where he stands."

It was the defection of Daniel Webster that completed the conversion of Emerson and turned him from an adherent into a propagandist of abolition. Not pity for the slave, but indignation at the violation of the Moral Law by Daniel Webster, was at the bottom of Emerson's anger. His abolitionism was secondary to his main mission, his main enthusiasm. It is for this reason that he stands on a plane of intellect where he might, under other circumstances, have met and defeated Webster. After the 7th of March, 1850, he recognized in Webster the embodiment of all that he hated. In his attacks on Webster, Emerson trembles to his inmost fibre with antagonism. He is savage, destructive, personal, bent on death.

This exhibition of Emerson as a fighting animal is magnificent, and explains his life. There is no other instance of his ferocity. No other nature but Webster's ever so moved him; but it was time to be moved, and Webster was a man of his size. Had these two great men of New England been matched in training as they were matched in endowment, and had they then faced each other in debate, they would not have been found to differ so greatly in power. Their natures were electrically repellent, but from which did the greater force radiate? Their education differed so radically that it is impossible to compare them, but if you translate the Phi Beta Kappa address into politics, you have something stronger than Webster,—something that recalls Chatham; and Emerson would have had this advantage,—that he was not afraid. As it was, he left his library and took the stump. Mr. Cabot has given us extracts from his speeches:—

"The tameness is indeed complete; all are involved in one hot haste of terror,—presidents of colleges and professors, saints and brokers, lawyers and manufacturers; not a liberal recollection, not so much as a snatch of an old song for freedom, dares intrude on their passive obedience. . . . Mr. Webster, perhaps, is only following the laws of his blood and constitution. I suppose his pledges were not quite natural to him. He is a man who lives by his memory; a man of the past, not a man of faith and of hope. All the drops of his blood have eyes that look downward, and his finely developed understanding only works truly and with all its force when it stands for animal good; that is, for property. He looks at the Union as an estate, a large farm, and is excellent in the completeness of his defence of it so far. What he finds already written he will defend. Lucky that so much had got well written when he came, for he has no faith in the power of self-government. Not the smallest municipal provision, if it were new, would receive his sanction. In Massachusetts, in 1776, he would, beyond all question, have been a refugee. He praises Adams and Jefferson, but it is a past Adams and Jefferson. A present Adams or Jefferson he would denounce. . . . But one thing appears certain to me: that the Union is at an end as soon as an immoral law is enacted. He who writes a crime into the statute book digs under the foundations of the Capitol. . . . The words of John Randolph, wiser than he knew, have been ringing ominously in all echoes for thirty years: 'We do not govern the people of the North by our black slaves, but by their own white slaves.' . . . They come down now like the cry of fate, in the moment when they are fulfilled."

The exasperation of Emerson did not subside, but went on increasing during the next four years, and on March 7, 1854, he read his lecture on the Fugitive Slave Law at the New York Tabernacle: "I have lived all my life without suffering any inconvenience from American Slavery. I never saw it; I never heard the whip; I never felt the check on my free speech and action, until the other day, when Mr. Webster, by his personal influence, brought the Fugitive Slave Law on the country. I say Mr. Webster, for though the bill was not his, it is yet notorious that he was the life and soul of it, that he gave it all he had. It cost him his life, and under the shadow of his great name inferior men sheltered themselves, threw their ballots for it, and made the law. . . . Nobody doubts that Daniel Webster could make a good speech. Nobody doubts that there were good and plausible things to be said on the part of the South. But this is not a question of ingenuity, not a question of syllogisms, but of sides. *How came he there?* . . . But the question which history will ask is broader. In the final hour when he was forced by the peremptory necessity of the closing armies to take a side,—did he take the part of great principles, the side of humanity and justice, or the side of abuse, and oppression, and chaos? . . . He did as immoral men usually do,—made very low bows to the Christian Church and went through all the Sunday decorums, but when allusion was made to the question of duty and the sanctions of morality, he very frankly said, at Albany, 'Some higher law, something existing somewhere between here and the heaven—I do not know where.' And if the reporters say true, this wretched atheism found some laughter in the company."

It was too late for Emerson to shine as a political debater. On May 14, 1857, Longfellow wrote in his diary, "It is rather painful to see Emerson in the arena of politics, hissed and hooted at by young law students." Emerson records a similar experience at a later date: "If I were dumb, yet would I have gone and mowed and muttered or made signs. The mob roared whenever I attempted to speak, and after several beginnings I withdrew." There is nothing "painful" here: it is the sublime exhibition of a great soul in bondage to circumstance.

The thing to be noted is that this is the same man, in the same state of excitement about the same idea, who years before spoke out in The American Scholar, in the Essays, and in the Lectures.

What was it that had aroused in Emerson such Promethean antagonism in 1837 but those same forces which in 1850 came to their culmination and assumed visible shape in the person of Daniel Webster? The formal victory of Webster drew Emerson into the arena, and made a dramatic episode in his life. But his battle with those forces had begun thirteen years earlier, when he threw down the gauntlet to them in his Phi Beta Kappa oration. Emerson by his writings did more than any other man to rescue the youth of the next generation and fit them for the fierce times to follow. It will not be denied that he sent ten thousand sons to the war.

In speaking of Emerson's attitude toward the anti-slavery cause, it has been possible to dispense with any survey of that movement, because the movement was simple and specific and is well remembered. But when we come to analyze the relations he bore to some of the local agitations of his day, it becomes necessary to weave in with the matter a discussion of certain tendencies deeply imbedded in the life of his times, and of which he himself was in a sense an outcome. In speaking of the Transcendentalists, who were essentially the children of the Puritans, we must begin with some study of the chief traits of Puritanism.

What parts the factors of climate, circumstance, and religion have respectively played in the development of the New England character no analysis can determine. We may trace the imaginary influence of a harsh creed in the lines of the face. We may sometimes follow from generation to generation the course of a truth which at first sustained the spirit of man, till we see it petrify into a dogma which now kills the spirits of men. Conscience may destroy the character. The tragedy of the New England judge enforcing the Fugitive Slave Law was no new spectacle in New England. A dogmatic crucifixion of the natural instincts had been in progress there for two hundred years. Emerson, who is more free from dogma than any other teacher that can be named, yet comes very near being dogmatic in his reiteration of the Moral Law.

Whatever volume of Emerson we take up, the Moral Law holds the same place in his thoughts. It is the one statable revelation of truth which he is ready to stake his all upon. "The illusion that strikes me as the masterpiece in that ring of illusions which our life is, is the timidity with which we assert our moral sentiment. We are made of it, the world is built by it, things endure as they share it; all beauty, all health, all intelligence exist by it; yet we shrink to speak of it or range ourselves by its side. Nay, we presume strength of him or them who deny it. Cities go against it, the college goes against it, the courts snatch any precedent at any vicious form of law to rule it out; legislatures listen with appetite to declamations against it and vote it down."

With this very beautiful and striking passage no one will quarrel, nor will any one misunderstand it.

The following passage has the same sort of poetical truth. "Things are saturated with the moral law. There is no escape from it. Violets and grass preach it; rain and snow, wind and tides, every change, every cause in Nature is nothing but a disguised missionary." . . .

But Emerson is not satisfied with metaphor. "We affirm that in all men is this majestic perception and command; that it is the presence of the eternal in each perishing man; that it distances and degrades all statements of whatever saints, heroes, poets, as obscure and confused stammerings before its silent revelation. *They* report the truth. *It* is the truth." In this last extract we have Emerson actually affirming that his dogma of the Moral Law is Absolute Truth. He thinks it not merely a form of truth, like the old theologies, but very distinguishable from all other forms in the past.

Curiously enough, his statement of the law grows dogmatic and incisive in proportion as he approaches the borderland between his law and the natural instincts: "The last revelation of intellect and of sentiment is that in a manner it severs the man from all other men; makes known to him *that the spiritual powers are sufficient to him if no other being existed;* that he is to deal absolutely in the world, as if he alone were a system and a state, and though all should perish could make all anew." Here we have the dogma applied, and we see in it only a new form of old Calvinism as cruel as Calvinism, and not much different from its original. The italics are not Emerson's, but are inserted to bring out an idea which is everywhere prevalent in his teaching.

In this final form, the Moral Law, by insisting that sheer conscience can slake the thirst that rises in the soul, is convicted of falsehood; and this heartless falsehood is the same falsehood that has been put into the porridge of every Puritan child for six generations. A grown man can digest doctrine and sleep at night. But a young person of high purpose and strong will, who takes such a lie as this half-truth and feeds on it as on the bread of life, will suffer. It will injure the action of his heart. Truly the fathers have eaten sour grapes, therefore the children's teeth are set on edge.

To understand the civilization of cities, we must look at the rural population from which they draw their life. We have recently had our attention called to the last remnants of that village life so reverently gathered up by Miss Wilkins, and of which Miss Emily Dickinson was the last authentic voice. The spirit of this age has examined with an almost pathological interest this rescued society. We must go to it if we would understand Emerson, who is the blossoming of its culture. We must study it if we would arrive at any intelligent and general view of that miscellaneous crop of individuals who have been called the Transcendentalists.

Between 1830 and 1840 there were already signs in New England that the nutritive and reproductive forces of society were not quite wholesome, not exactly well adjusted. Self-repression was the religion which had been inherited. "Distrust Nature" was the motto written upon the front of the temple. What would have happened to that society if left to itself for another hundred years no man can guess. It was rescued by the two great regenerators of mankind, new land and war. The dispersion came, as Emerson said of the barbarian conquests of Rome, not a day too soon. It happened that the country at large stood in need of New England as much as New England stood in need of the country. This congested virtue, in order to be saved, must be scattered. This ferment, in order to be kept wholesome, must be used as leaven to leaven the whole lump. "As you know," says Emerson in his Eulogy on Boston, "New England supplies annually a large detachment of preachers and schoolmasters and private tutors to the interior of the South and West. . . . We are willing to see our sons emigrate, as to see our hives swarm. That is what they were made to do, and what the land wants and invites."

For purposes of yeast, there was never such leaven as the Puritan stock. How little the natural force of the race had really abated became apparent when it was placed under healthy conditions, given land to till, foes to fight, the chance to renew its youth like the eagle. But during this period the relief had not yet come. The terrible pressure of Puritanism and conservatism in New England was causing a revolt not only of the Abolitionists, but of another class of people of a type not so virile as they. The times have been smartly described by Lowell in his essay on Thoreau:—

"Every possible form of intellectual and physical dyspepsia brought forth its gospel. Bran had its prophets. . . . Everybody had a Mission (with a capital M) to attend to everybody else's business. No brain but had its private maggot, which must have found pitiably short commons sometimes. Not a few impecunious zealots abjured the use of money (unless earned by other people), professing to live on the internal revenues of the spirit. Some had an assurance of instant millennium so soon as hooks and eyes should be substituted for buttons. Communities were established where everything was to be common but common sense. . . . Conventions were held for every hitherto inconceivable purpose."

Whatever may be said of the Transcendentalists, it must not be forgotten that they represented an elevation of feeling, which through them qualified the next generation, and can be traced in the life of New England to-day. The strong intrinsic character lodged in these recusants was later made manifest; for many of them became the best citizens of the commonwealth,—statesmen, merchants, soldiers, men and women of affairs. They retained their idealism while becoming practical men. There is hardly an example of what we should have thought would be common in their later lives, namely, a reaction from so much ideal effort, and a plunge into cynicism and malice, scoundrelism and the flesh-pots.

In their early life they resembled the Abolitionists in their devotion to an idea; but with the Transcendentalists self-culture and the æsthetic and sentimental education took the place of more public aims. They seem also to have been persons of greater social refinement than the Abolitionists.

The Transcendentalists were sure of only one thing,—that society as constituted was all wrong. In this their main belief they were right. They were men and women whose fundamental need was activity, contact with real life, and the opportunity for social expansion; and they keenly felt the chill and fictitious character of the reigning conventionalists. The rigidity of behavior which at this time characterized the Bostonians seemed sometimes ludicrous and sometimes disagreeable to the foreign visitor. There was great gravity, together with a certain pomp and dumbness, and these things were supposed to be natural to the inhabitants and to give them joy. People are apt to forget that such masks are never worn with ease. They result from the application of an inflexible will, and always inflict discomfort. The Transcendentalists found themselves all but stifled in a society as artificial in its decorum as the court of France during the last years of Louis XIV.

Emerson was in no way responsible for the movement, although he got the credit of having evoked it by his teaching. He was elder brother to it, and was generated by its parental forces; but even if Emerson had never lived, the Transcendentalists would have appeared. He was their victim rather than their cause. He was always tolerant of them and sometimes amused at them, and disposed to treat them lightly. It is impossible to analyze their case with more astuteness than he did in an editorial letter in The Dial. The letter is cold, but is a masterpiece of good sense. He had, he says, received fifteen letters on the Prospects of Culture. "Excellent reasons have been shown us why the writers, obviously persons of sincerity and elegance, should be dissatisfied with the life they lead, and with their company. . . . They want a friend to whom they can speak and from whom they may hear now and then a reasonable word." After discussing one or two of their proposals,—one of which was that the tiresome "uncles and aunts" of the enthusiasts should be placed by themselves in one delightful village, the dough, as Emerson says, be placed in one pan and the leaven in another,—he continues: "But it would be unjust not to remind our younger friends that whilst this aspiration has always made its mark in the lives of men of thought, in vigorous individuals it does not remain a detached object, but is satisfied along with the satisfaction of other aims." Young Americans "are educated above the work of their times and country, and disdain it. Many of the more acute minds pass into a lofty criticism . . . which only embitters their sensibility to the evil, and widens the feeling of hostility between them and the citizens at large. . . . We should not know where to find in literature any record of so much unbalanced intellectuality, such undeniable apprehension without talent, so much power without equal applicability, as our young men pretend to. . . . The balance of mind and body will redress itself fast enough. Superficialness is the real distemper. . . . It is certain that speculation is no succedaneum for life." He then turns to find the cure for these distempers in the farm lands of Illinois, at that time already being fenced in "almost like New England itself," and closes with a suggestion that so long as there is a woodpile in the yard, and the "wrongs of the Indian, of the Negro, of the emigrant, remain unmitigated," relief might be found even nearer home.

In his lecture on the Transcendentalists he says: ". . . But their solitary and fastidious manners not only withdraw them from the conversation, but from the labors of the world: they are not good citizens, not good members of society; unwillingly they bear their part of the public and private burdens; they do not willingly share in the public charities, in the public religious rites, in the enterprises of education, of missions foreign and domestic, in the abolition of the slave-trade, or in the temperance society. They do not even like to vote." A less sympathetic observer, Harriet Martineau, wrote of them: "While Margaret Fuller and her adult pupils sat 'gorgeously dressed,' talking about Mars and Venus, Plato and Goethe, and fancying themselves the elect of the earth in intellect and refinement, the liberties of the republic were running out as fast as they could go at a breach which another sort of elect persons were devoting themselves to repair; and my complaint against the 'gorgeous' pedants was that they regarded their preservers as hewers of wood and drawers of water, and their work as a less vital one than the pedantic orations which were spoiling a set of well-meaning women in a pitiable way." Harriet Martineau, whose whole work was practical, and who wrote her journal in 1855 and in the light of history, was hardly able to do justice to these unpractical but sincere spirits.

Emerson was divided from the Transcendentalists by his common sense. His shrewd business intellect made short work of their schemes. Each one of their social projects contained some covert economic weakness, which always turned out to lie in an attack upon the integrity of the individual, and which Emerson of all men could be counted on to detect. He was divided from them also by the fact that he was a man of genius, who had sought out and fought out his means of expression. He was a great artist, and as such he was a complete being. No one could give to him nor take from him. His yearnings found fruition in expression. He was sure of his place and of his use in this world. But the Transcendentalists were neither geniuses nor artists nor complete beings. Nor had they found their places or uses as yet. They were men and women seeking light. They walked in dry places, seeking rest and finding none. The Transcendentalists are not collectively important because their *Sturm und Drang* was intellectual and bloodless. Though Emerson admonish and Harriet Martineau condemn, yet from the memorials that survive, one is more impressed with the sufferings than with the ludicrousness of these persons. There is something distressing about their letters, their talk, their memoirs, their interminable diaries. They worry and contort and introspect. They rave and dream. They peep and theorize. They cut open the bellows of life to see where the wind comes from. Margaret Fuller analyzes Emerson, and Emerson Margaret Fuller. It is not a wholesome ebullition of vitality. It is a nightmare, in which the emotions, the terror, the agony, the rapture, are all unreal, and have no vital content, no consequence in the world outside. It is positively wonderful that so much excitement and so much suffering should have left behind nothing in the field of art which is valuable. All that intelligence could do toward solving problems for his friends Emerson did. But there are situations in life in which the intelligence is helpless, and in which something else, something perhaps possessed by a ploughboy, is more divine than Plato.

If it were not pathetic, there would be something cruel—indeed there is something cruel—in Emerson's incapacity to deal with Margaret Fuller. He wrote to her on October 24, 1840: "My dear Margaret, I have your frank and noble and affecting letter, and yet

I think I could wish it unwritten. I ought never to have suffered you to lead me into any conversation or writing on our relation, a topic from which with all persons my Genius warns me away."

The letter proceeds with unimpeachable emptiness and integrity in the same strain. In 1841 he writes in his diary: "Strange, cold-warm, attractive-repelling conversation with Margaret, whom I always admire, most revere when I nearest see, and sometimes love; yet whom I freeze and who freezes me to silence when we promise to come nearest."

Human sentiment was known to Emerson mainly in the form of pain. His nature shunned it; he cast it off as quickly as possible. There is a word or two in the essay on Love which seems to show that the inner and diaphanous core of this seraph had once, but not for long, been shot with blood: he recalls only the pain of it. His relations with Margaret Fuller seem never normal, though they lasted for years. This brilliant woman was in distress. She was asking for bread, and he was giving her a stone, and neither of them was conscious of what was passing. This is pitiful. It makes us clutch about us to catch hold, if we somehow may, of the hand of a man.

There was manliness in Horace Greeley, under whom Miss Fuller worked on the New York Tribune not many years afterward. She wrote: "Mr. Greeley I like,—nay, more, love. He is in his habit a plebeian, in his heart a nobleman. His abilities in his own way are great. He believes in mine to a surprising degree. We are true friends."

This anæmic incompleteness of Emerson's character can be traced to the philosophy of his race; at least it can be followed in that philosophy. There is an implication of a fundamental falsehood in every bit of Transcendentalism, including Emerson. That falsehood consists in the theory of the self-sufficiency of each individual, men and women alike. Margaret Fuller is a good example of the effect of this philosophy, because her history afterward showed that she was constituted like other human beings, was dependent upon human relationship, and was not only a very noble, but also a very womanly creature. Her marriage, her Italian life, and her tragic death light up with the splendor of reality the earlier and unhappy period of her life. This woman had been driven into her vagaries by the lack of something which she did not know existed, and which she sought blindly in metaphysics. Harriet Martineau writes of her: "It is the most grievous loss I have almost ever known in private history, the deferring of Margaret Fuller's married life so long. That noble last period of her life is happily on record as well as the earlier." The hardy Englishwoman has here laid a kind human hand on the weakness of New England, and seems to be unconscious that she is making a revelation as to the whole Transcendental movement. But the point is this: there was no one within reach of Margaret Fuller, in her early days, who knew what was her need. One offered her Kant, one Comte, one Fourier, one Swedenborg, one the Moral Law. You cannot feed the heart on these things.

Yet there is a bright side to this New England spirit, which seems, if we look only to the graver emotions, so dry, dismal, and deficient. A bright and cheery courage appears in certain natures of which the sun has made conquest, that almost reconciles us to all loss, so splendid is the outcome. The practical, dominant, insuppressible active temperaments who have a word for every emergency, and who carry the controlled force of ten men at their disposal, are the fruits of this same spirit. Emerson knew not tears, but he and the hundred other beaming and competent characters which New England has produced make us almost envy their state. They give us again the old Stoics at their best.

Very closely connected with this subject—the crisp and cheery New England temperament—lies another which any discussion of Emerson must bring up,—namely, Asceticism. It is probable that in dealing with Emerson's feelings about the plastic arts we have to do with what is really the inside, or metaphysical side, of the same phenomena which present themselves on the outside, or physical side, in the shape of asceticism.

Emerson's natural asceticism is revealed to us in almost every form in which history can record a man. It is in his philosophy, in his style, in his conduct, and in his appearance. It was, however, not in his voice. Mr. Cabot, with that reverence for which every one must feel personally grateful to him, has preserved a description of Emerson by the New York journalist, N. P. Willis: "It is a voice with shoulders in it, which he has not; with lungs in it far larger than his; with a walk which the public never see; with a fist in it which his own hand never gave him the model for; and with a gentleman in it which his parochial and 'bare-necessaries-of-life' sort of exterior gives no other betrayal of. We can imagine nothing in nature (which seems too to have a type for everything) like the want of correspondence between the Emerson that goes in at the eye and the Emerson that goes in at the ear. A heavy and vase-like blossom of a magnolia, with fragrance enough to perfume a whole wilderness, which should be lifted by a whirlwind and dropped into a branch of aspen, would not seem more as if it could never have grown there than Emerson's voice seems inspired and foreign to his visible and natural body." Emerson's ever exquisite and wonderful good taste seems closely connected with this asceticism, and it is probable that his taste influenced his views and conduct to some small extent.

The anti-slavery people were not always refined. They were constantly doing things which were tactically very effective, but were not calculated to attract the over-sensitive. Garrison's rampant and impersonal egotism was good politics, but bad taste. Wendell Phillips did not hesitate upon occasion to deal in personalities of an exasperating kind. One sees a certain shrinking in Emerson from the taste of the Abolitionists. It was not merely their doctrines or their methods which offended him. He at one time refused to give Wendell Phillips his hand because of Phillips's treatment of his friend, Judge Hoar. One hardly knows whether to be pleased at Emerson for showing a human weakness, or annoyed at him for not being more of a man. The anecdote is valuable in both lights. It is like a tiny speck on the crystal of his character which shows us the exact location of the orb, and it is the best illustration of the feeling of the times which has come down to us.

If by "asceticism" we mean an experiment in starving the senses, there is little harm in it. Nature will soon reassert her dominion, and very likely our perceptions will be sharpened by the trial. But "natural asceticism" is a thing hardly to be distinguished from functional weakness. What is natural asceticism but a lack of vigor? Does it not tend to close the avenues between the soul and the universe? "Is it not so much death?" The accounts of Emerson show him to have been a man in whom there was almost a hiatus between the senses and the most inward spirit of life. The lower register of sensations and emotions which domesticate a man into fellowship with common life was weak. Genial familiarity was to him impossible; laughter was almost a pain. "It is not the sea and poverty and pursuit that separate us. Here is Alcott by my door,— yet is the union more profound? No! the sea, vocation, poverty, are seeming fences, but man is insular and cannot be touched. Every man is an infinitely repellent orb, and holds his individual being on that condition. . . . Most of the persons whom I see in my own house I see across a gulf; I cannot go to them nor they come to me."

This aloofness of Emerson must be remembered only as blended with his benignity. "His friends were all that knew him," and, as Dr. Holmes said, "his smile was the well-remembered line of Terence written out in living features." Emerson's journals show the difficulty of his intercourse even with himself. He could not reach himself at will, nor could another reach him. The sensuous and ready contact with nature which more carnal people enjoy was unknown to him. He had eyes for the New England landscape, but for no other scenery. If there is one supreme sensation reserved for man, it is the vision of Venice seen from the water. This sight greeted Emerson at the age of thirty. The famous city, as he approached it by boat, "looked for some time like nothing but New York. It is a great oddity, a city for beavers, but to my thought a most disagreeable residence. You feel always in prison and solitary. It is as if you were always at sea. I soon had enough of it."

Emerson's contempt for travel and for the "rococo toy," Italy, is too well known to need citation. It proceeds from the same deficiency of sensation. His eyes saw nothing; his ears heard nothing. He believed that men travelled for distraction and to kill time. The most vulgar plutocrat could not be blinder to beauty nor bring home less from Athens than this cultivated saint. Everything in the world which must be felt with a glow in the breast, in order to be understood, was to him dead-letter. Art was a name to him; music was a name to him; love was a name to him. His essay on Love is a nice compilation of compliments and elegant phrases ending up with some icy morality. It seems very well fitted for a gift-book or an old-fashioned lady's annual.

"The lovers delight in endearments, in avowals of love, in comparisons of their regards. . . . The soul which is in the soul of each, craving a perfect beatitude, detects incongruities, defects, and disproportion in the behavior of the other. Hence arise surprise, expostulation, and pain. Yet that which drew them to each other was signs of loveliness, signs of virtue; and these virtues are there, however eclipsed. They appear and reappear and continue to attract; but the regard changes, quits the sign and attaches to the substance. This repairs the wounded affection. Meantime, as life wears on, it proves a game of permutation and combination of all possible positions of the parties, to employ all the resources of each, and acquaint each with the weakness of the other. . . . At last they discover that all which at first drew them together—those once sacred features, that magical play of charms—was deciduous, had a prospective end like the scaffolding by which the house was built, and the purification of the intellect and the heart from year to year is the real marriage, foreseen and prepared from the first, and wholly above their consciousness. . . . Thus are we put in training for a love which knows not sex nor person nor partiality, but which seeks wisdom and virtue everywhere, to the end of increasing virtue and wisdom. . . . There are moments when the affections rule and absorb the man, and make his happiness dependent on a person or persons. But in health the mind is presently seen again," etc.

All this is not love, but the merest literary coquetry. Love is different from this. Lady Burton, when a very young girl, and six years before her engagement, met Burton at Boulogne. They met in the street, but did not speak. A few days later they were formally introduced at a dance. Of this she writes: "That was a night of nights. He waltzed with me once, and spoke to me several times. I kept the sash where he put his arm around me and my gloves, and never wore them again."

A glance at what Emerson says about marriage shows that he suspected that institution. He can hardly speak of it without some sort of caveat or precaution. "Though the stuff of tragedy and of romances is in a moral union of two superior persons whose confidence in each other for long years, out of sight and in sight, and against all appearances, is at last justified by victorious proof of probity to gods and men, causing joyful emotions, tears, and glory, —though there be for heroes this *moral union,* yet they too are as far as ever from an intellectual union, and the moral is for low and external purposes, like the corporation of a ship's company or of a fire club." In speaking of modern novels, he says: "There is no new element, no power, no furtherance. 'T is only confectionery, not the raising of new corn. Great is the poverty of their inventions. *She was beautiful, and he fell in love.* . . . Happy will that house be in which the relations are formed by character; after the highest and not after the lowest; the house in which character marries and not confusion and a miscellany of unavowable motives. . . . To each occurs soon after puberty, some event, or society or way of living, which becomes the crisis of life and the chief fact in their history. In women it is love and marriage (which is more reasonable), and yet it is pitiful to date and measure all the facts and sequel of an unfolding life from such a youthful and generally inconsiderate period as the age of courtship and marriage. . . . Women more than all are the element and kingdom of illusion. Being fascinated they fascinate. They see through Claude Lorraines. And how dare any one, if he could, pluck away the coulisses, stage effects and ceremonies by which they live? Too pathetic, too pitiable, is the region of affection, and its atmosphere always liable to mirage."

We are all so concerned that a man who writes about love shall tell the truth that if he chance to start from premises which are false or mistaken, his conclusions will appear not merely false, but offensive. It makes no matter how exalted the personal character of the writer may be. Neither sanctity nor intellect nor moral enthusiasm, though they be intensified to the point of incandescence, can make up for a want of nature.

This perpetual splitting up of love into two species, one of which is condemned, but admitted to be useful—is it not degrading? There is in Emerson's theory of the relation between the sexes neither good sense, nor manly feeling, nor sound psychology. It is founded on none of these things. It is a pure piece of dogmatism, and reminds us that he was bred to the priesthood. We are not to imagine that there was in this doctrine anything peculiar to Emerson. But we are surprised to find the pessimism inherent in the doctrine overcome Emerson, to whom pessimism is foreign. Both doctrine and pessimism are a part of the Puritanism of the times. They show a society in which the intellect had long been used to analyze the affections, in which the head had become dislocated from the body. To this disintegration of the simple passion of love may be traced the lack of maternal tenderness characteristic of the New England nature. The relation between the blood and the brain was not quite normal in this civilization, nor in Emerson, who is its most remarkable representative.

If we take two steps backward from the canvas of this mortal life and glance at it impartially, we shall see that these matters of love and marriage pass like a pivot through the lives of almost every individual, and are, sociologically speaking, the *primum mobile* of the world. The books of any philosopher who slurs them or distorts them will hold up a false mirror to life. If an inhabitant of another planet should visit the earth, he would receive, on the whole, a truer notion of human life by attending an Italian opera than he would by reading Emerson's volumes. He would learn from the Italian opera that there were two sexes; and this, after all, is probably the fact with which the education of such a stranger ought to begin.

In a review of Emerson's personal character and opinions, we are thus led to see that his philosophy, which finds no room for the emotions, is a faithful exponent of his own and of the New England temperament, which distrusts and dreads the emotions. Regarded as a sole guide to life for a young person of strong conscience and undeveloped affections, his works might conceivably be even harmful because of their unexampled power of purely intellectual stimulation.

Emerson's poetry has given rise to much heart-burning and disagreement. Some people do not like it. They fail to find the fire in the ice. On the other hand, his poems appeal not only to a large number of professed lovers of poetry, but also to a class of readers who find in Emerson an element for which they search the rest of poesy in vain.

It is the irony of fate that his admirers should be more than usually sensitive about his fame. This prophet who desired not to have followers, lest he too should become a cult and a convention, and whose main thesis throughout life was that piety is a crime, has been calmly canonized and embalmed in amber by the very forces he braved. He is become a tradition and a sacred relic. You must speak of him under your breath, and you may not laugh near his shrine.

Emerson's passion for nature was not like the passion of Keats or of Burns, of Coleridge or of Robert Browning; compared with these men he is cold. His temperature is below blood-heat, and his volume of poems stands on the shelf of English poets like the icy fish which in Caliban upon Setebos is described as finding himself thrust into the warm ooze of an ocean not his own.

But Emerson is a poet, nevertheless, a very extraordinary and rare man of genius, whose verses carry a world of their own within them. They are overshadowed by the greatness of his prose, but they are authentic. He is the chief poet of that school of which Emily Dickinson is a minor poet. His poetry is a successful spiritual deliverance of great interest. His worship of the New England landscape amounts to a religion. His poems do that most wonderful thing, make us feel that we are alone in the fields and with the trees,—not English fields nor French lanes, but New England meadows and uplands. There is no human creature in sight, not even Emerson is there, but the wind and the flowers, the wild birds, the fences, the transparent atmosphere, the breath of nature. There is a deep and true relation between the intellectual and almost dry brilliancy of Emerson's feelings and the landscape itself. Here is no defective English poet, no Shelley without the charm, but an American poet, a New England poet with two hundred years of New England culture and New England landscape in him.

People are forever speculating upon what will last, what posterity will approve, and some people believe that Emerson's poetry will outlive his prose. The question is idle. The poems are alive now, and they may or may not survive the race whose spirit they embody; but one thing is plain: they have qualities which have preserved poetry in the past. They are utterly indigenous and sincere. They are short. They represent a civilization and a climate.

His verse divides itself into several classes. We have the single lyrics, written somewhat in the style of the later seventeenth century. Of these The Humble Bee is the most exquisite, and although its tone and imagery can be traced to various well-known and dainty bits of poetry, it is by no means an imitation, but a masterpiece of fine taste. The Rhodora and Terminus and perhaps a few others belong to that class of poetry which, like Abou Ben Adhem, is poetry because it is the perfection of statement. The Boston Hymn, the Concord Ode, and the other occasional pieces fall in another class, and do not seem to be important. The first two lines of the Ode,

> "O tenderly the haughty day
> Fills his blue urn with fire."

are for their extraordinary beauty worthy of some mythical Greek, some Simonides, some Sappho, but the rest of the lines are commonplace. Throughout his poems there are good bits, happy and golden lines, snatches of grace. He himself knew the quality of his poetry, and wrote of it,

> "All were sifted through and through,
> Five lines lasted sound and true."

He is never merely conventional, and his poetry, like his prose, is homespun and sound. But his ear was defective: his rhymes are crude, and his verse is often lame and unmusical, a fault which can be countervailed by nothing but force, and force he lacks. To say that his ear was defective is hardly strong enough. Passages are not uncommon which hurt the reader and unfit him to proceed; as, for example:—

> "Thorough a thousand voices
> Spoke the universal dame:
> 'Who telleth one of my meanings
> Is master of all I am.'"

He himself has very well described the impression his verse is apt to make on a new reader when he says,—

> "Poetry must not freeze, but flow."

The lovers of Emerson's poems freely acknowledge all these defects, but find in them another element, very subtle and rare, very refined and elusive, if not altogether unique. This is the mystical element or strain which qualifies many of his poems, and to which some of them are wholly devoted.

There has been so much discussion as to Emerson's relation to the mystics that it is well here to turn aside for a moment and consider the matter by itself. The elusiveness of "mysticism" arises out of the fact that it is not a creed, but a state of mind. It is formulated into no dogmas, but, in so far as it is communicable, it is conveyed, or sought to be conveyed, by symbols. These symbols to a sceptical or an unsympathetic person will say nothing, but the presumption among those who are inclined towards the cult is that if these symbols convey anything at all, that thing is mysticism. The mystics are right. The familiar phrases, terms, and symbols of mysticism are not meaningless, and a glance at them shows that they do tend to express and evoke a somewhat definite psychic condition.

There is a certain mood of mind experienced by most of us in which we feel the mystery of existence; in which our consciousness seems to become suddenly separated from our thoughts, and we find ourselves asking, "Who am I? What are these thoughts?" The mood is very apt to overtake us while engaged in the commonest acts. In health it is always momentary, and seems to coincide with the instant of the transition and shift of our attention from one thing to another. It is probably connected with the transfer of energy from one set of faculties to another set, which occurs, for instance, on our waking from sleep, on our hearing a bell at night, on our observing any common object, a chair or a pitcher, at a time when our mind is or has just been thoroughly preoccupied with something else. This displacement of the attention occurs in its most notable form when we walk from the study into the open fields. Nature then attacks us on all sides at once, overwhelms, drowns, and destroys our old thoughts, stimulates vaguely and all at once a thousand new ideas, dissipates all focus of thought and dissolves our attention. If we happen to be mentally fatigued, and we take a walk in the country, a sense of immense relief, of rest and joy, which nothing else on earth can give, accompanies this distraction of the mind from its problems. The reaction fills us with a sense of mystery and expansion. It brings us to the threshold of those spiritual experiences which are the obscure core and reality of our existence, ever alive within us, but generally veiled and sub-conscious. It brings us, as it were, into the ante-chamber of art, poetry, and music. The condition is one of excitation and receptiveness, where art may speak and we shall understand. On the other hand, the condition shows a certain dethronement of the will and attention which may ally it to the hypnotic state.

Certain kinds of poetry imitate this method of nature by calling on us with a thousand voices at once. Poetry deals often with vague or contradictory statements, with a jumble of images, a throng of impressions. But in true poetry the psychology of real life is closely followed. The mysticism is momentary. We are not kept suspended in a limbo, "trembling like a guilty thing surprised," but are ushered into another world of thought and feeling. On the other hand, a mere statement of inconceivable things is the *reductio ad absurdum* of poetry, because such a statement puzzles the mind, scatters the attention, and does to a certain extent superinduce the "blank misgivings" of mysticism. It does this, however, *without* going further and filling the mind with new life. If I bid a man follow my reasoning closely, and then say, "I am the slayer and the slain, I am the doubter and the doubt," I puzzle his mind, and may succeed in reawakening in him the sense he has often had come over him that we are ignorant of our own destinies and cannot grasp the meaning of life. If I do this, nothing can be a more legitimate opening for a poem, for it is an opening of the reader's mind. Emerson, like many other highly organized persons, was acquainted with the mystic mood. It was not momentary with him. It haunted him, and he seems to have believed that the whole of poetry and religion was contained in the mood. And no one can gainsay that this mental condition is intimately connected with our highest feelings and leads directly into them.

The fault with Emerson is that he stops in the ante-chamber of poetry. He is content if he has brought us to the hypnotic point. His prologue and overture are excellent, but where is the argument? Where is the substantial artistic content that shall feed our souls?

The Sphinx is a fair example of an Emerson poem. The opening verses are musical, though they are handicapped by a reminiscence of the German way of writing. In the succeeding verses we are lapped into a charming reverie, and then at the end suddenly jolted by the question, "What is it all about?" In this poem we see expanded into four or five pages of verse an experience which in real life endures an eighth of a second, and when we come to the end of the mood we are at the end of the poem.

There is no question that the power to throw your sitter into a receptive mood by a pass or two which shall give you his virgin attention is necessary to any artist. Nobody has the knack of this more strongly than Emerson in his prose writings. By a phrase or a common remark he creates an ideal atmosphere in which his thought has the directness of great poetry. But he cannot do it in verse. He seeks in his verse to do the very thing which he avoids doing in his prose: follow a logical method. He seems to know too much what he is about, and to be content with doing too little. His mystical poems, from the point of view of such criticism as this, are all alike in that they all seek to do the same thing. Nor does he always succeed. How does he sometimes fail in verse to say what he conveys with such everlasting happiness in prose!

> "I am owner of the sphere,
>   Of the seven stars and the solar year,
>   Of Cæsar's hand and Plato's brain,
>   Of Lord Christ's heart and Shakespeare's strain."

In these lines we have the same thought which appears a few pages later in prose: "All that Shakespeare says of the king, yonder slip of a boy that reads in the corner feels to be true of himself." He has failed in the verse because he has thrown a mystical gloss over a thought which was stronger in its simplicity; because in the verse he states an abstraction instead of giving an instance. The same failure follows him sometimes in prose when he is too conscious of his machinery.

Emerson knew that the sense of mystery accompanies the shift of an absorbed attention to some object which brings the mind back to the present. "There are times when the cawing of a crow, a weed, a snowflake, a boy's willow whistle, or a farmer planting in his field is more suggestive to the mind than the Yosemite gorge or the Vatican would be in another hour. In like mood, an old verse, or certain words, gleam with rare significance." At the close of his essay on History he is trying to make us feel that all history, in so far as we can know it, is within ourselves, and is in a certain sense autobiography. He is speaking of the Romans, and he suddenly pretends to see a lizard on the wall, and proceeds to wonder what the lizard has to do with the Romans. For this he has been quite properly laughed at by Dr. Holmes, because he has resorted to an artifice and has failed to create an illusion. Indeed, Dr. Holmes is somewhere so irreverent as to remark that a gill of alcohol will bring on a psychical state very similar to that suggested by Emerson; and Dr. Holmes is accurately happy in his jest, because alcohol does dislocate the attention in a thoroughly mystical manner.

There is throughout Emerson's poetry, as throughout all of the New England poetry, too much thought, too much argument. Some of his verse gives the reader a very curious and subtle impression that the lines are a translation. This is because he is closely follow-ing a thesis. Indeed, the lines are a translation. They were thought first, and poetry afterwards. Read off his poetry, and you see through the scheme of it at once. Read his prose, and you will be put to it to make out the connection of ideas. The reason is that in the poetry the sequence is intellectual, in the prose the sequence is emotional. It is no mere epigram to say that his poetry is governed by the ordinary laws of prose writing, and his prose by the laws of poetry.

The lines entitled Days have a dramatic vigor, a mystery, and a music all their own:—

> "Daughters of Time, the hypocritic Days,
>   Muffled and dumb like barefoot dervishes,
>   And marching single in an endless file,
>   Bring diadems and fagots in their hands.
>   To each they offer gifts after his will,
>   Bread, kingdoms, stars, and sky that holds them all.
>   I, in my pleached garden, watched the pomp,
>   Forgot my morning wishes, hastily
>   Took a few herbs and apples, and the Day
>   Turned and departed silent. I, too late,
>   Under her solemn fillet saw the scorn."

The prose version of these lines, which in this case is inferior, is to be found in Works and Days: "He only is rich who owns the day. . . . They come and go like muffled and veiled figures, sent from a distant friendly party; but they say nothing, and if we do not use the gifts they bring, they carry them as silently away."

That Emerson had within him the soul of a poet no one will question, but his poems are expressed in prose forms. There are passages in his early addresses which can be matched in English only by bits from Sir Thomas Browne or Milton, or from the great poets. Heine might have written the following parable into verse, but it could not have been finer. It comes from the very bottom of Emerson's nature. It is his uttermost. Infancy and manhood and old age, the first and the last of him, speak in it.

"Every god is there sitting in his sphere. The young mortal en-ters the hall of the firmament; there is he alone with them alone, they pouring on him benedictions and gifts, and beckoning him up to their thrones. On the instant, and incessantly, fall snowstorms of illusions. He fancies himself in a vast crowd which sways this way and that, and whose movements and doings he must obey; he fancies himself poor, orphaned, insignificant. The mad crowd drives hither and thither, now furiously commanding this thing to be done, now that. What is he that he should resist their will, and think or act for himself? Every moment new changes and new showers of deceptions to baffle and distract him. And when, by and by, for an instant, the air clears and the cloud lifts a little, there are the gods still sitting around him on their thrones,—they alone with him alone."

With the war closes the colonial period of our history, and with the end of the war begins our national life. Before that time it was not possible for any man to speak for the nation, however much he might long to, for there was no nation; there were only discordant provinces held together by the exercise on the part of each of a strong and conscientious will. It is too much to expect that national character shall be expressed before it is developed, or that the arts shall flourish during a period when everybody is preoccupied with the fear of revolution. The provincial note which runs through all our literature down to the war resulted in one sense from our dependence upon Europe. "All American manners, language, and writings," says Emerson, "are derivative. We do not write from facts, but we wish to state the facts after the English manner. It is the tax we pay for the splendid inheritance of English Literature." But in a deeper sense this very dependence upon Europe was due to our disunion among ourselves. The equivocal and unhappy self-assertive patriotism to which we were consigned by fate, and which made us perceive and resent the condescension of foreigners, was the logical outcome of our political situation.

The literature of the Northern States before the war, although full of talent, lacks body, lacks courage. It has not a full national tone. The South is not in it. New England's share in this literature is so large that small injustice will be done if we give her credit for all of it. She was the Academy of the land, and her scholars were our authors. The country at large has sometimes been annoyed at the self-consciousness of New England, at the atmosphere of clique, of mutual admiration, of isolation, in which all her scholars, except Emerson, have lived, and which notably enveloped the last little distinguished group of them. The circumstances which led to the isolation of Lowell, Holmes, Longfellow, and the Saturday Club fraternity are instructive. The ravages of the war carried off the poets, scholars, and philosophers of the generation which immediately followed these men, and by destroying their natural successors left them standing magnified beyond their natural size, like a grove of trees left by a fire. The war did more than kill off a generation of scholars who would have succeeded these older scholars. It emptied the universities by calling all the survivors into the field of practical life; and after the war ensued a period during which all the learning of the land was lodged in the heads of these older worthies who had made their mark long before. A certain complacency which piqued the country at large was seen in these men. An ante-bellum colonial posing, inevitable in their own day, survived with them. When Jared Sparks put Washington in the proper attitude for greatness by correcting his spelling, Sparks was in cue with the times. It was thought that a great man must have his hat handed to him by his biographer, and be ushered on with decency toward posterity. In the lives and letters of some of our recent public men there has been a reminiscence of this posing, which we condemn as absurd because we forget it is merely archaic. Provincial manners are always a little formal, and the pomposity of the colonial governor was never quite worked out of our literary men.

Let us not disparage the past. We are all grateful for the New England culture, and especially for the little group of men in Cambridge and Boston who did their best according to the light of their day. Their purpose and taste did all that high ideals and good taste can do, and no more eminent literati have lived during this century. They gave the country songs, narrative poems, odes, epigrams, essays, novels. They chose their models well, and drew their materials from decent and likely sources. They lived stainless lives, and died in their professors' chairs honored by all men. For achievements of this sort we need hardly use as strong language as Emerson does in describing contemporary literature: "It exhibits a vast carcass of tradition every year with as much solemnity as a new revelation."

The mass and volume of literature must always be traditional, and the secondary writers of the world do nevertheless perform a function of infinite consequence in the spread of thought. A very large amount of first-hand thinking is not comprehensible to the average man until it has been distilled and is fifty years old. The men who welcome new learning as it arrives are the picked men, the minor poets of the next age. To their own times these secondary men often seem great because they are recognized and understood at once. We know the disadvantage under which these Humanists of ours worked. The shadow of the time in which they wrote hangs over us still. The conservatism and timidity of our politics and of our literature to-day are due in part to that fearful pressure which for sixty years was never lifted from the souls of Americans. That conservatism and timidity may be seen in all our past. They are in the rhetoric of Webster and in the style of Hawthorne. They killed Poe. They created Bryant.

Since the close of our most blessed war, we have been left to face the problems of democracy, unhampered by the terrible complications of sectional strife. It has happened, however, that some of the tendencies of our commercial civilization go toward strengthening and riveting upon us the very traits encouraged by provincial disunion. Wendell Phillips, with a cool grasp of understanding for which he is not generally given credit, states the case as follows:—

"The general judgment is that the freest possible government produces the freest possible men and women, the most individual, the least servile to the judgment of others. But a moment's reflection will show any man that this is an unreasonable expectation, and that, on the contrary, entire equality and freedom in political forms almost invariably tend to make the individual subside into the mass and lose his identity in the general whole. Suppose we stood in England to-night. There is the nobility, and here is the church. There is the trading class, and here is the literary. A broad gulf separates the four; and provided a member of either can conciliate his own section, he can afford in a very large measure to despise the opinions of the other three. He has to some extent a refuge and a breakwater against the tyranny of what we call public opinion. But in a country like ours, of absolute democratic equality, public opinion is not only omnipotent, it is omnipresent. There is no refuge from its tyranny, there is no hiding from its reach; and the result is that if you take the old Greek lantern and go about to seek among a hundred, you will find not one single American who has not, or who does not fancy at least that he has, something to gain or lose in his ambition, his social life, or his business, from the good opinion and the votes of those around him. And the consequence is that instead of being a mass of individuals, each one fearlessly blurting out his own convictions, as a nation, compared to other nations, we are a mass of cowards. More than all other people, we are afraid of each other."

If we take a bird's-eye view of our history, we shall find that this constant element of democratic pressure has always been so strong a factor in moulding the character of our citizens, that there is less difference than we could wish to see between the types of citizenship produced before the war and after the war.

Charles Follen, that excellent and worthy German who came to this country while still a young man and who lived in the midst of the social and intellectual life of Boston, felt the want of intellectual freedom in the people about him. If one were obliged to describe the America of to-day in a single sentence, one could hardly do it better than by a sentence from a letter of Follen to Harriet Martineau written in 1837, after the appearance of one of her books: "You have pointed out the two most striking national characteristics, 'Deficiency of individual moral independence and extraordinary mutual respect and kindness.'"

Much of what Emerson wrote about the United States in 1850 is true of the United States to-day. It would be hard to find a civilized people who are more timid, more cowed in spirit, more illiberal, than we. It is easy to-day for the educated man who has read Bryce and Tocqueville to account for the mediocrity of American literature. The merit of Emerson was that he felt the atmospheric pressure without knowing its reason. He felt he was a cabined, cribbed, confined creature, although every man about him was celebrating Liberty and Democracy, and every day was Fourth of July. He taxes language to its limits in order to express his revolt. He says that no man should write except what he has discovered in the process of satisfying his own curiosity, and that every man will write well in proportion as he has contempt for the public.

Emerson seems really to have believed that if any man would only resolutely be himself, he would turn out to be as great as Shakespeare. He will not have it that anything of value can be monopolized. His review of the world, whether under the title of Manners, Self-Reliance, Fate, Experience, or what-not, leads him to the same thought. His conclusion is always the finding of eloquence, courage, art, intellect, in the breast of the humblest reader. He knows that we are full of genius and surrounded by genius, and that we have only to throw something off, not to acquire any new thing, in order to be bards, prophets, Napoleons, and Goethes. This belief is the secret of his stimulating power. It is this which gives his writings a radiance like that which shone from his personality.

The deep truth shadowed forth by Emerson when he said that "all the American geniuses lacked nerve and dagger" was illustrated by our best scholar. Lowell had the soul of the Yankee, but in his habits of writing he continued English tradition. His literary essays are full of charm. The Commemoration Ode is the high-water mark of the attempt to do the impossible. It is a fine thing, but it is imitative and secondary. It has paid the inheritance tax. Twice, however, at a crisis of pressure, Lowell assumed his real self under the guise of a pseudonym; and with his own hand he rescued a language, a type, a whole era of civilization from oblivion. Here gleams the dagger and here is Lowell revealed. His limitations as a poet, his too much wit, his too much morality, his mixture of shrewdness and religion, are seen to be the very elements of power. The novelty of the Biglow Papers is as wonderful as their world-old naturalness. They take rank with greatness, and they were the strongest political tracts of their time. They imitate nothing; they are real.

Emerson himself was the only man of his times who consistently and utterly expressed himself, never measuring himself for a moment with the ideals of others, never troubling himself for a moment with what literature was or how literature should be created. The other men of his epoch, and among whom he lived, believed that literature was a very desirable article, a thing you could create if you were only smart enough. But Emerson had no literary ambition. He cared nothing for belles-lettres. The consequence is that he stands above his age like a colossus. While he lived his figure could be seen from Europe towering like Atlas over the culture of the United States.

Great men are not always like wax which their age imprints. They are often the mere negation and opposite of their age. They give it the lie. They become by revolt the very essence of all the age is not, and that part of the spirit which is suppressed in ten thousand breasts gets lodged, isolated, and breaks into utterance in one. Through Emerson spoke the fractional spirits of a multitude. He had not time, he had not energy left over to understand himself; he was a mouthpiece.

If a soul be taken and crushed by democracy till it utter a cry, that cry will be Emerson. The region of thought he lived in, the figures of speech he uses, are of an intellectual plane so high that the circumstances which produced them may be forgotten; they are indifferent. The Constitution, Slavery, the War itself, are seen as mere circumstances. They did not confuse him while he lived; they are not necessary to support his work now that it is finished. Hence comes it that Emerson is one of the world's voices. He was heard afar off. His foreign influence might deserve a chapter by itself. Conservatism is not confined to this country. It is the very basis of all government. The bolts Emerson forged, his thought, his wit, his perception, are not provincial. They were found to carry inspiration to England and Germany. Many of the important men of the last half century owe him a debt. It is not yet possible to give any account of his influence abroad, because the memoirs which will show it are only beginning to be published. We shall have them in due time; for Emerson was an outcome of the world's progress. His appearance marks the turning-point in the history of that enthusiasm for pure democracy which has tinged the political thought of the world for the past one hundred and fifty years. The youths of England and Germany may have been surprised at hearing from America a piercing voice of protest against the very influences which were crushing them at home. They could not realize that the chief difference between Europe and America is a difference in the rate of speed with which revolutions in thought are worked out.

While the radicals of Europe were revolting in 1848 against the abuses of a tyranny whose roots were in feudalism, Emerson, the great radical of America, the arch-radical of the world, was revolting against the evils whose roots were in universal suffrage. By showing the identity in essence of all tyranny, and by bringing back the attention of political thinkers to its starting-point, the value of human character, he has advanced the political thought of the world by one step. He has pointed out for us in this country to what end our efforts must be bent.

# William James

NONE OF US will ever see a man like William James again: there is no doubt about that. And yet it is hard to state what it was in him that gave him either his charm or his power, what it was that penetrated and influenced us, what it is that we lack and feel the need of, now that he has so unexpectedly and incredibly died. I always thought that William James would continue forever; and I relied upon his sanctity as if it were sunlight.

I should not have been abashed at being discovered in some mean action by William James; because I should have felt that he would understand and make allowances. The abstract and sublime quality of his nature was always enough for two; and I confess to having always trespassed upon him and treated him with impertinence, without gloves, without reserve, without ordinary, decent concern for the sentiments and weaknesses of human character. Knowing nothing about philosophy, and having the dimmest notions as to what James's books might contain, I used occasionally to write and speak to him about his specialties in a tone of fierce contempt; and never failed to elicit from him in reply the most spontaneous and celestial gayety. Certainly he was a wonderful man.

He was so devoid of selfish aim or small personal feeling that your shafts might pierce, but could never wound him. You could not "diminish one dowle that's in his plume." Where he walked, nothing could touch him; and he enjoyed the Emersonian immunity of remaining triumphant even after he had been vanquished. The reason was, as it seems to me, that what the man really meant was always something indestructible and persistent; and that he knew this inwardly. He had not the gift of expression, but rather the gift of suggestion. He said things which meant one thing to him and something else to the reader or listener. His mind was never quite in focus, and there was always something left over after each discharge of the battery, something which now became the beginning of a new thought. When he found out his mistake or defect of expression, when he came to see that he had not said quite what he meant, he was the first to proclaim it, and to move on to a new position, a new misstatement of the same truth,—a new, debonair apperception, clothed in non-conclusive and suggestive figures of speech.

How many men have put their shoulders out of joint in striking at the phantasms which James projected upon the air! James was always in the right, because what he meant was true. The only article of his which I ever read with proper attention was "The Will to Believe," a thing that exasperated me greatly until I began to see, or to think I saw, what James meant, and at the same time to acknowledge to myself that he had said something quite different. I hazard this idea about James as one might hazard an idea about astronomy, fully aware that it may be very foolish.

In private life and conversation there was the same radiation of thought about him. The center and focus of his thought fell within his nature, but not within his intellect. You were thus played upon by a logic which was not the logic of intellect, but a far deeper thing, limpid and clear in itself, confused and refractory only when you tried to deal with it intellectually. You must take any fragment of such a man by itself, for his whole meaning is in the fragment. If you try to piece the bits together, you will endanger their meaning. In general talk on life, literature, and politics James was always throwing off sparks that were cognate only in this, that they came from the same central fire in him. It was easy to differ from him; it was easy to go home thinking that James had talked the most arrant rubbish, and that no educated man had a right to be so ignorant of the first principles of thought and of the foundations of human society. Yet it was impossible not to be morally elevated by the smallest contact with William James. A refining, purgatorial influence came out of him.

I believe that in his youth, James dedicated himself to the glory of God and the advancement of Truth, in the same spirit that a young knight goes to seek the Grail, or a young military hero dreams of laying down his life for his country. What his early leanings towards philosophy or his natural talent for it may have been, I do not know; but I feel as if he had first taken up philosophy out of a sense of duty,—the old Puritanical impulse,—in his case illumined, however, with a humor and genius not at all of the Puritan type. He adopted philosophy as his lance and buckler, —psychology, it was called in his day,—and it proved to be as good as the next thing,—as pliable as poetry or fiction or politics or law would have been,—or anything else that he might have adopted as a vehicle through which his nature could work upon society.

He, himself, was all perfected from the beginning, a selfless angel. It is this quality of angelic unselfishness which gives the power to his work. There may be some branches of human study—mechanics perhaps—where the personal spirit of the investigator does not affect the result; but philosophy is not one of them. Philosophy is a personal vehicle; and every man makes his own, and through it he says what he has to say. It is all personal: it is all human: it is all non-reducible to science, and incapable of being either repeated or continued by another man.

Now James was an illuminating ray, a dissolvent force. He looked freshly at life, and read books freshly. What he had to say about them was not entirely articulated, but was always spontaneous. He seemed to me to have too high an opinion of everything. The last book he had read was always "a great book"; the last person he had talked with, a wonderful being. If I may judge from my own standpoint, I should say that James saw too much good in everything, and felt towards everything a too indiscriminating approval. He was always classing things up into places they didn't belong and couldn't remain in.

Of course, we know that Criticism is proverbially an odious thing; it seems to deal only in shadows,—it acknowledges only varying shades of badness in everything. And we know, too, that Truth is light; Truth cannot be expressed in shadow, except by some subtle art which proclaims the shadow-part to be the lie, and the non-expressed part to be the truth. And it is easy to look upon the whole realm of Criticism and see in it nothing but a science which concerns itself with the accurate statement of lies. Such, in effect, it is in the hands of most of its adepts. Now James's weakness as a critic was somehow connected with the peculiar nature of his mind, which lived in a consciousness of light. The fact is that James was non-critical, and therefore divine. He was forever hovering, and never could alight; and this is a quality of truth and a quality of genius.

The great religious impulse at the back of all his work, and which pierces through at every point, never became expressed in conclusive literary form, or in dogmatic utterance. It never became formulated in his own mind into a statable belief. And yet it controlled his whole life and mind, and accomplished a great work in the world. The spirit of a priest was in him,—in his books and in his private conversation. He was a sage, and a holy man; and everybody put off his shoes before him. And yet in spite of this,—in conjunction with this, he was a sportive, wayward, Gothic sort of spirit, who was apt, on meeting a friend, to burst into foolery, and whose wit was always three parts poetry. Indeed his humor was as penetrating as his seriousness. Both of these two sides of James's nature—the side that made a direct religious appeal, and the side that made a veiled religious appeal—became rapidly intensified during his latter years; so that, had the process continued much longer, the mere sight of him must have moved beholders to amend their lives.

I happened to be at Oxford at one of his lectures in 1908; and it was remarkable to see the reverence which that very un-revering class of men—the University dons—evinced towards James, largely on account of his appearance and personality. The fame of him went abroad, and the Sanhedrim attended. A quite distinguished, and very fussy scholar, a member of the old guard of Nil-admirari Cultivation,—who would have sniffed nervously if he had met Moses—told me that he had gone to a lecture of James's "though the place was so crowded, and stank so that he had to come away immediately."—"But," he added, "he certainly has the face of a sage."

There was, in spite of his playfulness, a deep sadness about James. You felt that he had just stepped out of this sadness in order to meet you, and was to go back into it the moment you left him. It may be that sadness inheres in some kinds of profoundly religious characters,—in dedicated persons who have renounced all, and are constantly hoping, thinking, acting, and (in the typical case) praying for humanity. Lincoln was sad, and Tolstoi was sad, and many sensitive people, who view the world as it is, and desire nothing for themselves except to become of use to others, and to become agents in the spread of truth and happiness,—such people are often sad. It has sometimes crossed my mind that James wanted to be a poet and an artist, and that there lay in him, beneath the ocean of metaphysics, a lost Atlantis of the fine arts; that he really hated philosophy and all its works, and pursued them only as Hercules might spin, or as a prince in a fairy tale might sort seeds for an evil dragon, or as anyone might patiently do some careful work for which he had no aptitude. It would seem most natural, if this were the case between James and the metaphysical sciences; for what is there in these studies that can drench and satisfy a tingling mercurial being who loves to live on the surface, as well as in the depths of life? Thus we reason, forgetting that the mysteries of temperament are deeper than the mysteries of occupation. If James had had the career of Molière, he would still have been sad. He was a victim of divine visitation: the Searching Spirit would have winnowed him in the same manner, no matter what avocation he might have followed.

The world watched James as he pursued through life his search for religious truth; the world watched him, and often gently laughed at him, asking, "When will James arise and fly? When will 'he take the wings of the morning, and dwell in the uttermost parts of the sea'?" And in the meantime, James was there already. Those were the very places that he was living in. Through all the difficulties of polyglot metaphysics and of modern psychology he waded for years, lecturing and writing and existing,—and creating for himself a public which came to see in him only the saint and the sage, which felt only the religious truth which James was in search of, yet could never quite grasp in his hand. This very truth constantly shone out through him,—shone, as it were, straight through his waistcoat,—and distributed itself to everyone in the drawing-room, or in the lecture-hall where he sat. Here was the familiar paradox, the old parable, the psychological puzzle of the world. "But what went ye out for to see?" In the very moment that the world is deciding that a man was no prophet and had nothing to say, in that very moment perhaps is his work perfected, and he himself is gathered to his fathers, after having been a lamp to his own generation, and an inspiration to those who come after.

# President Eliot

FOR HALF A CENTURY President Eliot was one of the great personal figures in American life. He was known to every man in America and to many people in Europe. Everyone has an interest in such a character; especially in America, where men are too much alike and great individuals are a rarity. Every one of us bears a relation of some sort to any great character who has lived in the immediate past. This must be my excuse for setting down a few remarks and hair-brained reminiscences which recall President Eliot to my mind. Many of them are, perhaps, links in my own history rather than in his.

There is another good reason for writing about Eliot. He was not a political figure, nor an artist, nor a thinker: he was the embodiment of a mood of the American people, a sincere, important, and yet passing mood: and he belongs to a class of men who fill a great place in the public eye and are suddenly and ungratefully forgotten;—the class of worthies. Twenty-five years from now, young men will be shamelessly asking, "Who was President Eliot?" And therefore many monographs and sketches of him ought to be written at once.

Eliot's prominence is connected with the rise of the new education, that system or that blind battling for light, which began in America during the seventies, when the opinion prevailed that the commercial growth of the United States,—our growth in population and in wealth,—compelled the pulling down of the old buildings and old curricula, and the making of all things anew. I have heard William James say, "Yes, yes, we must have large things first, size first; the rest will come." This was the unspoken philosophy, the inner compelling, dumb thought of the epoch; and Eliot, when he was chosen President of Harvard in 1870, dedicated his life to the idea. He was shouldering, as it turned out, not only Harvard College but the higher education of the whole country. Before his day no one used to ask who was President of Harvard University. At the close of his day the President of Harvard was a national figure, and the Presidents of all the other Colleges in the country were persons to be reckoned with. Let us not, however, credit too much to any one man. Transformations in the popular imagination use men, choose figure-heads, subdue individuals to their will. Eliot was the nonpareil schoolmaster to his age,—an age that worshiped the schoolmaster and clung to him. The recent rise of Woodrow Wilson in political life is connected with the same deep educational impulse.

I will begin by recalling a few of the social conditions in Cambridge thirty years ago; for while such matters seem to be superficial, they really result from causes that are deep and old, causes of national significance.

In my undergraduate days (1880-1884) there was a tacit understanding at Harvard that social intercourse between the faculty and the students was bad form. Louis Dyer was at that time a young assistant professor, and he had either been to Oxford, or else he had read about Oxford. He held the belief that it was well for the boys to meet the tutors and professors; and he used to give smoking-parties in his room and to make himself personally agreeable to the students. The boys thought this a clumsy sort of joke, and the College authorities thought it—I don't know what—but they soon stamped him out; and he went abroad and afterwards lived for many years in Oxford, beloved by all, surrounded by the academic atmosphere which he had once foolishly tried to improvise at Harvard. I have often thought of Dyer, and of his gentleness, and of the way he blew the cigarette smoke out of his nose. He was a little like one of those mild mythological animals in "Alice in Wonderland," sweet as summer, and, as it were, harmless,—in fact, a creature that presented a strange contrast to the cynical professors and the brute students at Harvard College. He faded away with his charming grin and, by good luck, I saw him again at Oxford twenty-five years later, a few weeks before his death. Louis Dyer represented the "false dawn" of the social idea at Harvard. This idea was vigorously carried out by the authorities a few years later when they made the discovery that something was wrong at Harvard, that nobody loved anybody there, and that the thing to do was to give weekly teas at Brook's Hall, to ask everyone, to get ladies from Boston, Bishops from anywhere, social people at any cost, social talent to bridge the gulf between instructors and instructed. Nobly they labored. It was shoulder-to-shoulder, never say die, love one love all, more tea, more ladies. The whole movement was sincere in the extreme; it was a real dawn, somewhat grotesque and naïve, —(as if Phœbus should take down the shutters, and Aurora bang the doors open and proclaim the day;) but Harvard has been a more human place ever since. Indeed, what Harvard truly needed was the outside world,—ladies, Bishops and tea. Perhaps all institutions need these same things.

There was one comic element about this social revival at Harvard, —viz., the flying-wedge endeavor to make out that President Eliot had been Phœbus all along, and was standing effulgent with social love in his heart, loving the boys, encouraging the professors, shedding influence. Now as a matter of fact, President Eliot was the spiritual father of the glacial era theretofore in progress, he was the figure-head of those previous dreadful times; and I have sometimes stopped to shake hands with him because I thought it was right;— and also, I confess, because I thought it would cause him pain. Such is the silliness of the undergraduate mind. The trustees, the ladies, Bishops and steerers of Harvard, having received new warmth themselves from what Milton calls the "mellowing year," got at President Eliot and thawed him out. They told him he was the best fellow in the world, they told the world that he had a heart of gold and was a misunderstood person;—and the thing was done. President Eliot responded to the treatment; he glowed, he beamed. He really did have a warm place in him, and they moved this round in front where people could see it and feel it; and, by Jove, the New Legend was launched.

There was something in this legend, too. Besides the warmth that comes from success and from middle-life, there had always been more geniality in Eliot than most people supposed. If the same process of incaloration that Eliot received from his friends could have been applied to Emerson, to Hawthorne, and to James Russell Lowell, they would have glowed also. Indeed, while Lowell was in England where he was properly petted, he grew forthcoming and hearty,—qualities he soon lost upon returning to America and experiencing the formal and reverential manners of his compatriots. I make no doubt that George Ticknor, Robert C. Winthrop, John Quincy Adams, yes, Edward Everett himself would have turned a rosy hue and put forth green branches if they could have been x-rayed with warm social feeling, coming from a hot source of divine love. But such a thing was not known in their day. I have an instinctive suspicion that it was Alice Freeman Palmer who introduced this elemental heat into Boston in the late eighties, but upon this subject I am imperfectly informed.

The Doctor Eliot who first swam into my undergraduate ken as the martinet who stalked across the yard, and who was traditionally regarded as an important, hostile, and sinister influence,—a sort of Dickens-like haunted-man,—was a very remarkable person. His voice was remarkable,—a low vibrant, controlled, melodious voice that seemed to have so much reverence in it, the voice, you would say, of a cultivated man. And yet President Eliot had not the point of view of a cultivated man, nor had he reverence for cultivation *per se*. He regarded cultivation somewhat as Michael Angelo regarded the painting of the Venetian school,—as a thing fit for women. Life was greater than culture. No ideals except ideals of conduct had reality for him. Literature and philosophy and *all that* were the names of things in bottles to him. I'm not sure that there was not in him a touch of jealousy, a Puritan dread of the Humanities. With this was combined a truly unique pity for poverty in any student, and a truly pious belief in education as a means of self-advancement. And let us pause here to note that in all this Eliot was a sincere, spontaneous representative of the average American. By some accident which separated him from his own class,—for New England possessed many men with the old-fashioned feeling for the Humanities,—he became representative of the country at large.

If there was about Doctor Eliot an absence of cultivation, there was the presence of force. The voice was force; its vibrations were the vibrations of force. The modulations of it were modulations of force, the melody was the melody of force. Behind it there was a two-handed engine of human pertinacity, an intellect very accurately limited and a genius for the understanding of men.

I will give an instance of his clairvoyance in matters of character. When I was halfway through college my family lost money. I was on the verge of leaving Harvard. News of the situation somehow reached Eliot, and he sent for me and offered me tutoring. It appeared that a certain young loafer (whom I will not name, as he became through the incident and has remained ever since, a valued friend) required the services of a mental puncher of some sort to force him to work. It must be remembered that I did not belong to the working classes in college; and never dreamed of tutoring anyone. I really was not competent to do proper tutoring. But this kind of a boosting job was within my powers. I had not known that it was within my powers, but Doctor Eliot knew it; and I did such wonders with my young renegade, and he gained such unheard-of marks in the ensuing examinations, that both he and I have lived on the memory of those intellectual triumphs ever since. At the time I speak of there must have been a thousand undergraduates in the academic department, and Doctor Eliot had the reputation of not knowing one man from another. This anecdote is one out of hundreds. In every walk of life, in all his dealings with men, Doctor Eliot was doing such things every day. His greatness lay in his handling of men.

He had his policies, which, as I conceive, were to make Harvard large and well-known. Besides this matter he had his "Elective System," which I have never understood, but which seems to have been a corollary from the axiom "size first." It was imagined that a university must be a place where everything was taught, and that all sorts of departments ought to be opened at once. It was perfectly natural that America, looking at Germany, and bent upon swallowing the whole of learning at one gulp, should invent some sort of great fair, where the students were to come and take their fill, following their own election under some sort of supervision. The thing which nobody seems to have thought of was the relation which any foreign University bears to the average literacy of the country it serves. Perhaps our pedagogues neglected this consideration with their eyes open. They conceived that a University need provide opportunities merely, and that the students would do the rest. Now in Germany, where every student is already a highly educated person, who knows what he wants and knows how to work, such a system is admirable. But in America, where the boys come up to college with broken sets of rudimentary reminiscence, and without knowing what they want or how to get it, the great need in any University is the need of good teaching. We have found this out since those days; and we have discovered it largely through the strong-handed, logical power with which Harvard pursued the other path and took the consequences. So, also, in the endeavor to introduce research work, and to put a premium on the original thesis, it was surely natural to imitate Germany, and to forget that not even the immensely high average of general education among the Germans is sufficient to prevent much of their research work from being a stench in the nostrils,—an agony under the long-suffering moon. A special thesis should be the work of a ripe scholar,—if possible of a man who also knows the world. But ought we to set a man to making original researches in anthropology and Hindu-metaphysics when he has had no experience of life and only a class-room knowledge of books?

Eliot's greatness, however, lay not in his conceptions,—which were simple enough, and sometimes, as many have thought, mistaken; but in his power to carry them through. The circumstances required the construction of a one-man machine. It may be remarked parenthetically that all rapid changes in society come about through the creation of a one-man machine. This is the only way in which executive business on a large scale can be done quickly. A true University, on the other hand, can never rest upon the will of one man. A true University always rests upon the wills of many divergent-minded old gentlemen, who refuse to be disturbed, but who growl in their kennels. Now Eliot was a servant of his age, and his age commissioned him to refashion Harvard within a lifetime.

Administrative talent means the power to serve unseen masters, to know by instinct what can be done and to do it, to weigh opponents, thwarting some, conciliating others; deceiving some, destroying others. And all the while in the background of the great administrator's mind lie the great forces which he is really serving, —the political forces, the millions of clients, the practical world of his day. A thinker may reach mankind through his books: he may live in ideas which are realized only in a later generation or are never realized at all. He is bound to his age by no ties except metaphysical ties. But an administrator, however able, can accomplish only that which the work-a-day world of his day will permit him to accomplish. If he tries to do more he will be turned out of office. In the case of Doctor Eliot the subjection of the administrator to his age was especially apparent; for Eliot's first great need was a need of money; and money could only come from State Street and from Wall Street, and could only be expended in ways which the business men of America approved. The money question is the key to Doctor Eliot's career, merely because it is the key to his epoch. His very extraordinary nature could, I believe, have ruled a seventeenth-century theocracy. He cared nothing for money; he cared merely for power. But power in the United States between 1870-1910 meant money power: therefore Eliot's nature took on a financial hue.

I remember being surprised and a little shocked at the first speech I ever heard from him. It was, I think, at a great Harvard function in Memorial Hall, perhaps in connection with the 250th Anniversary of the College. Eliot seemed to dwell upon nothing but money. Figures were in every climax; not figures of speech, but Arabic, decimal symbols of value. And his words were music to the audience; every statement was greeted with applause. I came to reflect afterwards that it was only by such music as this that the wine could be drawn from the cask. Eliot in his financial rhapsodies drew golden tears down Pluto's cheek, and he built his College. The music was crude: it was not Apollo's lute: it was the hurdy-gurdy of pig-iron and the stockyards. To this music rose the walls of Harvard, and of all our Colleges,—our solemn temples, theaters, clinics, dormitories, museums. So also of the somewhat Corybantic advertising that Eliot inaugurated and which still continues in milder form, the clubs, parades, intelligence offices and boat rides, the Harvard Brigade that beats up trade for the College, —foolish would be the man who should blame any individual for these things (as I have often done). They are the symbols of contemporary America,—inevitable, necessary, the portals of the future. As for Eliot's share in all of them, all one can say is, "What wonderful manipulation of an era, what masterly politics!" If you find in Pindar's odes the intimate longings of the Greek nature, you will find in Eliot's reports the throb of the American heart; you will find in his propaganda the genius of the American people of his epoch. These are the reasons why Eliot became one of the great figureheads of the age.

One can never really explain a man, or track talent to its lair; and all attempts to do so are works of the imagination. No one can follow the currents of influence that run between a man and his antagonists, or between a man and his followers. All that we ever really do in such cases is to state the problem. I have always been surprised at the influence exercised by Eliot over his contemporaries, some of whom seemed to be his equals in moral force and his superiors in power of thinking. They regarded him as divinely commissioned, and they stood aside. They withheld their judgment in a manner which I thought almost immoral; but I see now that this was merely a phenomenon of the epoch.

These men adored Eliot; to them he was great and good and magnanimous,—a being superior to themselves.

Such an ascendency was not gained in a moment, but grew up during many years, and resulted from many different qualities in Doctor Eliot. It was accomplished by the glamour of his personality, by the general belief in his righteousness, and in his humility, by his appeal to ethnic loyalty (Harvard and New England), and most of all, it was accomplished through the fact that Eliot was a man of destiny and these other men were inquirers. There were, of course, quarrels in the camp of Harvard; there was opposition; there was hostility as deep as life on the part of many strong personalities. But there never was a death-grapple (I mean defiance, resignations, pamphlets), between Eliot and a man of the first rank. Those whom he could not control, he side-shunted in some way that left them harmless. The men of the first rank he hypnotized. To be sure, they didn't quite know, as we do to-day, what was happening, and what conditions would be left behind; *but they would have let him do anything*. I have listened to some of these men in open-mouthed wonder when they expounded their views on President Eliot. The aged Emerson was one of Eliot's admirers. They put Emerson on the Board of Trustees of Harvard and he used to wander about Cambridge casting his innocent benediction upon the work of reorganization. "But why, but why," asks the casual observer, "do I detect a note of disapproval in this description of what was happening at Harvard?" In order to answer this question one must recur to general ideas. A college is the home of scholastic influence, and scholasticism means leisure. Leisure is a plant of slow growth, hard to domesticate in any hurried, new and commercial society. Cultivated men are men of whims and tastes, of enthusiasms and of special talents. Cultivation cannot be dragooned. It must be humored. The little sprouts and spears of true university life that had slowly and painfully taken root about Harvard Square during two hundred years, were destroyed at the behest of our great ignorant National Board of Improvements. It was heartrending, but inevitable. If Eliot had not done it, the age would have found a man that would. The way this system works in crushing talent is somewhat as follows:—Let us suppose that there is, in a certain University, a young instructor of promise in the field of English literature. Shall he be advanced? Of course he shall. But it appears that he has opinions with regard to the new gymnasium that are opposed to the views of the Control. He can write and speak: he is a forcible person. How then can we advance him? His advancement would put our whole administration in jeopardy. On the contrary, let him understand that in this college there is no future for him; then he will quickly depart and leave us to carry on our important projects. Can we leave an ivy-mantled tower in the midst of our New Boulevard? This is the way that progress looks upon cultivation. It is a strange thing how vice always strikes at the heart. Not only vice, but mere error works a blight: some policy which seems harmless, or seems to be mistaken in only one of its aspects, turns out to involve death-doing consequences. Sometimes a lack of tact—or what seems a mere lack of tact—comes between a character and its destiny; or a man dies from a cold in the head. So this harmless-seeming error in the choice of young professors did, in fact, generate a poison which deadened the whole of education.

What is the most important thing in education? It is the relation between teacher and pupil. Here is the focus of the whole matter; this tiny crucible must boil, or your whole College will be cold. The Business Era chilled this heart-center of University life in America; because, during this Era, natural law operated to bring the youngest scholars under the control of unenthusiastic instructors. Persons of individual power were the very ones who were discharged. Thus the instructors,—without anyone's being aware of it,

—were being picked out *because of* their unenthusiasm. So terrible is natural law.

There is, however, a truer and more awful aspect of the matter. The system stamped out private mind in our colleges. It attacked the soul of the individual instructor through its control over his livelihood. This is the great historic crime of the world, the crime of churches, empires, tyrannies; and it has been the great crime of our commercial epoch in America. It has been a successful crime and it has impoverished the intellect and chilled the character of our teaching classes for a generation.

Let us return to Doctor Eliot. Every generation is a secret society, and has incommunicable enthusiasms, tastes and interests which are a mystery both to its predecessors and to posterity. There is a Zeitgeist at the bottom of all hero-worship. Heroes are created by the puffing up of faith out of the soil,—a spontaneous exhalation from contemporary, spiritual conditions. The essence of hero-worship seems to be this:—the worshiper is convinced that what the hero is about to do is *for the best:* the worshiper backs and indorses his champion by instinct and before the act. A slight paralysis of the judgment in the worshiper is what creates the situation. How this paralysis arises it is impossible to say; but anyone who has ever felt the joy of even a momentary paralysis of the judgment,—of even a momentary belief in any hero,—can understand the rise of all heroes. The pleasure that lives in the spontaneous act of worship brings the hero into existence. Those men who evoke such worship must be allowed their special rank. This does not mean, however, that these men will permanently interest the world. The only thing it certainly proves in them is an inordinate and tremendous vitality.

Everything about Eliot was vital. His wonderful low voice, his benignant smile, a smile that was assured, well-poised and habitual, could not be forgotten. To talk with him was to be played upon by a fountain of genial force. It was not quite natural force. Perhaps you felt just a touch of *control,* as if you were being drawn in somewhere. Perhaps you questioned "Why this benevolence?" or feared he might be crediting you with almost too much assent to his own view of the world;—as a very motherly nurse might smile on a new-born babe with rather more approval than the child thought was called for by the circumstances. Yet the principal experience was one of pleasure. As for the general impression you had in your mind, when you thought of Eliot's position in the world of Boston; —a little nimbus of glory always seemed to enclose him. He was the victim of a general apotheosis. He was really a king of men in his generation.

It was interesting to see a man so distinctly of the past as Eliot was, both in externals and in internals, take the lead in the nineteenth century. He had the formality of manner which belonged to 1820,—the formality of the man who never was young, but must have been a precisian in his earliest days. He had the temperament of the ecclesiastic, of the Archbishop, the missionary, the General of an Order. What is it that such men accomplish? They unify, they spread a standard. They are great yeomen, who brand wild cattle and build fences. The savage, terrible hordes of America waked up in 1870, to the importance of salvation by education. Perhaps they valued education too highly, and in their ignorance demanded more than even education can give. Yet these hordes were ingenuous in their desire to be saved. As the Frankish tribes in the sixth century submitted to Rome, so the Americans in the nineteenth submitted to Massachusetts. The creatures were received and taxed, schooled and attended to. Some lowering of old standards, some loss of cultivation (let us hope only temporary), ensued as a matter of course. Yet the whole process was important, significant, big with influence upon the future. The Pope during this epoch was Charles William Eliot.

It is hard to get far enough away from the canvas to take any general view of such a subject as education. Education means everything.

I remember the expectations with which I entered College, the vistas of Classical reading, of historical discussion, of scientific thought that rose in my mind when I thought of Harvard. I supposed that all of this delightful exploration into the universe would go forward accompanied by the genial assistance of elder people and by the joyous emulation of younger ones. Not school hours and recitations, but afternoon walks, suppers and excursions, conversation and experimental essay, the critique, the daring paraphrase, lived in my mind as the probable stage-settings and vehicles of academic education. I suppose I had read about such things in books and memoirs. After the first cold douche and shock of arrival in Harvard College was past, however, I became as hardened as the rest. By the time I came to know Louis Dyer he seemed to me to be a quixotic person. Just as your nicely-brought-up little boy comes back out of the street and utters vulgar bombast in the drawing room, so did I adopt the tone of Harvard College and patronize (I remember the feeling), yes, patronize this excellent gentleman, Louis Dyer, who was trying to recall me to my own tastes and beliefs.

The ladies'-tea era and the young men's Christian era, which I have mentioned, did not come into blossom while I was an undergraduate, but a few years later, and as a reaction from the awful bleakness that was just setting in in my day. No one can deny the wholesomeness of this drawing-room movement, yet no one can doubt its inadequacy. Young college men can get a great deal from drawing rooms and from tea, and from bishops; but their real social needs are best supplied by hard-thinking, highly-educated men, not too much older than themselves, who live and work and think with them. Such men impart their ideals, their knowledge, their benevolence, to the students in the very act and process of college life and work. The sudden discovery by certain philanthropists that the social side of education was all but extinct at Harvard, led to the formation of brigades and brotherhoods whose members went out and brought in the half-frozen students, much as the Salvation Army sends out persons with stretchers to bring in the victims of alcoholism.

The times called for such emergency work, and perhaps some deep instinct told the educators that if they should direct their steps straight toward Humanity, they would find the humanities.

In recent years it has been discovered on all hands that what our colleges need is "inspired teachers." Harvard gave a prize to an essay on this subject not long ago. But how to find such teachers is the question. They cannot be ordered by the gross from the factory. They must be discovered, one by one, and brought home from the woods and swamps, like orchids. They must be placed in a conservatory, not in a carpenter-shop; and they must be honored and trusted. They must be allowed to teach their own subjects in their own ways, and to hold and express private opinions about University management. Such men can never be introduced into our colleges except through a widespread "inspiration" on the part of everyone in the country as to what education means. I think I see a College president of the old style, after he has obtained a finely recommended, young "inspiring" teacher, and has discovered that the teacher's "inspiration" slops over into practical matters, and affects College management. The president would regard himself as false to his trust unless he took immediate steps to restrict, curtail and qualify that young man's inspirations. No, no! There will be no volcanic change in university conditions in America. The elements that control the situation are elements which change very slowly. The American people must come to value learning for its own sake before we can hope for scholars as the managers of our education.

When a Museum of Fine Arts is founded in a Western city it is at first managed by business men, because there are no experts at hand. As time goes on, however, trained scholars and competent persons are gradually found, to whom the institution is entrusted for management. This illustration may give us an allegory of the whole recent history of American education. Business men have run the colleges because business was predominant. The time is coming when our colleges will be run by scholars because the people trust the scholars. We already see the beginning of this epoch in instances which require no citation; and we may be content as to the general direction in which the forces are moving.

# Julia Ward Howe

THE GREAT DOCTOR HOWE, whose figure towers over little Boston, was a man in middle life, and was well understood by Europe and America to be one of the world's wise men, when he married a New York girl of remarkable beauty, wit and wealth. This was in the year 1843. It made little difference to Dr. Howe where he lived, or what circle he moved in; but when he threw in his fortunes with the anti-slavery outcasts and Beacon Street looked askance at him, it made this difference to his wife, that she never really became a Bostonian. She lived, however, to become one of the best known personalities in the town, and to have a little court of her own. There was something about her which attracted individuals of all conditions, from foreign patriots,—the residuaries of Dr. Howe's revolutionary interests,—to the most modern representatives of every social reform. Her own people had been bankers, with harps and marble statues in their salons. Singing, and Italian lessons, and the provincial splendors of early New York had been hers; and after her marriage with Dr. Howe, she had traveled with him abroad and had seen many of the celebrities of Europe at a time when genius was in bloom there.

Apart from all this, she was in herself a daughter of the great liberal epoch of the nineteenth century which produced Bright, Garrison, Garibaldi and a whole race of lesser social missionaries who felt that they were marching to music, and who never doubted that clouds would break and truth triumph in the end,—men and women whose idealism and whose belief in the destinies of mankind bound them into a sort of brotherhood in world politics. She had, at any rate, lived among the heroes of her time, and she retained to the end a bigness and heroic outlook upon life which belonged to the epoch of her youth. Furthermore she was a poetess. In early married life she published a volume or two of verse, which were read and admired by the world of American letters, and the luster of which never quite left her. Neither she nor her circle ever forgot that there were laurels on her brow.

It must be remembered also that she continued in her own person the traditions of the Transcendentalists, whose school of thought became submerged in the welter of the anti-slavery struggle. She was a friend and disciple of Emerson and felt, as indeed every Transcendentalist felt, that she had a metaphysical creed to expound. If the writings of this school have left little that is powerful except the Essays of the master himself, nevertheless the spirit of the Oversoul became expressed in the lives of many of his contemporaries. I have known people who wrote philosophy very ill, who yet seemed to have received a kind of heavenly message from stepping in and out of Emerson's library. This species of Emersonianism clung to Mrs. Howe.

Some serene element of the successful person, who lives above circumstance, shone out of her conversation,—which was, by the way, extremely unlike the Concord school of talk. She was always a doughty, gallant battler in the drawing-room, with the old style of attack. She feutered her lance, as was the custom of the forties, and rode her charger straight at the opponent.

The accidents of the world, which had swept away wealth and had left her only a modest little house, and a scanty income, had taken nothing from her. She had always lived in mansions of her own. Her guests were kings and queens to her. If the door had been opened by a charity girl with a wooden leg, and the meal had consisted of a chop on a trencher, the guest would still have felt that he was being welcomed with reverence and was feasting with Hafiz and Melchior. There are people in whom spiritual experiences dissolve self-consciousness, so that all humanity walks for them on the same social plane. Such was the ideal of the antique philosophers, and Mrs. Howe, in a certain way, reminded one of those ancients. Ben Franklin had the same quality in his old age,—a quality which

no one ought to attain to in youth; for youth is properly dedicated
to error. When Mrs. Howe was young, she was so high-spirited and
self-willed that she sometimes became a problem to her friends.
Old ladies have told me about her romanticism and her uncontrolla-
bility. I knew her only in old age, and when her chief characteristic
was an unfailing gayety. It was strange that a woman of causes,
whose main business was to worry politicians, arouse the people
and do in fact the most unpleasant things a woman can do, never
should have betrayed those traces of the work which are seen in almost all public spirited women.

Mrs. Howe was liberal, spontaneous, feminine. Her supreme endowment was her health. She had the domed brow and the bon-
homie of a woman who has never been sick. Such people are ever
younger than their children; for their children soon grow up into
sad, practical men and women, while they themselves retain the
buoyancy of youth. The world cannot teach them sorrow. Mrs.
Howe thus became the pet of her numerous children, at the same
time that she was the Mother Superior of the latest generation of
nonconformist philanthropy in Boston. She accepted both posts with
enthusiasm.

Her power of enjoyment was a natural advantage, like a large
fortune or a great talent, and it was really this force that made her
beloved. If she had a weakness, it was the weakness of almost all
leaders, the habit of accepting adulation from insignificant people,
whom she suffered to rest in the belief that she was a prophetess.
But she did this so innocently, and humbly, that I cannot feel sure
that her own hopes and illusions as to her greatness were not a part
of her charm.

The marvel of her was that she could never have been influenced
by Boston. She was not even irritated by the self-sufficiency of
Bostonians, by that slight mental cramp in them which is a grief to
many of their sincerest admirers. Of course everybody in Boston
knew her. One couldn't help knowing her. The policemen knew
her; the school-children sang her "Battle Hymn of the Republic";
the statesmen, scholars, scientists, and publicists for a generation
regarded her as one of their cherished institutions and as a pillar of
the crumbling world. Individual Beacon Street knew her, but not
collective Beacon Street. To collective Beacon Street she was *persona
non grata*. I remember being a little shocked at the way certain very

nice people used to speak of her; though in retrospect, the prejudice which good society has against non-conforming greatness, appears in the light of agreeable local color.

I have often lain awake at night wondering what was the matter with Boston. At such times, anecdotes creep out of corners in my memory and throw doubtful gleams of light on possible solutions. But I cannot catch and chain these ideas. One of my classmates, a modest youth from South Carolina, when he was a Freshman at Harvard, walked into the bosom of a great Boston drawing-room with his overshoes on. All the family were seated about,—the aged and distinguished grandparents, the model father, the benignant mother, and many appropriate children of all ages. My friend was unconscious of his predicament, young and modest. Summoning all of his imperfect Southern breeding, he did his best with the hard beginnings of cheerful talk. But he felt an oppression in the air, then a wave of sympathy,—a sense of humiliation,—a waiting fear. He saw that the younger members of the family were in hurried consultation about something, which he prophetically knew concerned himself. The suspense became unbearable, and at last an appropriate child of the family group drew him aside and whispered to him the awful truth. My friend told me the story the next day, and I knew instantly, and I know now, that the solution of Boston lay beneath my hand if I had but the wit to see it. But what is it?

Clarence King told me that he happened to be in Boston in 1870, when Bret Harte first appeared upon the extreme Western horizon, with his "Luck of Roaring Camp," and the rest of his wonderful earliest work in his hand. King at once became an object of interest in Boston because he knew Bret Harte, and was taken to lunch with the famous Saturday Club at the Parker House, where Longfellow, Holmes, Emerson, Lowell and the other immortals resorted for pie and for celestial converse. Mr. Longfellow, who was the most gracious gentleman that ever lived, turned to King and asked in regard to Bret Harte—"But is he a genius?" Longfellow pronounced the word "ge-ni-us," and quietly paused for a reply. King said, "Why as to that, Mr. Longfellow, everybody knows that the country possesses no *three-syllabled genius* outside of Massachusetts." "Did they laugh?" I asked of King. "Not a smile," he said. "But afterwards, Dr. Holmes came round during the coffee and cigars and pressed my hand quietly and told me that that was a good thing I had said to Longfellow."

In this anecdote, we get very near the secret. Why didn't those gentlemen laugh? They were the wittiest set in America, fond of laughing, collected at lunch for the very purpose of joking. Yes, but not at *themselves;* and not in response to the jest of a new, raw outsider. Had Dr. Holmes himself made the quip, it would have been repeated all over Boston. But they were not prepared to laugh before knowing whether Clarence King was a wit. Where was his certificate? And who let him in, anyway?

The great, terrible, important powers of the world, like social caste and religious domination, always rest on secrets. A man is born on the wrong side of the street and can therefore never enter into certain drawing-rooms, even though he be in every way superior to everyone in those drawing-rooms. When you try to find out what the difference is between him and the rest, and why he is accursed, you find that the reason is a secret. It is a secret that a certain kind of straw hat is damnable. Little boys know these things about other little boys. The world is written over with mysterious tramp-languages and symbols of Masonic hieroglyphics. I know these things because I belong to the Masonic Lodge of Massachusetts. By the accident of birth I am inside Boston (Æschylus says that relationship is a tremendous force). I am inside of Boston, and I am going to divulge the meaning of every Masonic symbol which I can decipher.

Boston has always been a hieratic aristocracy. Its chief rulers were parsons in the eighteenth century, and business men in the nineteenth. But you may take it for granted that there was always a pharisaical clique in the middle of Boston, a clique of elders. The anthropologists have no doubt a name for the gang-instinct and cryptic passion that binds thieves together, and fills the words "he is one of us" with so much religious power. Now, amid all the downfall of Puritanism, and of the old Boston cultivation, the inner core of a loyalty to a local priesthood still rules the city; and, on the whole, rules it well. Social Boston is a religious society, so also is business Boston, so is sporting Boston, so is literary Boston. If you know the town well, you will often find persons there who are not of the caste. Their countenances do not fall at the mention of Moses and Aaron, and they wear no phylacteries. You will generally find that such people are mere sojourners in Boston; their fathers and grandfathers came from elsewhere.

One should immerse one's self occasionally in some hieratic influence in order to understand how vulgar and disgusting any merely personal virtue appears in the eyes of the faith. The devout Protestant is, to the devout Catholic, a gross and boorish person.

The nature of Mrs. Howe's social talents was not acceptable to the taste of Boston. Her house was full of Persians, Armenians, and the professors of strange new faiths. I think it was her followers rather than herself that displeased the Bostonians. She sat at the gate and entertained all men, including a lot of people who Boston thought ought not to be entertained. But there she sat, nevertheless, —all courage, all wit and all benignity, and so will the image of her ever remain in the minds of the thousands of those who knew her.

# Mr. Brimmer

MARTIN BRIMMER was the finest gentleman that I have ever known intimately; and I never met him without feeling that I myself was a boor, but that this was of no consequence, because his breeding and goodness sufficed to cover my nakedness. I might gambol or even wallow, but he would blossom in the perfection of self-effacing courtesy.

He was the best of old Boston; for he was not quite inside the Puritan tradition and was a little sweeter by nature and less sure he was right than the true Bostonian is. He was a lame, frail man, with fortune and position; and one felt that he had been a lame, frail boy, lonely, cultivated, and nursing an ideal of romantic honor. There was a knightly glance in his eye and a seriousness in his deep voice that told of his living, and of his having lived always, in a little Camelot of his own. He was not quixotic, but he was independent. There were portcullises and moats and flowered gardens around him. He was humble with a kind of Hidalgo humility, —the humility of a magnificent impoverished Portuguese Duke. There was nothing sanctimonious about his mind, and this is what really distinguished him from the adjacent Bostonian nobility.

In looking at the eighteenth century portraits of Puritan Elders, I have often reflected that the Puritans were traders. Whatever they may have been when they first landed, they soon became keen-eyed and practical, hard and cold. Their resemblance to the old Venetian merchants may be traced in the Doge's Palace, where the cold,

Yankee faces loom down familiarly on the shuddering American tourist. I could attach to almost every portrait in Venice an honored Puritan name; and, with a little study and reflection, I could tell how each pictured aristocrat must have made his money. There was in Mr. Brimmer nothing of that austere look which comes from holding on to property and standing pat. And besides this, he was warm; not, perhaps, quite as warm as the Tropics, but very much warmer than the average Beacon Street mantle-pieces were. He would discourse and laugh heartily about these mantel-pieces,— instead of turning haughty and assuming a look of profaned intimacy, if anyone noticed the absence of fire in them. There was a spark of fight too in Mr. Brimmer; as I found to my cost once, when I received a letter from him beginning, "Sir," in the old dueling style, and more beautiful in its chirography than anything a merely democratic age can produce.

At the time I knew him best, he was no longer young, and was the figure-head of philanthropy, art and social life in Boston. Mrs. Brimmer loved *luxe*. Her banquets were as dignified and well mounted as such things can possibly be; and the banquets were followed by ceremonial receptions of intimate friends: dear people they were, too. The whole procedure was accompanied by a certain gorgeousness and parade, which used to terrify me, and not me only; for the whole of Boston was at that time awed by the splendor of these parties, yet proud of their grand manner. When I went to London a few years later, I saw some old-fashioned coachmen with round wigs,—I think they were made of glass,—and I suggested that Mrs. Brimmer ought to put some of these wigs on her coachmen;—but this was never done. The wigs, however, were on the banquets; and the old-fashioned family servants, the inner domestic reality of everything in the household, made it a most notable establishment.

Mr. Brimmer ate no more than a bird, and smoked thin, straw-colored cigars. He cared nothing for luxury, but moved in it as an old lord might move in a castle, just because it was there: to him it was his attic. His clothes were remarkable. They came from England, and were of the finest stuffs, and of the ancientest models; and they hung upon him negligently. This, by the way, was characteristic of the true old Bostonians. They got their clothes from Poole; but they never tried them on. Yet, instead of making a ridiculous figure in the garments, they dignified their apparel. They wore their clothes well; and I have seen octogenarian millionaires, with youthful hose well saved upon their shrunk shanks, pacing Beacon Street like old masters. Say what you will, there was something strong about the old Commonwealth; and, as it melted slowly into modern times, I watched and treasured the apparition. It was a great relief to me, as a college lad who was passing through many wrestlings of the spirit over shirts and pumps, and who thought there might exist some dreadful law of correctness in the higher circles of society,—it was a great relief to me, after I had conscientiously bought a white tie of the proper contemporary cut, to find that Martin Brimmer had done no such thing. Here was the finest gentleman I had ever seen; but when he wanted a tie, he caused a valet to open a trunk and to pull from the bottom of it a tie of seventeen years before. Mr. Brimmer put on the tie none too carefully; and came down stairs with a grave courtesy. The Italian nieces adjusted his tie, the red silk drawing-room with the statue of Story's Cleopatra was thrown open, and the great world of little Boston arrived with its arms outspread.

Mrs. Brimmer afforded ideal contrasts to her husband. She was large, imposing, handsome, blonde and infantile. Her cheeks had never been roughly visited by the winds of heaven. Indeed she was one of those people whom the world instinctively surrounds with a hedge of protection. Her dearest friends never quite told her the truth; and I am sure that, in childhood, her playmates must always have petted her and given her the prettiest string of beads. She was a queen-bee, twice as large and twice as handsome as other women; and she wore Damascened brocades and ostrich feathers, and had eyes as blue as the sky.

That age was an age of witticisms and of personal hits, which were recorded and handed about. To-day the taste for bon mots has waned, and if anyone should bring such a thing as a witticism into a drawing-room, people would balk at it and regard it as an old snuff-box. But in those days, sallies of wit were correct and conventional. Dr. Holmes and Tom Appleton and Judge Hoar were the professional wits of Boston, just as Evarts and Travers were the professional wits of New York. Behind these veterans there were hundreds of skirmishing humorists who made social life agreeable. Evening receptions were regarded as a natural form of amusement;

people stood in a pack, and ate and drank, and talked volubly till midnight. And they enjoyed it too. There was a zest in it. I don't know why the world has become so dull of recent years, and society so insipid. People in Boston in the Eighties knew how to enjoy themselves.

There seems to exist a great invisible sponge that is always passing forward and back across society and wiping out coteries and traditions. It never succeeds in obliterating all of cultivation or all of happiness, yet it seems forever on the point of doing so. One of the staple illusions of middle life is the vision of a Vanishing Past. The experience must be classed with youth's illusions of an oncoming Roseate Future: both visions are normal. Indeed it is the vision of the Vanishing Past that has caused me to write these sketches. I am afraid that I may forget those vivid scenes of youth unless I write them down. They have risen in my memory recently, as the mirage rises,—ever at a fixed distance from the beholder; and I fear they may disappear again as I move farther away from them. Perhaps there is nothing of monumental interest in these balls, weddings and tea parties that I attended in Boston as an undergraduate, —except as all things have historic interest. Boston was a family,— a club,—and is so still. Some people resent the family atmosphere of Boston; but I always liked it. The people there speak of "Cousin John" and expect you to know to whom they refer. But this is charming! Someone has said that Boston was the only city in the world where when two ladies meet in the street, one says, "How is he?" The great business of Bostonians was to place values upon everything in the world, with conscientious accuracy. Professor Norton once said to me on the steps of Sanders Theatre, after a performance of Beethoven's "Eroica Symphony," that, after all, the "Sentiment" of the funeral march was a little "forced." This was charming, too. Of course it is not great or of the great world. And yet I know that in Paris and Berlin, in Oxford and Munich, there are constantly arising cliques and coteries that go on in the same sort of exclusive way. A sect arises whose pursuit it is to praise Cimabue or damn Handel. I knew of a French artist of whom great things were expected, who could only laugh when Michael Angelo was named. Michael Angelo made him laugh. He could do nothing but laugh. It was Boston's foible to set metes and bounds to everything: that was the game which we played; but it was a good game, and the players were among the best-hearted people in the world.

Mr. Brimmer's cultivation was, as has been seen, not of the Bostonian brand. He had no pose of any kind, no ambition. His cultivation was unconscious.

He was as much at home with a Turk as with an Englishman, and had the natural gravity which marks the Asiatic. He could, upon occasion, be severe and masterful; and at such times his thin jaw would protrude beneath his falling mustache. In that age the wandering Englishman of fashion was apt to drop in upon an American dinner-party in his traveling jacket. One such offender Mr. Brimmer caused to ascend in the elevator to become arrayed in a suit from the antique and honorable wardrobe of the house, before being admitted to the feast. I am sure that the host spoke with the sweetness of King Arthur and Galahad in making the suggestion to the stranger.

Mr. Brimmer's most powerful quality was his patience. He could endure and go on enduring almost to eternity. To a man of his delicate physique and inner sensitiveness, the jolting of life must ever have been painful; and he seemed often to be in pain; but whether it was physical pain or mental pain was hard to guess. Of all the virtues the virtue of patience is most foreign to youth: his power of patience impressed me and awed me. I am quite sure that if I should see him again I should be as much at the mercy of his superiority and of his quietude as I was at the age of twenty-three.

I will not attempt to describe Mr. Brimmer's public activities. Everyone revered him and regarded him as a model citizen, the benefactor and manager of museums and colleges. I only knew his social life. He must always have stood by himself: he seemed not to belong to any of the existing Bostonian types. He told me that, at some period during the war, when the cause of the North looked particularly hopeless, he had been at a dinner where many of the most prominent men in Boston were gathered to consider the military situation. It was a formal occasion, at which men gave their views *seriatim*. He was the only man present who thought the war could be pushed to a successful issue. Perhaps in every generation there are solitary men, who live like sentinels within their own thoughts, watching the world. Their very lack of personal aim makes them significant. They exert an influence that is peculiarly indefinable. They qualify other men.

The Brimmers had no children; but their household, and indeed the whole little kingdom that went with it, was greatly warmed and caused to glow by the presence of the two Italian nieces. Each of these girls grew up to be a remarkable woman, and died early, leaving a great gap behind her, and people looking up into heaven. I must speak of them in this place, however, not so much for their own sakes as because they were a part of Mr. and Mrs. Brimmer. They were the life of the establishment; and all the horses and carriages, banquets and ceremonies, all the empty childless wealth of the Brimmer household was glorified by their presence. These young ladies were in reality only half Italian, but they looked wholly Italian, and they were in themselves thoroughly foreign. The woman of northern Europe is, after all, a washed-out affair. Compared to the Mediterranean woman, she is a drudge and a good creature merely. The southern woman is an independent spirit. In spite of the Greek theories as to the suppression of the sex, Phædra, Medea and Sappho were as little suppressed as it is possible to be. They had freedom of thought and of conduct. Shakespeare's women owe their charm to this quality of freedom. He filched the type out of southern stories, and he dressed it in northern innocence. These two girls then, who looked like figures out of the Vita Nuova, brought with them from Italy the daring of a country where a woman is as good as a man, while they inherited in their own natures and from their American ancestors a sort of Anglo-Saxon piety. They were orphans, devout Protestants, much traveled, very good looking, rounded and spontaneous, modest and yet frankly emotional, forthcoming and yet remote. I shall not forget the first time that I saw them both. It was at one of the great social functions I have spoken of and at the moment when the family were awaiting the arrival of the crowd. The girls stood before the fireplace, supporting the household like caryatids and moved about through the rooms like some new kind of nymphs;—but not at all like the nymphs of Diana, rather like nymphs of Ceres and Proserpina which the God Pan had let loose in Boston.

These young girls hung garlands about the declining years of their aunt and uncle, being as devoted as daughters could have been; and then they vanished, almost at the same time that the old people died. Thus the whole structure of that enchanted palace, with its gates and gardens, its old servants, and stately banquets, its rose bushes and aviaries, and with the old Knight Brimmer and the two beautiful Italian girls,—seemed to fall together and disappear in a night. How they arose, I never knew, nor how they vanished.

The following lines were written at the time of his death:

> The mask of life is fallen. Behold the man!
> Such was he, and so is. How easily
> Do all the accidents of earth drop off.
> And as they fall, the Immortality
> The soul departs to, shines through the clay.
> Severe, calm, dominant: a general.—
> Frail, yet the very manifest of Power.—
> A look of life-long conquest on his brow.
> Christ Militant, Thy soldier as he lies!
> Not for our eyes this bearing, but for Thine.

# Mrs. Whitman

SOCIAL TALENT is a true and a rare thing; and though it may contain some tincture of ambition, as talent always does, this is but a small part of the phenomenon. The essence of it is a reverence for the talents of other people, a belief in the powers of others, a spiritual hospitality—which discovers that other people are remarkable and almost makes them so by lavishing an incredible faith upon their development.

The earliest reputation that Mrs. Whitman achieved was that of being an unknown lady from some savage town,—Baltimore, perhaps,—who had appeared in Boston. It was not many years, however, before she had become a center of social influence, and of that peculiar kind of social influence in which there are strands of art, idealism,—intellect. The reason for her enduring conquest was that her chief interest always lay with the young. Thus the future was with her.

The discovery must every day be made afresh that conversation is the life of literature, and perhaps of all the fine arts. Writing is a sort of conventional lie, and a rather dangerous one. The very greatest men never write at all. But there is an essential truth about conversation, which is due to its fluid non-conclusiveness. Talk leaves every question open: and every question really is open. This is what is meant by the so-called "art of conversation." Plato knew the secret, and often resorts to a sort of laborious equivocation in order to keep life in his dialogues. The man who writes always wants to conclude something instead of being content to lay it bare. But ideas sprout best after they have arisen and have been plowed under in conversation. Without this, they are apt to spread with a sickly luxuriance into unprunable philosophy,—dogmatic, difficult and falser than flippancy itself.

I have sometimes thought that one difference between French and German literature is that the Frenchman is always in a parlor; while the German, on the other hand, lives in the mining-camp of his profession. Of course there are German poets and novelists who deal with social life; but the hewers and diggers of the race are always encroaching; they occupy history, they invade journalism, they set up their barracks around philosophy. They have destroyed the German language; and all this because they work in silence. Good style is founded on speech. It is a weakness in our colleges that the students are always scribbling in the lecture rooms. The fountain pens should be taken from them at the doors of the class rooms. Examinations ought to be oral where possible, and nothing ought to be found on an examination paper except what has been threshed out in open discussion. If we could go one step further and forbid the professors to read their remarks from manuscript, we should take a long stride towards the life of the intellect.

It must be my excuse for this long preface that Mrs. Whitman was one who, somehow, represented a rediscovery of the importance of conversation. It was the intrinsic nature of the woman rather than any special intention that led her to take the course she did. Clever men love to be appreciated, and when, as rarely happens, a woman is found with so much enthusiasm for intelligence that she turns a special reflector upon anyone possessing it and gives him the shock and glow of recognition, the clever men will flock about her, and a sort of salon will arise. It was not men alone whom Mrs. Whitman fascinated by her sympathy. She subdued every sort of person, especially old ladies, especially young school girls, especially her own incorruptible contemporaries, who had never known such a creature before, but who sooner or later lay in chains to her resourceful personality.

I remember a curious Bostonian cockfight at her studio, where Professor Royce and Judge Oliver Wendell Holmes were pitted against each other to talk about the Infinite. Royce won, of course, —somewhat after the manner of Gladstone,—by involving the subject in such adamantine cobwebs of voluminous rolling speculation that no one could regain his senses thereafter. He not only cut the ground from under everyone's feet; but he pulled down the sun and moon, and raised up the ocean, and everyone was shipwrecked and took to small planks and cups of tea.

Mrs. Whitman was surrounded by geniuses. I didn't always believe in the rest of them, but I believed that somehow I must be a good one,—not so great as she believed, but still something quite considerable in my own way. She had an unterrified way of dealing with social life that would have made her a force in any community. If James Russell Lowell came to town, she would give a dinner party of twelve young people to meet him. He played up considerably upon one such occasion, though in a manner that was more historically interesting than socially pleasant. This was at the end of his life, when he wore a high hat with British obstinacy, and looked askance at the Common. He exactly resembled the portraits which we see of him on the calendars. And when some nice Senior from Harvard ventured to launch a very decent remark in his direction, Mr. Lowell corrected his grammar and delivered a lecture upon the uses of "shall" and "will." This was "Seeing Boston" with a vengeance; and yet who would not be glad to carry about with him the recollection of the megaphone?

Mrs. Whitman used, in entertaining, to mingle old and young together. To do this is the first requisite of agreeable society, and the only way of civilizing the younger generation. Wherever the practice falls into disuse, the boys and girls will run to seed as they grow up. Young people are naturally barbarians; and unless they are furnished with examples of good manners they soon become negligent, unashamed and illiterate. They forget those reserves which embody the traditions of centuries, and which add charm and intensity to social enjoyment. They would forget reading and writing, history, clothes, the multiplication table and how to tell time, if they were entirely abandoned by their elders. Well-bred older persons unconsciously dominate the imagination of the young, and inform them as to many matters without uttering a word. In this way good traditions are preserved. The civilizing process goes forward in the drawing rooms of every country in Europe; but in America the practice prevails of leaving the young people to themselves. The consequence is that the children of our nicest families often behave as if they had never seen an educated person or entered a drawing room. The young savages are at Coney Island now, and will be at Hayti to-morrow, unless the custom is revived of bringing old and young together for the amusements of life.

This lack of social training in our young people is, by the way, merely a sample of our great national defect. If one were to give, in a single word, the difference between Europe and America, the word would be training. What we need most in every department of life,—in scholarship, in science, in journalism, in administrative business and in the decorative arts,—is training. Neither aptitude, intellect, nor ambition; neither love nor religion is lacking to us. Our great need is a need of training.

It was not through any pedagogic theory, however, that Mrs. Whitman was led to mingle old and young at her parties. She was devoted to the individuals that she asked to her house; and that was the whole secret of their being there.

There are people whose interests and affections lie in the world of personality, to whom the whole of life is made up of people. Mrs. Alice Freeman Palmer (whom I never met) was such a woman. Not thoughts, not ideas, not religions, but people made the universe for her; and this gave her incommunicable, unimaginable access to people's hearts. She held the keys of them,—thousands of keys to thousands of individuals,—and they each felt themselves to be understood when they met her; they felt as it were, in contact with the power that made them. This sort of entry into people's minds Mrs. Whitman also had, though it was in a field of life quite different from Mrs. Palmer's field. Her province was both wider and narrower than Mrs. Palmer's. But for each of these women, people made up life. If you will consider the great permanent, practical needs of the world, you will see that one of them is the need of such focal personalities as these. Our University towns to-day are little Meccas for young enthusiasm. How sad is it to see the ignorant freshmen wandering about Harvard Square—and to find the same men again as Seniors, often wandering back to their distant homes, having found the cribs at Harvard but not having found anyone who could teach them how to draw down the fodder. Benevolence alone will not make a teacher, nor will learning alone do it. The gift of teaching is a peculiar talent, and implies a need and a craving in the teacher himself.

It would be impossible to say how much a whole generation, of whom I was one, owed to Mrs. Whitman; for her activity introduced us to one another and brought us forward. She would take no end of trouble. For years after many of us had left Boston, upon hearing that one of us was to pass through the town, she would improvise a meeting of the twenty persons the visitor most desired to see there. When she died a whole society seemed to be suddenly extinguished. Vesuvius had covered the town of Boston, and we went about poking among the ashes to find each other in holes, corners and side streets.

I find again and again in writing these memories that the most telling personalities I have known often, upon reflection, vaguely suggest tragedy. But tragedy is too strong a word;—perhaps renunciation or apparent failure would be better. The men and women who make the best boon companions seem to have given up hope of doing something else. They have, perhaps, tried to be poets and painters; they have tried to be actors, scientists and musicians. But some defect of talent or of opportunity has cut them off from their pet ambition, and has thus left them with leisure to take an interest in the lives of others. Your ambitious man is selfish. No matter how secret his ambition may be, it makes him keep his thoughts at home. He is putting pennies in the slot for himself every few moments. What sort of a man is that, then, to open one's heart to? He would be sure to advise you to take a liver-pill and to think no more of the matter. But the heartbroken people,—if I may use the word in a mild, benevolent sense,—the people whose wills are subdued to fate, give us consolation, recognition and welcome. There is nothing that we can do for such natures in return save to accept the situation and be thankful.

# PART THREE

PART THREE

# Society

Our institutions have survived, the perils of boss rule are past, and we may look back upon the system with a kind of awe, and recognize how easily the system might have overthrown our institutions and ushered in a period which history would have recorded as the age of the State Tyrants.

Let us imagine that some State like Pennsylvania, on which the boss system had been so firmly fixed that a boss was able to bequeath his seat in the United States Senate to his son, had shown forth an ambitious man, a ruler who realized that his function was not one of business, but one of government; let us imagine that a President of the Pennsylvania Railroad, some man of great capacity, had undertaken to rule the State. He would, by his position as State boss, have been able gradually to do away with the petty bosses and petty abuses. He would give the State a general cities law, good schools, clean streets, speedy justice; every necessary municipal improvement. Gas, water, boulevards would be supplied with an economy positively startling to a generation accustomed to jobs. He would destroy the middlemen as Louis XI destroyed the nobles, and give to his State, for the first time in the history of the country, good government. A benign tyranny, with every department in the hands of experts, makes the strongest form of government in the world. Every class is satisfied. Pennsylvania would have been famous the world over. Its inhabitants would have been proud of it; foreigners would have written books about it; other States would have imitated it.

Meanwhile the power of self-government would have been lost.

Biennial sessions of the Legislature are already a favorite device for minimizing the evils of Legislatures. But the dictator would have desired to discourage popular assemblies. The whole business world would have backed the boss, in his plan for quinquennial or decennial sessions. Once give way to the laziness, once cater to the inertia and selfishness of the citizen, and he sinks into slumber.

Our feeble and floundering citizens' movements in New York during the last ten years show us how hard it is to recover the power of self-government when once lost; how gradual the gain, even under the most stimulating conditions of misrule. Given thirty years of able administration by a single man, and the boss system would have sunk so deep into the popular mind, the arctic crust of prejudice and incompetence would have frozen so deep, that it might easily take two hundred years for the community to come to life. Recovery could only come through the creeping in of abuses, through the decentralization of the great tyranny. And as each abuse arose, the population would clamor to the dictator and beg him to correct it. After a while a few thinkers would arise who would see that the only way to revive our institutions was by the painstaking education of the people. The stock in trade of these teachers would be the practical abuses, and very often they would be obliged to urge upon the people a course which would make the abuses temporarily more acute.

We have escaped an age of tyrants, because the eyes of the bosses and their masters were fixed on money. They were not ambitious. Government was an annex to trade. To certain people the boss appears as a ruler of men. If proof were needed that he is a hired man employed to do the dirty work of others, what better proof could we have than this: No one of all the hundreds of bosses thrown up during the last thirty years has ever lifted himself out of his sphere, or even essayed to rule.

That devotion of the individual to his bank account which created the boss and saved us from the dictator must now be traced back into business.

For the sake of analysis it is convenient now to separate and again not to separate the influences of business proper from the influences of dishonesty, but in real life they are one thing. Dishonesty is a mere result of excessive devotion to money-making. The general and somewhat indefinite body of rules which are considered "honest" change from time to time. I call a thing dishonest when it offends my instinct. The next man may call it honest. The question is settled by society at large. "What can a man do and remain in his club?" That gives the practical standards of a community. The devotion of the individual to his bank account gives the reason why the financier and his agent, the boss, could always find councilmen, legislators, judges, lawyers, to be their jackals, or to put the equation with the other end first, it is the reason why the legislators could always combine to blackmail the capitalist: this political corruption is a mere spur and offshoot of our business corruption. We know more about it, because politics cannot be carried on wholly in the dark. Business can. The main facts are known. Companies organize subsidiary companies to which they vote the money of the larger company—cheating their stockholders. The railroad men get up small roads and sell them to the great roads which they control—cheating their stockholders. The purchasing agents of many great enterprises cheat the companies as a matter of course, not by a recognized system of commissions—like French cooks—but by stealth. So in trade, you cannot sell goods to the retailers, unless you corrupt the proper person. It is all politics. All our politics is business and our business is politics.

There is something you want to do, and the "practical man" is the man who knows the ropes, knows who is the proper person to be "seen." The slang word gives a picture of the times—to "see" a man means to bribe him.

But let no one think that dishonesty or anything else begins at the top. These big business men were once little business men.

To cut rates, to have a different price for each customer, to substitute one article for another, are the prevailing policies of the seller. To give uncollectible notes, to claim rebates, to make assignments and compromises, to use one shift or another in order to get possession of goods and pay less than the contract price, are the prevailing aims of the buyer.

It is unquestionably possible for an incorruptible man to succeed in business. But his scruples are an embarrassment. Not everybody wants such a man. He insists on reducing every reckoning to pounds sterling, while the rest of the world is figuring in maravedis. He must make up in ability what he lacks in moral obliquity.

He will no doubt find his nook in time. Honesty is the greatest luxury in the world, and the American looks with awe on the man who can afford it, or insists upon having it. It is right that he should pay for it.

The long and short of the matter is that the sudden creation of wealth in the United States has been too much for our people. We are personally dishonest. The people of the United States are notably and peculiarly dishonest in financial matters.

The effect of this on government is but one of the forms in which the ruling passion is manifest. "What is there in it for me?" is the state of mind in which our people have been existing. Out of this come the popular philosophy, the social life, the architecture, the letters, the temper of the age; all tinged with the passion.

Let us look at the popular philosophy of the day. An almost ludicrous disbelief that any one can be really disinterested is met at once. Any one who takes an intelligent interest in public affairs becomes a "reformer." He is liked, if it can be reasonably inferred that he is advancing his own interests. Otherwise he is incomprehensible. He is respected, because it is impossible not to respect him, but he is regarded as a mistaken fellow, a man who interferes with things that are not his business, a meddler.

The unspoken religion of all sensible men inculcates thrift as the first virtue. Business thunders at the young man, "Thou shalt have no other gods but me." Nor is it a weak threat, for business, when it speaks, means business. The young doctor in the small town who advocates reform loses practice for two reasons: first, because it is imagined that he is not a serious man, not a good doctor, if he gives time to things outside his profession; second, because the carriage-maker does not agree with him and regards it as a moral duty to punish him. The newsdealer in the Arcade at Rector Street lost custom because it was discovered that he was a Bryan man. The bankers would not buy papers of him. Since the days of David, the great luxury of the powerful has been to be free from the annoyance of other persons' opinions. The professional classes in any community are parasites on the moneyed classes; they attend the distribution. They cannot strike the hand that feeds them. In a country where economic laws tend to throw the money into the hands of a certain type of men, the morality of those men is bound to affect society very seriously.

The world-famous "timidity" of Americans in matters of opinion, is the outward and visible sign of a mental preoccupation. Tocqueville thought it was due to their democratic form of government. It is not due to democracy, but to commercial conditions. In Tocqueville's day it arose out of the slavery question, solely because that question affected trade.

In describing the social life of Boston, Josiah Quincy says of George Ticknor's hospitality: "There seemed to be a cosmopolitan spaciousness about his very vestibule. He received company with great ease, and a simple supper was always served to his evening visitors. Prescott, Everett, Webster, Hillard, and other noted Bostonians, well mixed with the pick of such strangers as happened to be in the city, furnished a social entertainment of the first quality. Politics, at least American politics, were never mentioned."

It was at such "entertainments" as this that the foreign publicists received their impressions as to the extinction of free speech in America. Politics could not be mentioned; but this was not due to our democratic form of government, but to the fact that Beacon Street was trading with South Carolina. "Politics" meant slavery, and Beacon Street could not afford to have values disturbed—not even at a dinner party.

We have seen that our more recent misgovernment has not been due to democracy, and we now see that the most striking weakness of our social life is not and never has been due to democracy.

Let us take an example: A party of men meet in a club, and the subject of free trade is launched. Each of these men has been occupied all day in an avocation where silence is golden. Shall he be the one to speak first? Who knows but what some phase of the discussion may touch his pocket? But the matter is deeper. Free speech is a habit. It cannot be expected from such men, because a particular subject is free from danger. Let the subject be dress reform, and the traders will be equally politic.

This pressure of self-interest which prevents a man from speaking his mind comes on top of that familiar moral terrorism of any majority, even a majority of two persons against one, which is one of the ultimate phenomena of human intercourse.

It is difficult to speak out a sentiment that your table companions disapprove of. Even Don Quixote was afraid to confess that it was he who had set the convicts at liberty, because he heard the barber and curate denounce the thing as an outrage. Now the weight of this normal social pressure in any particular case will depend on how closely the individuals composing the majority resemble each other. But men, lighted by the same passion, pursuing one object under the similar conditions, of necessity grow alike. By a process of natural selection, the self-seekers of Europe have for sixty years been poured into the hopper of our great mill. The Suabian and the Pole each drops his costume, his language, and his traditions as he goes in. They come out American business men; and in the second generation they resemble each other more closely in ideals, in aims, and in modes of thought than two brothers who had been bred to different trades in Europe.

The uniformity of occupation, the uniformity of law, the absence of institutions, like the church, the army, family pride, in fact, the uniformity of the present and the sudden evaporation of all the past, have ground the men to a standard.

America turns out only one kind of man. Listen to the conversation of any two men in a street car. They are talking about the price of something—building material, advertising, bonds, cigars.

We have, then, two distinct kinds of pressure, each at its maximum, both due to commerce: the pressure of fear that any unpopular sentiment a man utters will show in his bank account; the pressure of a unified majority who are alike in their opinions, have no private opinions, nor patience with the private opinions of others. Of these two pressures, the latter is by far the more important.

It cannot be denied that the catchwords of democracy have been used to intensify this tyranny. If the individual must submit when outvoted in politics, he ought to submit when outvoted in ethics, in opinion, or in sentiment. Private opinion is a thing to be stamped out, like private law. A prejudice is aroused by the very fact that a man thinks for himself; he is dangerous; he is anarchistic.

But this misapplication of a dogma is not the cause but the cloak of oppression. It is like the theory of the divine right of Kings—a thing invoked by conservatism to keep itself in control, a shibboleth muttered by men whose cause will not bear argument.

We must never expect to find in a dogma the explanation of the system which it props up. That explanation must be sought for in history. The dogma records but does not explain a supremacy. Therefore, when we hear some one appeal to democratic principle for a justification in suppressing the individual, we have to reflect how firmly must this custom be established, upon what a strong basis of interest must it rest, that it has power so to pervert the ideas of democracy. A distrust of the individual running into something like hatred may be seen reflected in the press of the United States. The main point is that Americans have by business training been growing more alike every day, and have seized upon any and every authority to aid them in disciplining a recusant.

We have then a social life in which caution and formalism prevail, and can see why it is that the gathering at the club was a dull affair.

We must now add one dreadful fact: Many of these men at the club are dishonest. The banker has come from a Directors' meeting of a large corporation, where he has voted to buy ten thousand shares of railroad stock which he and his associates bought on foreclosure at seventeen three weeks before, but which now stands at thirty, because the quotations have been rigged. The attorney for the corporation is here talking to Professor Scuddamore about the new citizens' movement, which the attorney has joined, for he is a great reformer, and lives in horror of the wickedness of the times. Beyond him sits an important man, whose corporation has just given a large sum to a political organization. Next to him is a Judge, who is a Republican, but fond of a chat with political opponents. With them is the editor of a reform paper, whose financial articles are of much importance to the town. A very eminent lawyer is in conversation with him. This lawyer has just received a large fee from the city for work which would not have brought him more than one-fifth of the amount if done for a private client. He is, by the way, a law partner of the latest tribune of the people, a man of stainless reputation. Here is also another type of honor, the middle-aged practitioner of good family, who has one of the best heads in town. He knows what all these other men are, and how they make their money; yet he dines at their houses, and gets business from them. On his left is a man much talked of ten years ago, a rare man to be seen here. He was ambitious, and became the hope of reform. But, unfortunately, he also had a talent for business. He became rich and cynical, and you see that he is looking about, as if in search of another disappointed man to talk to. There also is a great doctor, visiting physician of three hospitals, one of which is in receipt of city funds, and he knows the practice of packing the hospitals before inspection day in order to increase the appropriation. The man who endowed the hospital sits beyond. All these wires end in this club-room. Now start your topic—jest about free silver, make a merry sally on Mayor Jones. Start the question: "Why is the last reform commissioner of the gas works not in jail?" and see what a jovial crew you are set down with.

You will find as to any new topic, that each one requires time to adjust his cravat to it. You are in a company of men who are so anxious to be reasonable, to be "just," that it will require them till judgment day to make up their minds on any point. Nor is it easy to say how any one of them ought to behave. Is it dishonest to draw dividends from a corporation which you believe to be corruptly managed; to wink at bribery done in the interest of widows and of orphans? Must you cut a client because he owns a judge? What proof have you of any of these things? Do you demand of any one of these men that he shall offend or denounce the rest, and, short of that, what course should he take?

The point here made is not an ethical one as to how any one of these men ought to adjust himself to the corruption about him, but the sociological point—that a civilization based upon a commerce which is in all its parts corruptly managed will present a social life which is unintelligent and mediocre, made up of people afraid of each other, whose ideas are shopworn, whose manners are self-conscious.

The ill-concealed dependence of these men on each other is not resentful. They are the most good-natured men in the world. But they are unenlightened. Without free speech free thought can hardly exist. Without free speech you cannot gather the fruits of the mind's spontaneous workings. When a man talks with absolute sincerity and freedom he goes on a voyage of discovery. The whole company has shares in the enterprise. He may strike out some idea which explains the sphinx. The moral consequences of circumspect and affable reticence are even worse than the intellectual ones. "Live and let live," says our genial prudence. Well enough, but mark the event. No one ever lost his social standing merely because of his offences, but because of the talk about them. As free speech goes out the rascals come in.

Speech is a great part of social life, but not the whole of it. Dress, bearing, expression, betray a man, customs show character, all these various utterances mingle and merge into the general tone which is the voice of a national temperament; private motive is lost in it.

This tone penetrates and envelops everything in America. It is impossible to condemn it altogether. This desire to please, which has so much of the shopman's smile in it, graduates at one end of the scale into a general kindliness, into public benefactions, hospitals, and college foundations; at the other end it is seen melting into a desire to efface one's self rather than give offence, to hide rather than be noticed.

In Europe, the men in the pit at the theatre stand up between the acts, face the house, and examine the audience at leisure. The American dares not do this. He cannot stand the isolation, nor the publicity. The American in a horse car can give his seat to a lady, but dares not raise his voice while the conductor tramps over his toes. It violates every instinct of his commercial body to thrust his private concerns into prominence. The American addresses his equal, whom he knows familiarly, as Mr. Jones, giving him the title with as much subserviency as the Englishman pays to an unknown Earl.

Mere financial dishonesty is of very little importance in the history of civilization. Who cares whether Cæsar stole or Cæsar Borgia cheated? Their intellects stayed clear. The real evil that follows in the wake of a commercial dishonesty so general as ours is the intellectual dishonesty it generates. One need not mind stealing, but one must cry out at people whose minds are so befuddled that they do not know theft when they see it. Robert Walpole bought votes. He deceived others, but he did not deceive himself.

We have seen that the retailer in the small town could not afford to think clearly upon the political situation. But this was a mere instance, a sample of his mental attitude. He dare not face any question. He must shuffle, qualify, and defer. Here at last we have the great characteristic which covers our continent like a climate—intellectual dishonesty. This state of mind does not merely prevent a man having positive opinions. The American is incapable of taking a real interest in anything. The lack of passion in the American—

noticeable in his books and in himself—comes from the same habitual mental distraction; for passion is concentration. Hence also the
flippancy, superficiality, and easy humor for which we are noted.
Nothing except the dollar is believed to be worthy the attention of
a serious man. People are even ashamed of their tastes. Until recently, we thought it effeminate for a man to play on the piano.
When a man takes a living interest in anything, we call him a
"crank." There is an element of self-sacrifice in any honest intellectual work which we detect at once and score with contumely.

It was not solely commercial interest that made the biographers
of Lincoln so thrifty to extend and veneer their book. It was that
they themselves did not, could not, take an interest in the truth
about him. The second-rate quality of all our letters and verse is
due to the same cause. The intellectual integrity is undermined.
The literary man is concerned for what "will go," like the reformer
who is half politician. The attention of every one in the United
States is on some one else's opinion, not on truth.

The matter resolves itself at last into Pilate's question: What is
truth? We do not know, and shall never know. But it seems to involve a certain focussing and concentration of the attention that
brings all the life within us into harmony. When this happens to
us, we discover that truth is the only thing we had ever really
cared about in the world. The thing seems to be the same thing, no
matter which avenue we reach it by. At whatever point we are
touched, we respond. A quartet, a cathedral, a sonnet, an exhibition
of juggling, anything well done—we are at the mercy of it. But as
the whole of us responds to it, so it takes a whole man to do it.
Whatever cracks men up and obliterates parts of them, makes them
powerless to give out this vibration. This is about all we know of
individualism and the integrity of the individual. The sum of all
the philosophies in the history of the world can be packed back into
it. All the tyrannies and abuses in the world are only bad because
they injure this integrity. We desire truth. It is the only thing we
desire.

# The Negro Question

I COME HERE WITH SOME reluctance this evening; because I do not wish to be obliged to make up my mind about the race question. In making up one's mind, one closes one's mind; and this race question,—which is no more than the struggle between Good and Evil put into visible shape,—can only be settled from moment to moment by any one of us. In so far as we ourselves are perfect, we settle it for the moment.

The history of the United States down to about 1870 is a history of this particular struggle between good and evil. Our constitutional questions, Secession, the Civil War, Reconstruction,—all the heat and agony of our political life during seventy years, came out of this Negro question. Since 1870, the Negro question has ceased to be the pivot upon which our whole civilization turned, and has sunk to the position of being the chief among the great problems before us. It is a problem that has been clearly recognized and is being nobly met by the whites and by the blacks alike. Christianity, training, and education—these things are the solution, these things are the need of all of us. If we keep our individual minds clear of all rancor, time will do the rest.

I believe that no race ever had a better hero than the colored race has to-day in Booker Washington. He is the embodiment of what all of us ought to be in regard to this question: not only the Negro but the white man looks upon him with reverence, and learns from him to be patient, to put away animosity, to have faith in God, to pursue inflexibly processes which operate slowly.

The two races in America are spiritually in contact and can only improve in unison. Therefore when an Association of this kind is formed for "the advancement of the colored race," it might just as well be called "for the advancement of the white race." I suppose that you all understand this.

There is a great law governing the meeting of races. When a powerful race meets a helpless race, two things happen. First there is a carnival of crime. Cruelty and oppression take place: some men in each race become evil and hard-hearted. But the reverse also happens thereafter; goodness and mercy are developed: certain men become saints and heroes. Now in America we had two hundred and fifty years of the epoch during which both races were being injured by contact with one another, both were being made miserable, both brutalized, and in consequence of this very epoch of slavery our whole land to-day is still full of hard, hard hearts.

But the tide seems now to be running the other way, and the pressure created by the living together of the two races seems to be generating virtue. The educators and missionaries, the philanthropists and thinkers have sprung up in America and have devoted themselves to the Negro question. They form a sort of army. There are apostles and servants of Christ among us who have been called into being through this very question, and whose existence gives dignity to our whole civilization. They have not solved the question as yet. The depravity of the blacks and the lynchings by the whites have not ceased. Burnings of Negroes at the stake still draw upon our nation the contempt and horror of mankind. But the spirit that is to put an end to these things has already been born.

True reform comes slowly; and no race was ever freed except by its own efforts,—no man saved except through himself. Therefore, when I hear of the struggles which the poor Negroes are making in the South, to civilize and to educate themselves, when I hear of how they eke out illiberal public grants with mites saved out of their poverty, of how they are long suffering and reasonable,—I say to myself, This was worth waiting for. These people are saving themselves. They will obtain the money which they need, and will use it rightly. The same thought is of harder application to the lynching question. The communities where lynching occurs can only recover their power of self-government through their own efforts. The flower must grow out of the soil. The man on the spot who is a part of the community where lynching is threatened, must risk his life or lay his life down freely in defense of law. A mere willingness on the part of one man to do this will generally stop a lynching. And you will observe that this spirit is beginning to manifest itself among our people, and will end by preventing the atrocities.

I used to bewail the present legacy of the slave trade as much as the original iniquity of it. The fact that the Negroes are here at all seemed almost to overpunish America for the crime of their importation. I used to think that the consequences which that crime entailed in the perpetuation among us of passions fierce and base, and in the mingling of races that are better apart, were pure evils, —ghastly never-ending punishments. But now I believe that it is foolish to argue in such a manner as this about historic things. The subject is beyond our comprehension. What we think the greatest evils in our minute lives often bring to us the greatest blessings. It may be so with nations.

The race question certainly puts each of us to the alternative of becoming a great deal holier, a great deal kinder, a great deal deeper in character, or else of being brutalized to some extent. We have not yet got free from some of the intellectual consequences of slavery. The old cruelty of the plantation is gone, and yet I sometimes hear rich people in club-rooms arguing about the Negro question in a spirit, and from a point of view, that indicates an intellectual injury. My own friends sometimes show scars of the mind in dealing with the Negro question. They become for a moment like sixteenth-century pirates,—their eyes glitter, and they talk tyranny. Yet these men are now mere relics. The newer age shows ever fewer of the type. Such meetings as this show that the American people are choosing the upward path. Hardly a day passes but we see new proofs that America will solve her race question in the only way it can be solved,—through herself becoming more gentle and more intelligent.

Our progress in this direction is slow; the path leads upward at a very small angle. But let us remember that slowness of growth is what America most needs in all directions. In everything we have grown up too quickly. To-day all things among us go crashing forward too quickly. We should not desire sudden changes, even for the better. Sudden changes signify short-lived events. Therefore, if we see steady improvement going forward anywhere, let us rejoice that it goes forward slowly, so that its roots may sink deep, and all nature may accommodate herself to the change. Thus will the good things become permanent.

Isaiah says in a text that is too seldom quoted: "He that believeth shall not make haste." Those words seem to suggest the very patience which is the national endowment of the Negro race. We see the virtue to-day in the meek and sturdy spirit with which the leaders of that race are building up schools and sending out missionaries. They are men of long wind and great faith. They refuse to be drawn into controversy or to take part in occasional excitement. They realize the nature of their work. They have studied their problem with the passion of their souls, and they understand it. And we, who belong to the white race, may herein find our best lesson. We also must have long wind and perfect faith. We must be as patient, and school ourselves as thoroughly as they.

# Coatesville

W E   A R E   M E T  to commemorate the anniversary of one of the most dreadful crimes in history—not for the purpose of condemning it, but to repent of our share in it. We do not start any agitation with regard to that particular crime. I understand that an attempt to prosecute the chief criminals has been made, and has entirely failed; because the whole community, and in a sense our whole people, are really involved in the guilt. The failure of the prosecution in this case, in all such cases, is only a proof of the magnitude of the guilt, and of the awful fact that everyone shares in it.

I will tell you why I am here; I will tell you what happened to me. When I read in the newspapers of August 14, a year ago, about the burning alive of a human being, and of how a few desperate, fiend-minded men had been permitted to torture a man chained to an iron bedstead, burning alive, thrust back by pitchforks when he struggled out of it, while around about stood hundreds of well-dressed American citizens, both from the vicinity and from afar, coming on foot and in wagons, assembling on telephone call, as if by magic, silent, whether from terror or indifference, fascinated and impotent, hundreds of persons watching this awful sight and making no attempt to stay the wickedness, and no one man among them all who was inspired to risk his life in an attempt to stop it, no one man to name the name of Christ, of humanity, of government! As I read the newspaper accounts of the scene enacted here in Coatesville a year ago, I seemed to get a glimpse into the uncon-

255

scious soul of this country. I saw a seldom revealed picture of the American heart and of the American nature. I seemed to be looking into the heart of the criminal—a cold thing, an awful thing.

I said to myself, "I shall forget this, we shall all forget it; but it will be there. What I have seen is not an illusion. It is the truth. I have seen death in the heart of this people." For to look at the agony of a fellow-being and remain aloof means death in the heart of the onlooker. Religious fanaticism has sometimes lifted men to the frenzy of such cruelty, political passion has sometimes done it, personal hatred might do it, the excitement of the amphitheater in the degenerate days of Roman luxury could do it. But here an audience chosen by chance in America has stood spellbound through an improvised *auto-da-fé,* irregular, illegal, having no religious significance, not sanctioned by custom, having no immediate provocation, the audience standing by merely in cold dislike.

I saw during one moment something beyond all argument in the depth of its significance. You might call it the paralysis of the nerves about the heart in a people habitually and unconsciously given over to selfish aims, an ignorant people who knew not what spectacle they were providing, or what part they were playing in a judgment-play which history was exhibiting on that day.

No theories about the race problem, no statistics, legislation, or mere educational endeavor, can quite meet the lack which that day revealed in the American people. For what we saw was death. The people stood like blighted things, like ghosts about Acheron, waiting for someone or something to determine their destiny for them.

Whatever life itself is, that thing must be replenished in us. The opposite of hate is love, the opposite of cold is heat; what we need is the love of God and reverence for human nature. For one moment I knew that I had seen our true need; and I was afraid that I should forget it and that I should go about framing arguments and agitations and starting schemes of education, when the need was deeper than education. And I became filled with one idea, that I must not forget what I had seen, and that I must do something to remember it. And I am here to-day chiefly that I may remember that vision. It seems fitting to come to this town where the crime occurred and hold a prayer-meeting, so that our hearts may be turned to God through whom mercy may flow into us.

Let me say one thing more about the whole matter. The subject

we are dealing with is not local. The act, to be sure, took place at
Coatesville and everyone looked to Coatesville to follow it up. Some
months ago I asked a friend who lives not far from here something
about this case, and about the expected prosecutions, and he replied
to me: "It wasn't in my county," and that made me wonder whose
county it was in. And it seemed to be in my county. I live on the
Hudson River; but I knew that this great wickedness that happened
in Coatesville is not the wickedness of Coatesville nor of to-day. It
is the wickedness of all America and of three hundred years—the
wickedness of the slave trade. All of us are tinctured by it. No
special place, no special persons, are to blame. A nation cannot practice a course of inhuman crime for three hundred years and then
suddenly throw off the effects of it. Less than fifty years ago domestic slavery was abolished among us; and in one way and another
the marks of that vice are in our faces. There is no country in Europe where the Coatesville tragedy or anything remotely like it
could have been enacted, probably no country in the world.

On the day of the calamity, those people in the automobiles came
by the hundred and watched the torture, and passers-by came in a
great multitude and watched it—and did nothing. On the next
morning the newspapers spread the news and spread the paralysis
until the whole country seemed to be helplessly watching this awful
murder, as awful as anything ever done on the earth; and the
whole of our people seemed to be looking on helplessly, not able to
respond, not knowing what to do next. That spectacle has been in
my mind.

The trouble has come down to us out of the past. The only reason that slavery is wrong is that it is cruel and makes men cruel and
leaves them cruel. Someone may say that you and I cannot repent
because we did not do the act. But we are involved in it. We are
still looking on. Do you not see that this whole event is merely the
last parable, the most vivid, the most terrible illustration that ever
was given by man or imagined by a Jewish prophet, of the relation
between good and evil in this world, and of the relation of men to
one another?

This whole matter has been an historic episode; but it is a part,
not only of our national history, but of the personal history of each
one of us. With the great disease (slavery) came the climax (the
war), and after the climax gradually began the cure, and in the

process of cure comes now the knowledge of what the evil was. I say that our need is new life, and that books and resolutions will not save us, but only such disposition in our hearts and souls as will enable the new life, love, force, hope, virtue, which surround us always, to enter into us.

This is the discovery that each man must make for himself—the discovery that what he really stands in need of he cannot get for himself, but must wait till God gives it to him. I have felt the impulse to come here to-day to testify to this truth.

The occasion is not small; the occasion looks back on three centuries and embraces a hemisphere. Yet the occasion is small compared with the truth it leads us to. For this truth touches all ages and affects every soul in the world.

# PART FOUR

PART FOUR

## EACH PLAY A WORLD

THERE IS a world in each of Shakespeare's plays,—*the* world, I should say,—so felt and so seen as the world never was seen before nor could be felt and seen again, even by Shakespeare. Each play is a little local universe. His stage devices he repeats, but the atmosphere of a play is never repeated. *Twelfth Night, As You Like It,* and *The Merchant of Venice* are very unlike one another. The unity that is in each of them results from unimaginable depths of internal harmony in each. The group of persons in any play (I am speaking of the good plays) forms the unity; for the characters are psychologically interlocked with one another. Prospero implies Caliban; Toby Belch implies Malvolio; Shylock, Antonio. The effects of all imaginative art result from subtle implications and adjustments. The public recognizes these things as beauty, but cannot analyse them. To the artist, however, they have been the bricks and mortar out of which the work was builded. We feel, for instance, in the *Midsummer Night's Dream,* that the fairies are somehow correlative to the artisans. They are made out of a complementary chemical. On the other hand, Theseus and Demetrius and Hippolyta, in the same play, are lay figures which set off as with a foil both the fairies and the artisans. Theseus, Hippolyta, and Demetrius are marionettes which give intellect and importance to Bottom and Flute, and lend body and life to the tiny fairies. All this miraculous subtlety of understanding on Shakespeare's part is unconscious. He has had no recipe, no *métier.*

The colouring of each play, its humour, its mood, is Shakespeare's mood as he wrote the play. The mood of desperate philosophic questioning in which he wrote *Hamlet* gives to the play its only unity. So *Macbeth* and *King Lear* are each beclouded by its own kind of passionate speculation. The story is, in each case, a mere thread to catch the crystals from an overcharged atmosphere of feeling. The tragedy of *Lear* is loftier, more abstract in thought, and at the same time more hotly human in feeling than *Macbeth*. It is in these worlds of mood that we must seek Shakespeare, and we must remain somewhat moody and dreamy ourselves during the search. If we take a pair of tongs to catch him, he will elude us.

In *Othello,* Shakespeare seems to have become interested in working out the destruction of a noble soul by means of a stage demon, a sort of Richard III in private life and without ambition. Iago has no motive, and Othello has no weakness; and the conjunction of the two persons is artificial. The idea is, nevertheless, elaborated with diabolical cunning on the playwright's part, and the picture of Othello remains the best picture of jealousy in literature; so that the play belongs at the head of all problem plays. If considered seriously, *Othello* is a plea for evil; but, properly taken, it is a sort of awful *jeu d'esprit.* An odious play it is, false to life and without overtones. Yet so gigantic is the mind that became interested in this odious problem, and so thoroughly equipped in playwriting, that the world, after three centuries, goes on being deceived and fascinated by the story. Shakespeare's interest in the play is a playwright's interest; and he happens not to weary of the problem or to stray from his main theme during the whole course of the story. *Othello* is like a Greek tragedy in that it is a masterpiece of artificial logic with a bad ending. But, of course, *Othello* is extremely unlike the Greek from every other point of view; as, for instance, it has many characters, a complexity of plot, a shifting of scene, a very hard and non-lyrical treatment, and endless Elizabethan hurly-burly. We must never forget that the radical difference between ancient and modern drama is that modern drama is always unfolding a story. We are kept wondering how the thing will turn out. Ancient drama, on the contrary, takes the plot for granted and focuses our whole attention upon the treatment.

The unexampled spontaneousness of Shakespeare is due to the flame of his own curiosity, that hums like a great fire through his plays, which are plays only incidentally,—they are really studies, the memorandum books of a man who is thinking,—water-colour sketches made by an amateur for his own pleasure, and then filed away never to be examined again. Shakespeare has lived in them as he wrote them; he knows not their limits; he has no intentions, no subsequent curiosity. In spite of their stage merits, they lose by being acted, as things delicate lose by being placarded. Compared to Molière's plays, they show imperfection everywhere. But there is so much genius in them,—as much, perhaps, as there is in the rest of literature outside of them,—that they belong to a superhuman world. No one ever wrote like this before. It is a new vehicle. There exists nothing with which to compare it. There was a good deal of truth in the early view which regarded Shakespeare as a gifted savage. He does not make the compromises or play the game of stage art. But he is following law of some sort, or he could not have become so popular. In multifarious appeal he has no fellow. The child loves his wit, the youth his passion, the middle-aged person his knowledge of the world, the old man his metaphysical power, and all men his benevolence.

What is a play? I do not know; but I am sure that these things are much more than plays: to me they are metaphysical treatises. There never was a creature like Hamlet, and never can be: Hamlet is a philosophical gimcrack. He shows the mind of an elderly man set upon the shoulders of a boy of eighteen, and turned loose in a tragic situation. What a monstrous apparatus of thought is here set up! There never was a man like Macbeth, and there never can be. An over-sensitive, morbid, middle-aged recluse commits a brutal murder in a barbarous Scotch castle, and then gives himself the horrors by plunging about in his double character of bloody borderer and lyric hypochondriac. Men are not like that. There never was a man like Richard III, or indeed like any other complete stage villain. The stage villain is a comparatively low form of artificial device. He is a metaphysical hypothesis, like the rest, invented for purposes of demonstration.

Perhaps we ought, in dealing with this whole subject, to begin by regarding all stage-land, from wheels and pulleys to poetic metaphors, as a congeries of things that are essentially and necessarily false and make-believe,—elaborately constructed things, which, properly used, flash a momentary illusion of truth into the sympathetic eye, but which will not stand inspection,—no, not for a moment. The people who write essays on Shakespeare's characters, treating them as real, have found a pretty amusement, which is about as valuable as the literary pastime of writing imaginary conversations between famous dead people. A stage character is always merely the fragment of a picture. Perhaps only a profile is shown; and yet its duty is done then and there. No more than this profile of the man ever existed, and we can never know what a full view of the face might reveal. If we add to Shakespeare's sketch by tacking on a bit of our own imagination, we shall produce a strange rag doll, just as the writers of imaginary conversations produce strange rag dolls.

When we come to *King Lear* we are in deep waters. In this play the passion and the tragedy develop so naturally, so unexpectedly, and so suddenly out of the halcyon opening of the drama that we are taken unaware. The clouds gather and the lightning plays about, and, lo! we are in the heights and depths of human experience. But how did we get there? What element has done this, and what does it all mean? Shakespeare neither knew nor cared. Hidden within *King Lear,* as in *Hamlet,* is a terrific metaphysical apparatus, a psychometer or dynamo of passion. It sets the machinery of our hearts in motion. The thing has been inserted into our minds and works its own will upon us. The comment, or chorus work, which in *Hamlet* and in *Macbeth* is done by the protagonists themselves, is in *King Lear* distributed to a jester, a pretended madman and a friend in disguise. Lear himself is not a double consciousness like Hamlet or Macbeth, but a passionate, feeble-minded, ignorant old man, who becomes pathetic chiefly through his age. But why is this pathos so deep? And why do the little dogs, Tray, Blanche, and Sweetheart, move us so profoundly? I suppose that Shakespeare himself has been greatly moved as he lived through the scenes in all these plays. He has not known just why the plots worked out as they did. He was evidently experimenting, and found that his themes worked up to these climaxes automatically. In *Timon of Athens* he worries and rages, yet nothing will come of it. In *Coriolanus* he works like a Trojan, and is as dull as Corneille.

If Shakespeare had only been an artist like Leonardo, who was always calculating effects and analysing causes, we might know something of his art. But the fact is that he knew nothing about the matter himself, and does not aid us. He does not know what has happened. Let us take an illustration of his ingenuousness. He reads Montaigne's essay on Sebondus,—that great, long, impassioned essay, in which Montaigne demonstrates the impotency of man, his inability to know anything whatever, his helplessness, and the absurdity of all human pretence to intellect. It is Essay No. XII in the Second Book, and we can all follow in Everyman's Library the very text which Shakespeare pondered. Shakespeare read this essay with a devouring curiosity, and absorbed its ideas,—which, after all, are ideas that are never long absent from any thoughtful mind. The *"Que sçay-je?"* of Montaine might be Shakespeare's own motto, were not Shakespeare too profoundly unconscious to have any motto. He reads Montaigne, and for a time he *becomes* Montaigne. For a time he sees the whole universe from the point of view of the sceptic; and while this influence is upon him he becomes interested in refurbishing the old stock play of *Hamlet.* Before he is aware, he has begun to use Hamlet as a stalking-horse for Montaigne's philosophy. He does not invent Hamlet as Goethe invents Mephistopheles. Hamlet is merely the result of the different problems and occupations of Shakespeare's private mind. Shakespeare's primary interest is an interest in life, not an interest in play-writing or in philosophy; these things are subsidiary toys, algebraical signs, to him. And when, as in *Hamlet,* it turns out that the playwright has made a monster, he never stops to consider the matter. For Shakespeare does not know that his own talent is a talent for thinking, that his own chief interest lies in speculation. He thinks he is telling a story, and he believes that all these ideas are in the story: he sees them in the tale itself.

There are writers who write for themselves. They have a curiosity, they have a passion for study and for statement, and a joy in the process of writing. Their writings are personal memoirs. Saint-Simon and Samuel Pepys are men of genius by reason of the passionate interest they take in their themes. They give us the very heart of a man on every page. Writing is to them the same thing as living. It is articulate living. Now, curiously enough, Shakespeare belongs to this class of writers. While using a most abstract and impersonal vehicle, he became early in life so interested in his themes that his personal mind was absorbed into his work, and his personal experiences and reflections were at the disposal of his artistic requirements. The vehicle which he used is ostensibly an abstract vehicle, perhaps the most abstract literary form that exists; for the author of a play has apparently no voice at all. And yet Shakespeare expressed his most intimate personal experiences with such fluency that you might say his vehicle rules him. As the man in the street ruminates and is greatly at the mercy of accident for the turn in his thought, so Shakespeare. His theme runs away with him in the good plays, and refuses to run away with him in the bad plays. He has so many different planes of brilliancy that he can "pull off," as they say, almost anything; but he is never aiming at anything in particular when he begins. For instance, in the *Taming of the Shrew* he has on the background of his canvas a superficial old Italian comedy of manners and of horse-play. He botches a boisterous, amusing and not beautiful play out of it. How coarse is his brush here! The subject has amused him and excited his wit; but first-rate comedy cannot be made out of this material,—at least, so it seems. In *Romeo and Juliet,* Shakespeare's enormous romanticism is excited, as it is in *Antony and Cleopatra.* The subject enchants him. There is a dream quality in all he writes here which is at the bottom of the popularity of these plays. But he is still at the mercy of his dream. In *Julius Cæsar* the interest of the play fails after the assassination; the drama breaks in two. Why did not Shakespeare use the assassination as a climax, and so save this play? Because his old training in chronicle-plays suggested another course. When Shakespeare sits down to write a play about Julius Cæsar, he seizes North's *Plutarch* in his left hand and begins to write immediately. He is not thinking of how to make a drama. He is thinking about the man Cæsar and his history. And some French writer, whose name I forget, has said that the few words spoken by Cæsar in this play give the best picture of Cæsar that exists. In *Winter's Tale* the whole action is broken in two by one of those twenty-years-after, dismal arrangements which are so hard to listen to; but Shakespeare's own romantic feeling saves the play. It is saved by Shakespeare's personal charm, by his love of Perdita and of the pastoral scenes, by his passionate sentiment for Hermione and the reconciliation, by his enjoyment of Paulina and the baby. What Shakespeare does is always makeshift,—or rather inspiration. Thus, *Winter's Tale,* which begins coldly and in one of his worst manners, turns, through the turn of the plot, and quite unconsciously to the poet, into a fervent palinode in praise of conjugal love. It is shot through with personal emotion, and drips with the dews of dawn. Some people can hardly bear the excessive sentiment of *Winter's Tale;* and I confess that the reconveyance of Hermione to the breast of Leontes taxes my powers of consumption. But Shakespeare himself revelled in this. Shakespeare had, indeed, a school-girl side, the side that delights in keepsakes, in twin cherries, in long-treasured, innocent, early, passionate thoughts of happiness. The intensity of his feeling increases with the innocence of the matter in hand. This virginity of feeling, which gave us Cordelia and Desdemona, Ophelia and Miranda, governs the climax of *Winter's Tale.*

It has become customary to say that we know nothing of Shakespeare the man. But indeed we know his mind more intimately than we know the mind of any other historic person. The man himself we know: it is his method that defies our comprehension. His method is not an intellectual thing at all, and has never been reduced to a shape in which it can be studied. His method is a part of his digestion and of his daily life. The thing he laid his hand to he transmutes. At an earlier or later period of his life, *King Lear* would have turned under his hands into a rural comedy, or into a golden drama, like *The Merchant of Venice.*

Power in expression arises out of artistic unity, whether in comedy or tragedy; and in Shakespeare's good plays the whole volume of the drama rolls along in its own envelope, and with a natural flow like a tide of the ocean. Every word and metaphor, every character and incident, is drenched in a particular tint and cloud-colour. The whole thing is like a solid body, so unitary is its complexity; and as it rolls it invades our minds with the force of nature—our own nature. The law of its behaviour suits our mind so exactly that the fable seems to be a part of ourselves: a child can understand it. This can be said of Shakespeare only at his easiest and best, for there is also a Shakespeare who lumbers and jolts about, poses, makes bad jokes, breaks off in the middle, is obscene and contradictory, dull and horrid. For Shakespeare was the most careless writer that ever lived, and it is this carelessness which left him so open to the whisperings of the Muse.

Even the bad plays have individuality; each has a psychological character of its own; they do not resemble one another in spirit. And the Shakespeare who moves in and out of the bad plays, appearing and disappearing like a silent scene-shifter who is not meant to be observed, resembles the Shakespeare of the great plays in the length of his stride. He is not always radiant or at home in the play. He is often queer, sour, and low-minded, like a sick man. We recognise his mind, however, through its preoccupation with abstract thoughts expressed in dazzling, concrete images.

## TROILUS AND CRESSIDA

THERE IS a history of criticism which will go on forever, and Shakespeare's relation to it is indubitably very important. But Shakespeare's direct influence upon the great body of men who know nothing about this whole branch of learning is what makes him Shakespeare. The Gospels are not encrusted in theology, because biblical criticism has never adhered to the New Testament. So literary and dramatic criticism do not stick to Shakespeare. There is some sort of *vis major* behind the Gospels, and there is a *vis major* behind much of Shakespeare which nothing touches. This power draws and fascinates the scholar; it chains him to his desk and to his thesis; it does not, as a rule, liberate his intellect. The scholar whose imagination is alive is a rarity. Indeed, scholarship proverbially kills the imagination; and therefore in striving to find what is our own in Shakespeare—who is the greatest storehouse of imagination in the world—we should be indifferent to scholarship. Everyone of us has a personal share in this wealth, a special relation to this mountainous loadstone of attracting intellect. No matter what we find, we cannot carry it away, nor can we ever force anyone else to perceive and value our discovery exactly as we do.

Coleridge discovered two different Shakespeares in *All's Well that Ends Well*. This is the right spirit in which to read Shakespeare,—this free-handed plundering of his meanings. We should read Shakespeare for pleasure, and only for pleasure. The plays were meant to be gay trifles, the perfume and the suppliance of a minute. Music and painting and poetry yield up their meanings in flashes and by accident; and just here is where the critics go mad: for they think to bore into the meaning of poetry as a mouse bores into a cheese. A man who sits down to read *The Tempest* for six months at a stretch is sure to make some discovery about the play. The professional scholars who attack ancient poetry and lost religions in this spirit of conquest are always rewarded: they find something. They develop a hobby, a thesis, an *idée fixe*. They become interested in a discovery of some sort; and the life of the subject closes its portals.

So, then, let us be unscholarly, careless, and above all let us take no stock in our own discoveries, but regard the world as Dream Stuff, while we examine the extremely unpleasant play of *Troilus and Cressida,*—a play that can never have been good; for it has no humour, no dramatic force, no sustained beauty. It has neither action nor plot, neither wit nor intention; and it is pervaded by a low moral tone. It is, indeed, a horrid jumble of distasteful impressions. And yet the play is intimately and convincingly Shakespeare's own. My reason for taking it up is that we seem to find in it broken bits of Shakespeare's art, botches and scraps of him, often so crudely done as to lay bare the artist's intention without accomplishing his end. By studying these stray passages we seem to get some insight into the way the poet's mind worked.

*Troilus and Cressida* is supposed to concern the Trojan War; but no war seems to be in progress in it. Certain characters, or caricatures, wander on and off the stage, or offend us by their different breaches of taste. The dressing up of the Homeric heroes in Elizabethan costume produces burlesque. The principal characters suggest the operetta, and the minor ones the music-hall. Ajax appears as a sort of Bardolph or Pistol; Pandarus as an Andrew Aguecheek; Thersites as a Shakespearian clown—*e.g.,* Launcelot Gobbo, Autolycus. Helen is addressed by Paris as "Nell." Ulysses walks upon the stage reading a letter. Hector, in speaking to Menelaus, refers to Helen as "your quondam wife," to which Menelaus replies, "Name her not now, sir; she's a deadly theme." "O pardon, I offend," says Hector. We find it hard to credit Shakespeare with the worst parts of the dialogue; but the man who adopted and republished the lines is almost as much a reprobate as the man who wrote them.

There are many speeches in the play that no one but Shakespeare could have written,—not a juvenile Shakespeare, either, but the Shakespeare of *King Lear* and *Macbeth,* the full-grown, miracle-minded man. These good things detach themselves like new paint from an old canvas; but the canvas is covered with truly Shakespearian work,—only bad, unpleasant work,—so that some scholars have supposed that *Troilus and Cressida* was a youthful piece worked over by the mature artist. Whether the play be old or new, and whether the kernel of it be Shakespeare's own or another's, we can observe in it the working of Shakespeare's intelligence. Not only is the awakened great genius there, but the deboshed penny-a-liner is there also, all through the play. Besides these two men there is, here and there, a half-awakened Shakespeare, a boozy, indifferent Orpheus, who gropes past his thought and lunges on, sometimes swinging out a phrase like a wreath of roses and then again heaving a brick. All the beauties in the play are detached and scrappy things. That Shakespeare took no coherent interest in the story whenever he wrote it, or wrote *at* it,—of this we feel sure.

The play opens with a couple of scenes in the pot-house vein between Pandarus, Troilus, and Cressida; and then the Grecian leaders come on with a few long speeches in Shakespeare's most magnificent rhetoric, larded with his most personal and peculiar faults. Indeed, in this play most of his bold misuses of language are *infelicitous*. But the wreaths of roses are there also. As to the meaning of the play, we should gather from the long opening speeches that the plot was to have something to do with the perils of a divided authority; for this idea is given out by Agamemnon and then expanded and worked up by Ulysses in two speeches, of which the first is didactic and stately, somewhat like Portia's on the quality of mercy, and the second is a description, in a vein to make Homer weep, of the buffoonery practised in the tent of Achilles. The perils of a divided authority provide a philosophic theme on which the profound psychologist Shakespeare has reflected much, and the poetry comes boiling out of him as from a spring. Then it stops.

Thersites, the most degraded and most monstrous of Shakespeare's clowns, is now given his whack at the audience, and Ajax is presented as the stupid man. Then follows a family scene between Hector, Troilus, and Priam, in which the merits of the war are discussed. Hector happens to remark of Helen: "She is not worth what she doth cost the holding." This awakens, or half awakens, the sleeping philosopher in Shakespeare, and he gropes in his dream for his favourite thought: "There's nothing good or bad but thinking makes it so." This thought always swims in deep waters; it is a most difficult thought to express, as the Pragmatists have recently found; and Shakespeare's delivery of it upon the present occasion is so clumsy that we hardly know where he stands on the argument.

> *Troilus.* What is aught but as 'tis valued?
> *Hector.* But value dwells not in particular will;
>   It holds his estimate and dignity
>   As well wherein 'tis precious of itself
>   As in the prizer. 'Tis mad idolatry
>   To make the service greater than the god,
>   And the will dotes that is inclinable
>   To what infectiously itself affects,
>   Without some image of the affected merit.

Here, as so often in Shakespeare, everything both on and off the stage is held up while the master talks to himself in his own half-intelligible lingo about the secret problems of his thought. There must somewhere exist, thinks Shakespeare, a reality of which our thought is the image. A very similar passage occurs when Troilus discovers the perfidy of Cressida and proceeds to reason in an uninspired way about abstractions. His Cressida could not act thus; then there must be two Cressidas:

> *Troilus.* . . . O madness of discourse,
>   That cause sets up with and against thyself!
>   Bi-fold authority! where reason can revolt
>   Without perdition, and loss assume all reason.

It may be remarked that all through Shakespeare we come upon passages which we must read twice, because we must find the key to them; and the key is generally something profound. A page or two earlier in this play Cressida says: "Blind fear that, seeing reason leads, finds safer footing than blind reason stumbling without fear. To fear the worst oft cures the worst." His mind is so full of these abstractions that he tumbles them out sometimes in paradox. In moments of great excitement he makes them sing. But in *Troilus and Cressida* there is nothing to stimulate him to the pitch where philosophy turns into music.

On the other hand, those easier thoughts and more familiar themes which are the give-and-take of drama live so within his mastery that any pebble sets them off, as, for instance, the thought of *honour*. At the close of the family scene Troilus speaks with the tongue of Henry V:

> *Troilus*. Why, there you touched the life of our design:
>    Were it not glory that we more affected
>    Than the performance of our heaving spleens,
>    I would not wish a drop of Trojan blood
>    Spent more in her defence. But, worthy Hector,
>    She is a theme of honour and renown,
>    A spur to valiant and magnanimous deeds,
>    Whose present courage may beat down our foes,
>    And fame, in time to come, canonise us:
>    For, I presume, brave Hector would not lose
>    So rich advantage of a promis'd glory
>    As smiles upon the forehead of this action
>    For the wide world's revenue.

Immediately upon this fluent and appropriate climax there follows more Thersites, and a scene in which Ajax is made the butt of sham flattery,—all most truly Shakespearian and most truly horse-play.

We now approach the great scene of the play, in which Ulysses endeavours to persuade Achilles to abandon his ill-humour and fight. It seems impossible that Shakespeare should have read any translation of Homer, though he is supposed to have read Chapman; for Shakespeare imagines that Achilles' wrath was the result of sheer, motiveless ill-temper. He neglects the splendid dramatic reason for the wrath, namely, that the girl Briseis had been reft from Achilles by Agamemnon. Ulysses, then, after gaining the attention of Achilles by a ruse, approaches him with an argument based upon a philosophic abstraction so intellectual that Plato would have pricked up his ears at it. But no one except a professional casuist would be apt to guess what Ulysses was talking about:

> *Ulysses*.                       A strange fellow here
>    Writes me: That man, how dearly ever parted,
>    How much in having, or without or in,
>    Cannot make boast to have that which he hath,
>    Nor feels not what he owes, but by reflection;
>    As when his virtues shining upon others
>    Heat them, and they retort that heat again
>    To the first giver.

Achilles' reply surprises us, because it is academic, lacking all heat and passion. He thinks Ulysses' idea is very suggestive, very helpful.

> *Achilles.*     This is not strange, Ulysses.
>   The beauty that is borne here in the face
>   The bearer knows not, but commends itself
>   To others' eyes: nor doth the eye itself,
>   That most pure spirit of sense, behold itself,
>   Not going from itself; but eye to eye oppos'd
>   Salutes each other with each other's form:
>   For speculation turns not to itself
>   Till it hath travell'd, and is married there
>   Where it may see itself. This is not strange at all.

Ulysses "distinguishes," as the logicians would say:

> *Ulysses.*    I do not strain at the position,
>   It is familiar, but at the author's drift. . . .

Ulysses now develops his proposition, which is that men receive their own spiritual fulfilment through the effect which they produce upon others. The thought here reaches its last attenuation. The two heroes seem to be absorbed in bending over a game of metaphysical checkers. Then Ulysses launches his great, beautiful exhortation, one of the most remarkable speeches in all Shakespeare:

> *Ulysses.* Time hath, my lord, a wallet at his back,
>   Wherein he puts alms for oblivion;
>   A great-siz'd monster of ingratitudes:
>   Those scraps are good deeds past; which are devour'd
>   As fast as they are made, forgot as soon
>   As done: perseverance, dear my lord,
>   Keeps honour bright: to have done, is to hang
>   Quite out of fashion, like a rusty mail
>   In monumental mockery. Take the instant way;
>   For honour travels in a strait so narrow,
>   Where one but goes abreast: keep then the path;
>   For emulation hath a thousand sons
>   That one by one pursue: if you give way,
>   Or hedge aside from the direct forthright,
>   Like to an enter'd tide, they all rush by,
>   And leave you hindmost;

Or, like a gallant horse fall'n in first rank,
Lie there for pavement to the abject rear,
O'errun and trampled on: then what they do in present,
Though less than yours in past, must o'ertop yours;
For time is like a fashionable host
That slightly shakes his parting guest by the hand,
And with his arms outstretch'd, as he would fly,
Grasps-in the comer: welcome ever smiles,
And farewell goes out sighing. O, let not virtue seek
Remuneration for the thing it was;
For beauty, wit,
High birth, vigour of bone, desert in service,
Love, friendship, charity, are subjects all
To envious and calumniating time.
One touch of nature makes the whole world kin,
That all with one consent praise new-born gawds,
Though they are made and moulded of things past,
And give to dust that is a little gilt
More laud than gilt o'er-dusted.
The present eye praises the present object:
Then marvel not, thou great and complete man,
That all the Greeks begin to worship Ajax;
Since things in motion sooner catch the eye
Than what not stirs. The cry went once on thee,
And still it might, and yet it may again,
If thou wouldst not entomb thyself alive,
And case thy reputation in thy tent;
Whose glorious deeds, but in these fields of late,
Made emulous missions 'mongst the gods themselves,
And drave great Mars to faction.

The head and flow of eloquence in this speech carries Shakespeare over into a senseless but magnificent eulogy of the secret service of Agamemnon's government, through whose clever work Achilles' attachment to one of Priam's daughters has been discovered. The eloquence is checked suddenly, however, by a ditch of bad taste, almost of obscenity, and ends in a few flat lines. Such is Shakespeare,—so unconscious, so indifferent; so at the mercy of

what is in progress before him and within him; so unprincipled
in his art; so gifted in his mind.

There is yet another page of the play on which shines a genius
like that of *Romeo and Juliet*. Something in the sudden and en-
forced parting of Troilus and Cressida reminds Shakespeare of the
tender agony of such partings, which he must himself have known
or he could not have written:

> *Troilus.* . . . . .
> We two, that with so many thousand sighs
> Did buy each other, must poorly sell ourselves
> With the rude brevity and discharge of one.
> Injurious time now with a robber's haste
> Crams his rich thievery up, he knows not how:
> As many farewells as be stars in heaven,
> With distinct breath and consign'd kisses to them,
> He fumbles up into a loose adieu:
> And scants us with a single famish'd kiss,
> Distasted with the salt of broken tears.

I have not cited the little golden bits that gleam through *Troilus
and Cressida*. Any reader can find them for himself. But there is no
foil of drama behind these stray jewels. The play constantly reminds
us of Shakespeare's other worlds. Perhaps it supplied him with no
controlling mood, and he was thus led to filch from his other
moods. One might think that the following lines must come out of
*Othello*. Troilus is warning Cressida not to forget him among the
dances and gaieties of the Grecian camp:

> . . . . . . .
> But I can tell that in each grace of these
> There lurks a still and dumb-discoursive devil
> That tempts most cunningly. But be not tempted.

I must cite also a clever remark about women which is put in the
mouth of Ulysses by the great observer and lover of women, Shakespeare. It is coldly and somewhat coarsely said, and is extremely
abstract, intellectual, world-wise; yet it records and pictures a certain
type of woman very perfectly:

*Ulysses.* . . . . . . .

> O! these encounterers, so glib of tongue,
> That give accosting welcome ere it comes,
> And wide unclasp the tables of their thoughts
> To every ticklish reader, set them down
> For sluttish spoils of opportunity,
> And daughters of the game.

Throughout the play we have been in contact with the power of abstract reasoning, clothed at times in images so bright and easy as to make it beautiful, fading at times into commonplace, and often replaced by feeble humour and empty talk. The fact that the theme does not interest the poet isolates the jets of his talent and in some degree analyses the man for us. There is, as it were, no character-interest in this play, no Iago, no Shylock, no Romeo; and there is no plot. I can find no unity in it, and yet it is full of the greatest talent for writing that a man ever possessed. This talent seems to roll about like a hulk in the trough of the sea.

But Shakespeare knew nothing of all this. He was as much at home in the mud as in the rainbow, and spent perhaps not so much time over his *Troilus and Cressida* as any one will who tries to understand the play. Shakespeare had no intentions, but wrote as Mozart wrote. Very unlike Mozart was he: for parts of Shakespeare are ugly, and much of him is whimsical, and some of him is perverted. But his work is all a natural product, like the silk-worm's thread. One can never be quite sure that even Thersites may not show under the microscope some beautiful pattern on his back, as Caliban does.

Perhaps half the error in the world results from providing other people with intentions; and perhaps the unique power of Shakespeare consists in the fact that he had none. He rolls in the waters of his thought, fathoms deep, without attempt to save himself, without interest or knowledge as to where he is or in what direction he moves. He is unconscious, like an infant; and opening his eyes on the nearest object, remembers the remotest with no consciousness of transition. His mind is like a windmill that makes no effort, but merely transmits natural force; and his thoughts hit us with the power of all nature behind them. They are ingenuous, spontaneous, almost unexamined.

## THE MELANCHOLY PLAYS

IN THE FULL TIDE of one of Shakespeare's great arguments, as in *Lear* or in *Hamlet,* the forces are stupendous, yet through the perfection of the invisible machinery of the play there is nothing which we can take hold of, saying, "Here lies the power." It is the same with all other very great works of art. They teach us, *themselves,* but will not answer questions as to how it is done. Thus it comes about that one can best study the minds of great artists in their lesser and imperfect works. Here we find problems not too complex and a velocity of thought not so high as to defy pursuit. It is for this reason that a chapter has been devoted to *Troilus and Cressida;* and for the same reason it is well to turn over the leaves of Shakespear's other minor plays by the light of whatever we happen to know, whether of life or of literature.

Shakespeare was subject to fits of gloomy depression, or he never could have left behind such sad documents as some of these minor plays. How far the melancholy is due to the plot, and how far to the poet's own circumstances, we can never know. But we may assume that Shakespeare's mood as we find it in any play was the mood which governed him in the choice of the story. *All's Well that Ends Well* falls into the list of plays that leave us sad. Melancholy moulders in the very title of it; for we feel that all is not well nor ever has been nor can be well again. There was not much in the box of life; and there has been a great pother about opening it and shutting it, and at last it is shut up with a triumphant and sudden major chord, but the box is empty. *All's Well that Ends Well* is one of the plays in which an Italian plot proves to be an indigestible morsel to the English playwright. Why could not Shakespeare have treated this plot in the spirit of the *Taming of the Shrew,* which makes no moral appeal? The reason is that behind Shakespeare's *Taming of the Shrew* there was an old Italian comedy which gave him his colouring, whereas in *All's Well* he is adapting an older English play, which had taken an Italian fable seriously. The plot is at war with the dramatist, and neither one comes off wholly victorious. In some of his Italian stories—as in *Romeo and Juliet*— Shakespeare transmutes all the characters into himself, and triumphs. But in others he fails. The tales of the Italian prelate Bandello, in which wives disguise themselves and seduce their husbands, soldiers stab and throw dice, widows climb in and out of windows, and all men wear masks and take life lightly, are so foreign to Northern sentiment, that in giving them life Shakespeare often equivocates. The plot of *All's Well* is as follows: A maid cures a sick king, who promises to give her whatever bridegroom she shall choose in marriage. She chooses Bertram, with whom she has long been in love, and who flees the court upon the announcement that he must wed her. The rest of the story consists in the lady's contriving a secret assignation with Bertram, unknown to the man himself, who thereupon repents, marries her, and "all's well." Such a degraded plot might well daunt a romantic spirit. Even the genius of Shakespeare has been foiled by this material. There is no character in *All's Well that Ends Well* that can attract us, except the old Countess Mother, who is a secondary subject, a still-life portrait, and Lafeu, the old lord, who is a happy thought, done with a few strokes by the great playwright. The other characters are rendered gloomy by the exigencies of the plot. Bertram has been carefully understood, from the Northern point of view, as a sneak; Helena is sentimentalised in a manner so at war with her conduct as to make her repellent; Parolles is a bore.

There are points in this play, as in all the others, in which Shakespeare never fails. You may call him up at once in the morning, after he has left the tavern at midnight, and he will give you the speech of the innocent young girl at any desired length and of unfailing beauty. So, in this play, the speeches of the heroine, Helena, at the beginning of the play are charming,—till we find out what her course of action is to be. She starts off, as it were, with being Miranda; but, having cured the King, she bargains for a husband as follows:

> *Helena.* Then shalt thou give me with thy kingly hand
> What husband in thy power I will command:
> Exempted be from me the arrogance
> To choose from forth the royal blood of France,
> My low and humble name to propagate
> With any branch or image of thy state;
> But such a one, thy vassal, whom I know
> Is free for me to ask, thee to bestow.

Miranda soon disappears in the Italian intrigue, and never comes out alive. In the end Helena plays the part of a bawd. Perhaps this plot might have been carried through as a fairy story; but Shakespeare treats it with naturalism. He is doing his best with the tale, and grinds away at Parolles and at the episode of the drum. Why is not all this genial and amusing, like Falstaff or *Twelfth Night?* Shakespeare's heart is not in it, nor his head, either. There is, in truth, nothing here to excite him. He is conscientiously and cleverly staging the story, which is artificial and mundane. There is no point at which he can deliver a metaphysical remark about the other world.—Yes, there is one; and the words are put into the mouth of Lafeu, who comments upon the King's recovery as follows:

"They say miracles are past; and we have our philosophical persons, to make modern and familiar things supernatural and causeless. Hence is it that we make trifles of terrors, ensconcing ourselves into seeming knowledge, when we should submit ourselves to an unknown fear."

The profundity of Lafeu's idea is astonishing, and amounts to this: every explanation of the miraculous is superficial; behind all there must be a deeper miracle, which is not explained. The King's recovery reminds Shakespeare of this whole field of thought; but the action of the play presses, and he moves on.

At the bottom of our distress over Helena in *All's Well* there lies a dramatic difficulty. What we call a character in a play is a result, and not a prefigured idea. Shakespeare's characters result from his plots; and where a story is too artificial, even Shakespeare can do no more than throw out occasionally a good idea which is neutralised by the sequel. No matter how great a painter may be, he cannot admit false lights into his canvas without spoiling its atmosphere. In romantic drama a character is a mere drawing in smoke, —perfect so long as it is untouched, but the merest breath will confuse it. Cordelia lives in her few speeches, and is as solid as marble. If the plot of *King Lear* had required some subsequent banality from Cordelia, Shakespeare would not have hesitated for a moment. He would have dashed it in and gone to dinner, and we of the twentieth century should have been made to feel a little gloomy by it.

In *Measure for Measure* there is a much severer gloom than in *All's Well*. Here is a comedy to make a man drown himself and have Shakespeare's name carved on his tomb. There is a running accompaniment of great intellect in this play, whose action goes forward in a twilight of blighted silver, with no sunlight in it. In the poetic scenes there is the rhetoric of Prospero without his power. In the comic interludes there is the manner of Eastcheap without its humour.

Here again, as in *All's Well*, the innocent woman receives the few streaming shafts from heaven in a couple of scenes of great tragedy. The rest of the play follows out in detail a painful intrigue, through which the villain, Angelo, is safely married off to his old neglected sweetheart, Mariana of the Moated Grange. In the somewhat sudden wind up, every one shakes hands all round in a fashion worthy of Dickens, and the curtain falls.

In *Measure for Measure* the suggestion of the wicked Judge, Angelo, that he shall pardon Isabella's brother, but at the price of her own honour, gives rise to a tragic situation of the first magnitude; and the play immediately soars into tragedy as naturally as if Lear were on the stage. Isabella is a novice in a convent. Her directness and promptitude of mind are as marked as her innocence. Shakespeare's good women never understand evil. When her brother's friend, Lucio, the man about town, explains to her that her brother, Claudio, has been condemned to death through the enforcement of the old law against adultery, she does not comprehend. Her innocence strikes poetry into the debauchee. He apologises for his plainness of speech:

> *Lucio.*
>> I hold you as a thing ensky'd, and sainted
>> By your announcement, an immortal spirit,
>> And to be talk'd with in sincerity,
>> As with a saint.

He explains the matter again, and in language which no one can mistake. She understands now, but is not sure.

> *Isabella.* Someone with child by him?—My cousin Juliet?

It is agreed that she shall intercede with the Judge, Angelo. At her second interview with Angelo, when he proposes the infamous bargain, she misunderstands for a long time, and then bursts into flame as naturally as a peasant woman might do:

> *Ang.*        Believe me, on mine honour,
>   My words express my purpose.
> *Isab.* Ha! little honour to be much believed,
>   And most pernicious purpose!—Seeming, seeming!—
>   I will proclaim thee, Angelo; look for 't:
>   Sign me a present pardon for my brother,
>   Or with an outstretched throat I'll tell the world
>   Aloud what man thou art.

It next becomes her duty to consult Claudio, her brother, about the whole matter. And Claudio is shaken by the fear of death. This is one of Shakespeare's besieging thoughts, and the young Claudio, a somewhat unideaed youth, speaks with the tongue of Hamlet's father:

> Ay, but to die, and go we know not where;
> To lie in cold obstruction, and to rot;
> This sensible warm motion to become
> A kneaded clod; and the delighted spirit
> To bathe in fiery floods, or to reside
> In thrilling regions of thick-ribbed ice;
> To be imprison'd in the viewless winds,
> And blown with restless violence round about
> The pendant world; or to be worse than worst
> Of those that lawless and incertain thoughts
> Imagine howling!—'tis too horrible.
> The weariest and most loathed worldly life,
> That age, ache, penury, and imprisonment
> Can lay on nature is a paradise
> To what we fear of death.
> *Isab.* Alas! alas!
> *Claud.*        Sweet sister, let me live.
>   What sin you do to save a brother's life,
>   Nature dispenses with the deed so far
>   That it becomes a virtue.

> *Isab.*                          O you beast!
> O faithless coward! O dishonest wretch!
> Wilt thou be made a man out of my vice?
> Is 't not a kind of incest, to take life
> From thine own sister's shame? What should I think?
> Heaven shield, my mother play'd my father fair;
> For such a warped slip of wilderness
> Ne'er issu'd from his blood. Take my defiance:
> Die; perish! Might but my bending down
> Reprieve thee from thy fate, it should proceed
> I'll pray a thousand prayers for thy death,
> No word to save thee.

Here is womanhood from queen to peasant, and drama from eternity to eternity. But there is not much of either in *Measure for Measure,*—not enough of either to drag the play in the great procession of Shakespeare's tragedies. For this same woman, Isabella, at the close of the play is made to simulate another woman in making (not keeping) an assignation. The innocent, fiery Isabella of the earlier act would never have consented to play out the licentious Italian comedy which Shakespeare casts her for in the last act. The spectator feels this, and resents the soil which Shakespeare has cast on his own creation. But for this slander, Isabella would have taken her place beside Desdemona and Imogen. But Shakespeare sometimes had bad taste; or, rather, he had no taste at all: for taste is conscious art.

While all these things have been going on in *Measure for Measure,* the rightful Duke has made a pretended abdication, and has been moving about in the disguise of a friar, ready to appear as *deus ex machina* at the proper moment. For some reason which I cannot fathom this device is dramatically ineffective. It would have been better if the old Duke had been kept entirely out of the way till the climax. But in that case we should have missed another most Shakespearian lecture on death which the Duke-as-Friar delivers in the jail to the condemned Claudio, and which colours the play.

> *Claud.* The miserable have no other medicine,
>     But only hope.
> I have hope to live, and am prepar'd to die.

> *Duke.* Be absolute for death; either death, or life,
> Shall thereby be the sweeter. Reason thus with life:—
> If I do lose thee, I do lose a thing
> That none but fools would keep; a breath thou art,
> Servile to all the skyey influences,
> That do this habitation, where thou keep'st,
> Hourly afflict. . . .

In this long speech, of which I give only the opening, Hamlet, Macbeth, Prospero, Touchstone, and many others peep out, but there is no new character. The speech is a gloomy and decorative bit of rhetoric, sincere only in that it somehow depicts Shakespeare's mood. As for Angelo himself, with his gravity, his sudden, unconvincing lust, and his final happy marriage, the plot precludes his being a human character at all. There is no such man. It must be observed, in closing *Measure for Measure,* that the whole play is marked by a quite unnecessary grossness,—the indecency which goes with melancholy and is a part of it.

Every one should read *Timon of Athens,* and see whether a moral can be drawn out of it. Shakespeare seems to have chosen the plot because he was in ill-humour, perhaps sick. Feeling thoroughly cynical, he seems to have expected to write a cynical play. The cynicism in *Timon,* however, is so evenly distributed among so many characters that all the dramatic effect of it is lost. The play is thus without idea, and its incidents are absurdly dull. A sort of malevolence exhales from it, but nothing that can be thought of as philosophy. Timon, after a life of senseless expenditure, grows poor, and is surprised to find that his creditors and the sycophants who had surrounded him in prosperity do not love him in his disgrace. He therefore leaves Athens and digs in the earth for roots. In digging he finds gold, and with this he subsidises Alcibiades, who is also in exile, to avenge the injuries of both by destroying Athens. The play is too Elizabethan, too near the charade, and too shallow to be interesting as a play; but it is full of truly Shakespearian touches in the language. Shakespeare's genius has evidently been unable to take hold of this material. It was his habit to seize his themes experimentally, and he never knew what was coming out of a plot. He began at once, without knowing just where he was to end, and he never found the same theme twice. His most tremendous effects are due to this method, and his "effects defective" also come by this cause. When tragedy unrolls out of his gossamer, it arrives as a gift of nature,—born, not made. It has the brilliancy of the humming-bird and the edge of the sword-lily's leaf. *Romeo and Juliet* has in it the morn and liquid dew of youth. When the subject yields no tragedy, as in *Coriolanus*,—why, then you may take what you get. There was nothing in the subject, as it turns out. We can blame nobody for our disappointments in the Melancholy Plays. No one is responsible.

## SHAKESPEARE'S INFLUENCE

CONTACT with Shakespeare's large, impersonal mind makes us bigger. A man does not need to read a play through in order to receive the poet's influence, which is like an electric stimulation and affects our whole being, though we receive it through the finger-tips. If one could find two boys of twelve who were exactly alike, and if one of them should begin to read Shakespeare with interest, he would become more intelligent than the other lad within fifteen minutes. The acceptability of Shakespeare to the young is one of his divinest qualities. There is, as it were, a ready-made world which Shakespeare slides into our minds long before we are capable of receiving the real world. This Shakespearian world is healthier, happier, and infinitely cleverer than the real world. Its eloquence is running at a high speed, and the smallest contact with any word in it makes our entire system stand erect.

Shakespeare's intelligence was completely developed. There were matters that did not interest him; but everything that he knew was co-ordinated. He always speaks from the same pulpit. This is not obvious,—indeed, it is the last thing that many people would say about him,—because we do not know where that pulpit was, nor how he got into it. But his phrases always come from the same personality, from the same intellectual outlook. It is as if the human soul consisted of an infinite series of concentric spheres, one inside the other, and Shakespeare's voice always caused the same sphere to resound. When we hear the ring of it we cry, "Shakespeare!" in our sleep. He is a metaphysical unity, and all his characters are merely Shakespeare—Shakespeare with rays of humour about his head, or with an old cloak from some royal coronation upon his shoulders. We cannot distinguish between the man and the artist. The man and the artist are one.

It is this disappearance of the man into the artist, by the way, that has so puzzled the world about Shakespeare's personality. People are ever searching for the mask, and there is no mask. Ambition is what reveals men, and he had no ambition. Motive is what shows men's contours, and he had no motive. He had no desire to conceal himself, but he vanishes in a witticism because he is all wit. During his lifetime he was so logically perfect in his indifference that no one especially noticed his existence; and he passed through life as a pleasant fellow of no great importance, leaving such a minimum of personal reminiscences in the minds of his contemporaries that people now think him a mystery. The real mystery, however, is one which the knowledge of personal facts could not solve for us.

He has left the most powerful record of the kind of man he must have been by leaving a vacuum. His life and mind are a monument to the unknowable. The vanishing-point is in every moment of his thought and in every line of his work, and he has vanished into it. The average man is puzzled by this outcome. He thinks that the infinite is an algebraical term or a poetic sentiment; and Shakespeare presents him with the infinite in flesh and blood.

There are certain very categorical minds, often very strong minds, that feel a challenge in this whole phenomenon of Shakespeare's unknowability. They are excited and almost angered by it. They must and will understand. Hence the prodigious literature of quack discovery about Shakespeare. Now the quack is a man whose sentiment is not satisfied unless he discovers something that is not there. If he should find a true thing, it would coalesce with the rest of truth and somewhat defeat his ambition; he would never be satisfied with it. Each one of the new pundits has therefore a theory of his own and betrays a kind of megalomania in regard to it. All this false learning is a by-product of Shakespeare's metaphysical influence, much as the ten thousand dogmas of Christianity are the result of Christ's thought as it acts upon minds which resent the abstraction of that thought.

Shakespeare belongs to the Renaissance. We feel this quite distinctly in considering his relation to religion. Like the great pagan painters of the Italian Renaissance, he knows only so much of religion as his art teaches him,—as his art made necessary. There are some kinds of painting which imply religion. Paul Veronese, through sheer æsthetic necessity, paints a saint, paints a Pentecost. Guido Reni paints a Crucifixion which touches the sphere of religious truth. In such cases the artistic illumination suffices for the artistic need; but one step beyond it the artist does not go. So in Shakespeare there are decorative phrases of a religious beauty which is lent to him by the thing in hand,—I mean by the spiritual *mise en scène*.

For instance:

> "In those holy fields
> Over whose acres walked those blessed feet,
> Which fourteen hundred years ago were nailed
> For our advantage on the bitter cross."

Again:

> "He gave his honours to the world again,
> His blessed past to heaven, and slept in peace."

This kind of religious feeling in Shakespeare is a sort of feudal tapestry with which he adorns his banqueting-hall. Perhaps the political conditions of his day helped to banish religious motives from his stage. One suspects in him also an instinctive avoidance of such motives on grounds of personal feeling. At any rate, the absence of religious motive colours the plays and gives them their quality.

Shakespeare uses religious metaphors in much the same way that he uses mythology; indeed, I should say that the pagan symbolism was dearer to him than the Christian. His whole work is tinged with the atmosphere of an imaginary antiquity, which comes to him from translations of Ovid, Plutarch, and Virgil, and which bears the same relation to classic feeling that the backgrounds in quattrocentist pictures bear to ancient Rome. He never came near enough to the Latin writers to be influenced by them in style or purpose.

It is worth while to read the modest essay entitled *Life of Shakespeare* by Nicholas Rowe, Shakespeare's first editor, which was published in 1709, and which, on the whole, gives almost as good an account of the poet as the later critics have been able to work out. Rowe preserves a tradition, which the English scholars have somewhat neglected, that Shakespeare "died a Papist." That the poet should have accepted the final ministrations of a priest seems to chime in with what one finds in the plays. The tradition accords with the decorative piety of Shakespeare's spirit, and with the only doctrinal prejudice which we can certainly perceive in his work, —namely, his dislike of the Puritans. He could hardly have been a "good" Catholic, or we should have found it out in a hundred ways; but he was a romantic sceptic with a fondness for the dramatic beauties of the old religion. His Ghost in *Hamlet* is purgatorial and doctrinal,—just enough so for stage purposes. His marriages in the *Comedy of Errors* and in *Romeo and Juliet* are—well, they are really pagan, with a few candles and a vague Mother Church from No-Man's-Land standing behind. So also his burials are scenic. The dirge over Imogen, on the other hand, is pantheistic. This is his own sort of religion,—and a sweet rhapsody it is. So in most of his discourses on death the romanticism and the scepticism reveal to us Shakespeare's personal church.

With Shakespeare died the Renaissance in England. The psalm-singing weavers of whom he makes fun—and not good-natured fun, either—were to rule the land within a few years after his death. That they should cut so little figure in these plays, which teem with the national life, does not prove the non-existence of the pious weavers, but only that Shakespeare's thought did not receive them. It shows how special and peculiar is the world in which lives the artist,—even the greatest artist. Every artist is an *imperium in imperio,* a cathedral with perhaps a dead town at its feet, or, as in this case, a Renaissance palace with a live town at its feet.

With regard to the miraculous nature of life, Shakespeare never forgets it: it is everywhere. He resents the mere notion of rationalism. He will not have it that any explanation is true. Throughout *Hamlet* and *The Tempest*—indeed, in all his plays—he shows his acquaintance with hypnotism, telepathy, and the power of prayer,— with the potency of unseen forces which rule the world. "Spirits are not finely touched save to fine issues." The thing in hand is a part of something else; men are projections of other powers, and what we see is due to the operation of something behind. His moralising largely consists in drawing our attention to these phenomena. "Canst thou who dost command the beggar's knee command the health of it?" All these manifestations of spirit he knows not as theories or beliefs. He knows them in the raw, and sees them freshly as he speaks.

It is just because Shakespeare insists on leaving matters in the mist in which they are born that his thought endures. Persons who schematise the Unknowable codify themselves, and pass by with the age they live in. The crucible of Shakespeare turns all to vapour, and leaves a Shakespearian cosmos which is at every point true to itself. He thus gives us an instantaneous vision of a single one of the infinite concentric worlds that slumber in each of us.

Shakespeare's Universe is so at one with itself that it controls our attention like Greek art; and it is almost as far from the world of religion as Greek art is. That consciousness of the presence of God which invades men's emotions and almost extinguishes the visible world for them is not in Shakespeare. Moreover, that desire to communicate and spread the consciousness of God to others, which accompanies the experience, is very far from Shakespeare. It would be distasteful to him. He is with the primal intellect in such matters; and those views which are brought back and re-delivered to the intellect only after the intellect has suffered a thorough plunge, and has been for a time drowned in religious emotion, are unknown to him.

I confess that the intellect often comes back melted and distorted from the drowning experiences of religion, and that religion has thus sent down through the centuries a track of distorted intellect, side by side with the track of sanctity, of benevolence, and of natural power. Nevertheless, the emotional consciousness of God is one of the most important factors in human history. It moulds and changes humanity. This influence did not pass through Shakespeare, and to transmit it is no part of his function. Thus it appears that the profoundest experience of half mankind—to wit, religion—is not within the range of Shakespeare's sympathies; and yet he remains the greatest dramatist of the world. How does this come about? It comes about through the rarity of great genius, and through the vastness of range in human life.

We can perhaps best realise the matter by turning to some entirely different field of thought. We see, for instance, in Beethoven or in Bach a talent comparable to Shakespeare's, exercised in a world quite different from Shakespeare's world.

The great artist is, indeed, a rare person. There have been only a handful of them in the history of western Europe. And it is a notable thing that these great artists, while each one speaks from his own sphere, do not attack one another. Shakespeare does not attack Plato; nor Bach, Shakespeare. Even Chinese mysticism looms at us from the old pictures with meanings which are native to our Western sentiment.

All forms of great art are cognate and support one another. Shakespeare is probably the strongest personal influence of a purely intellectual kind in the world. He is one of the great sages of humanity who teach something to the master-intellects of each generation. And besides this, he is by far the most popular poet in the world, and teaches metaphysics to millions who do not know they are learning, but find in him merely a fellow-being who loves and understands them.

# Index